VOICES OF AMERICA

Jewish Pioneers of St. Paul 1849–1874

VOICES OF AMERICA

Jewish Pioneers of St. Paul 1849–1874

Gene H. Rosenblum

ARCADIA PUBLISHING

ISBN 978-0-7385-1862-6

Published by Arcadia Publishing
Charleston, South Carolina

Printed in the United States of America

Library of Congress Catalog Card Number: 2001089394

For all general information contact Arcadia Publishing at:
Telephone 843-853-2070
Fax 843-853-0044
E-Mail sales@arcadiapublishing.com
For customer service and orders:
Toll-Free 1-888-313-2665

Visit us on the Internet at www.arcadiapublishing.com

Contents

About the Author

Gene H. Rosenblum is a retired St. Paul real estate attorney. He is a graduate of the University of Minnesota with a B.A. degree, and the William Mitchell College of Law (formerly the St. Paul College of Law) with a Juris Doctor degree. He has served as an assistant to the Mayor of St. Paul, and Assistant Corporation Counsel for the City of St. Paul. He has served two terms on the St. Paul Heritage Preservation Commission. He also has been "of counsel" to the Attorney General of the State of Minnesota.

He is a past president of Ira Weil Jeffrey B'nai B'rith Lodge, and a former member of the Board of Governors of the old District No. 6, B'nai B'rith.

He is one of the founders of the Jewish Historical Society of the Upper Midwest, and served on its board for a number of years. He is also the past president of the B'nai B'rith Rochester Chaplaincy at the Mayo Clinic, and has served on the board of the Temple of Aaron congregation.

He has written various articles in the Jewish Digest and the American Jewish World. He has also written of Judge Isaac Nunez Cardozo in an article called "Western Grandee," in the Western States Jewish History magazine, published by the Western States Jewish History Association.

He is married, has two children, one grandson, and five great-grandsons.

INTRODUCTION

One of the most difficult tasks of students of the history of Jews in many of America's large and small communities is to determine who was a Jew.

Traditionally, a Jew is a person who was born of a Jewish mother. However, many of the early Jews in American history disavowed their heritage, or were so ambivalent that they did not regard themselves as Jews. Many individuals in our history lived a life similar to Abram S. Elfelt: he was born a Jew, participated in the Jewish community as a president of Minnesota Lodge of B'nai B'rith, then intermarried, and was buried on a Saturday, contrary to Jewish tradition. Such noted scholars as Rabbi Gunther Plaut, former rabbi of Mt. Zion Temple, whose *Jews in Minnesota* is a classic work, and Professor Hyman Berman, professor of history at the University of Minnesota, claim that Jacob Jackson Noah, who served as Minnesota's first Clerk of the Minnesota Supreme Court, was the first Jewish attorney in Minnesota. My research shows that although he went on to have a distinguished career as Assistant Secretary of War under President Rutherford B. Hayes, his only real contacts with the Jewish community were very minimal at best.

There were two connections: his father was the famous Major Mordecai Manual Noah, former U.S. Consul in Tunis. As a young man in St. Paul in December of 1851, Noah gave a lecture entitled: "Political, Social, and Prospective Conditions of the Jews Throughout the World." That was it.

In between, his political career soared, and he used his father's fame to his advantage. Noah never participated in Jewish communal life. Instead he avoided the small Jewish community in St. Paul. He was an ambitious young man. He married a Tennessee girl, and in 1857, became a father to a son named Horace. When the Civil War came along, he resigned his office and left his young family to command a military unit in the war. After the Civil War, he did not return to Minnesota. He left for Tennessee, and later Washington D.C. When he died, he was buried as an Episcopalian.

The same problem is true with Maurice Auerbach, a prominent banker who married Senator Henry Rice's daughter, or Dr. Arthur Ancker, who founded St. Paul's first public hospital. Both were descendants of a long Jewish ancestry. Neither ever acknowledged their heritage.

A better case can be made for Judge Isaac Nunez Cardozo, who was born to a prominent Sephardic Jewish family and lived a full Jewish life. He was appointed as the first United States Commissioner for the Federal District and Circuit Courts of Minnesota in 1858, and was active in both religious life and the legal profession.

In my research of probate records, state and federal census records, city directories, newspaper accounts, obituaries, membership lists of synagogues, social clubs, and even organizations such as B'nai B'rith, I have tried to be as accurate as possible. Whether I have succeeded is for the reader who is familiar with many of the persons or families named to determine. In any event, most of the pioneer Jews in St. Paul, Minnesota, made substantial contributions to our community in many ways. This book is a tribute to them.

Gene H. Rosenblum, December 2000

These Were the Pioneers

(Spouses name in Parenthesis)

A

Aron Aaronheimer(Arnheimer)
Isaac Ansel
Sig Adler (Sophia Cardozo)
Mr. A. Applebaum
Morris Appel(Apple)
Alexander Appel
Joseph Abeles
Julius Abeles
Julius Austrian(Hannah Leopold)
Marx Austrian (Caroline Wilner)
Edward Austrian
Albert Austrian
Nathan Abrahamson

B

Isaac Bondy
Sarah Bondy
Solomon Bergman (Julia Schlesinger)
David Bergman
Oscar Bergman
Clarence Bergman
Nathan Bernheim
Caroline Bernheim
Emmanuel Bernheim
Louis Bernheim
Pauline Bernheim
Solomon Becker
S.E. Beckert
Rabbi J. Burgheim
A. Braun
Ferdinand Becker
Joseph Bergfeld
Charles Bergfeld
Abraham Blum
Aaron Blum
Isaac Blum
Charles Blum
Nathan Blumenthal
Nathan Bergfeld
Charles Bernstein
Robert Burton
S. Blasco

C

Isaac Nunez Cardozo (Rachel Seixas)
Henry Cali (Cole)(Fanny)
Dr. Isaac N. Cohen
H. Cahn
Eva Cardozo
Rebecca Cardozo
Nellie (Ellen) Cardozo
Julius Cohn
Moses Coddon
George N. Cardozo (Rachel)
Phineas N. Cardozo
Benjamin N. Cardozo
William Cardozo
Simon Cardozo
Ralph N. Cardozo
Benjamin Calmenson
Levi Cardozo
Cain Calmenson
Moses Calmenson
Louis Calmenson
Philip Calmenson
Samuel Calmenson
Gutman Caplan
Samuel Coddon
Isaac Coddon
Nathan Coddon
Nathan B. Cohen

E

Abram Elfelt
Charles Elfelt
Edwin Elfelt
S. Ettlinger

F

Max Frankel(Josephine Newman)
Rudolph Frankel
Michael Frankel
Louis Frankel
Hiram D. Frankel
Edwin L. Fryer
Anna Fryer
Eva Frank
Charles Fantle

G

M. Gundelfinger
Abraham Greenwald
A. Goldberg
Simon Greenwald
Fanny Lion Goodman
Daniel Goodman
Frances Goodman
Laura Goodman
Norman Goodman
Reuben Goldstein
Abraham Goldstein
David Goodman
David Goldman
David Greenblatt
Louis Goodkind
Benjamin Goodkind
William Goodkind
Wolf Goodman
Jacob Goldstein

H

G. Hirshler
H. Hirschberg
Hirsch Heimann (Teresa)
Isadore Heiman
Charles Hostetter (Annie Lowenstein)
Benjamin Hostetter
Sidney Hostetter
William Hostetter
Florence Hostetter
Abram Hostetter
Michael Harris
Gustave Heineman
Albert Heineman
Edward Heineman
Sigmund Hanauer
Gustave Hanauer

I

Leopold Isaacs

J

S. Josephs
Simon Jacoby
Simon Jacobs

K

Abraham Koritowsky
Joseph Kahn
Mrs. Solomon Kahn
Jennie Koenigsberg
Isaac Koenigsberg
Abraham Kaufman
Mortiz Kafka

L

David Lowitz
Elias Lowitz
Kaimon Lion (Dina)
Nathan Lion
Aaron Lovenstein
Levi Lovenstein
Mrs. Ann Lovenstein
B. Lichtenstern
Samuel Levy
Michael Levy
Abraham Leopold
Samuel Levi
Jacob Levi
Harry L. Levy
Henry Levy
Jessie Levy

M

Ralph Marchinsky
Marx (Max) Marx
S. Meyers
Reverend Emanuel Marcuson
Aaron Meyer
Rosa Lion Miller
Henry Marx

Morris Marx
Elizabeth Marx
Julius Mendelsohn
Louis Mendelsohn
Solomon Moses
David Mayer
Aaron Mark
Abraham Marchofsky
Jacob Mannheimer
Robert Mannheimer
Emil Mannheimer
Abraham Mark
Joseph Mark
Abraham Marks

N

Jacob Newman
J. Newman
Bernard Neuman

O

Ansel Oppenheim (Josie Greve)
Joseph Oppenheim
James Oppenheim
Herman Oppenheim
L. Phillips
Benjamin Plechner
Charles Polski
Moses Polski
Louis Pavian

R

M. Rice
Isadore Rose
Emmanuel Rose
Albert N.(Napoleon) Rose
Isaac E. Rose
Nathan S. Rose
Benjamin Rose
Eva Rose
Hyman Rose
Leopold Rose
Simon Rose
Joseph Rosenfield
Jascha Rosenholtz
Mayer Rosenholtz
Simon Rosenfels
Samuel Rudowsky

S

Meyer L Salomon
W. Schreiber
S. Schuster
Zipporah Seixas
Harry C. Seixas
Isaac B. Seixas
Gershom C. Seixas
Jacob C. Seixas
Abbie I Seixas
Rebecca Seixas
Sarah Sternberg
Alexander Sternberg
Samuel Sternberg
Herman (Ike)Sternberg
Joseph H. Smith
Sylvester Sulzbach
Moses Sulzbach
David Sulzbach
Gustave Sulzbach
Nathan Solomon
Henry T. Sattler
David C. Sattler
Jacob.B. Sattler
Leopold Schlesinger
Henry J. Strouse
Ephraim Skorish

U

Joseph Ullmann (Amelia)

W

Max Warshauer
Rabbi Leopold Winterer
Zsigo Weiss
Philip Weiss
Philip E. Weiss
Sigmund Weiss
Adolph Weiss
Herman Weiss
Max Wittleshofer

NOTE: We have listed the first generation pioneers, as well as their children, where known. Also, some of the names listed as pioneers may or may not have been of the Jewish faith, but they were related to prominent Jewish pioneer families by marriage.

ACKNOWLEDGMENTS

In 1978, after being encouraged and endorsed by Russell Fridley of the Minnesota Historical Society and Virginia Kunz of the Ramsey County Historical Society, I submitted an application to the National Endowment for the Humanities for a grant to do the history of the pioneer Jews in St. Paul, Minnesota. The application required submitting a work program and a proposed manuscript. There was a shortage of funds in the National Endowment for the Humanities and for other reasons, the grant was never made.

Thereafter, I submitted approximately 40 copies of the manuscript to various community leaders, and forgot about it.

In August 2000, Dr. Rhoda Lewin of Minneapolis, an old friend and my former editor when I worked on the *University of Minnesota Daily*, and a member of the Academic Council of the American Jewish Historical Society, contacted me and encouraged me to submit my manuscript to Arcadia Publishing of Chicago for their *Voices of America Series*. Their suggestion: flesh out the manuscript with pictures.

Thanks to Bonnie Wilson and the assistance of the staff of the Minnesota Historical Society, as well as Priscilla Farnham and Mollie Stillman of the Ramsey County Historical Society, Linda Schloff of the Jewish Historical Society of the Upper Midwest, and Andy Kraushaar of the Wisconsin State Historical Society. With their help I have been able to produce a pictorial history of the pioneer Jews in St. Paul, Minnesota, and a vivid snapshot of the pioneering era and the times in which they lived, from 1849–1874.

I also want to give special thanks to Mordecai Specktor of the American Jewish World, who allowed me access to photos from his archives. Also I want to thank Jane Steinman and Warren Steiner of Mt. Zion Synagogue, who opened up their picture archives and allowed me to use some very old lithographic plates.

I want to especially thank Eli Skora of the United Jewish Fund and Council of St. Paul, whose endorsement and sponsorship went a long way in helping to finalize publication.

Finally, I want to thank my wife, Nancy, whose patience and support encouraged me to bring this book to a satisfactory completion.

United Jewish Fund and Council

THE JEWISH FEDERATION OF GREATER ST. PAUL

February 7, 2001

The United Jewish Fund and Council of St. Paul, the St. Paul Federation, is proud and honored to lend its non-profit status to sponsor the publication of this historic work by Gene H. Rosenblum. Jewish Pioneers of St. Paul *is a book all of us will want to have in our home libraries. He has, with great precision, given us through words and historic pictures the remarkable evolution of the Jewish people of St. Paul, Minnesota, from their immigrant beginnings in the 1840s before Minnesota became a state, and through the first 25 years of growth. It is a story of the early Jewish families. Our mission has always been to stimulate the cultural, economic and everyday life of the Jewish community of St. Paul, Minnesota. Although an intermediate size community, St. Paul's Jewish community has always been a leader. This book is a tribute to them.*

Sincerely,

Eli Skora,
Executive Director

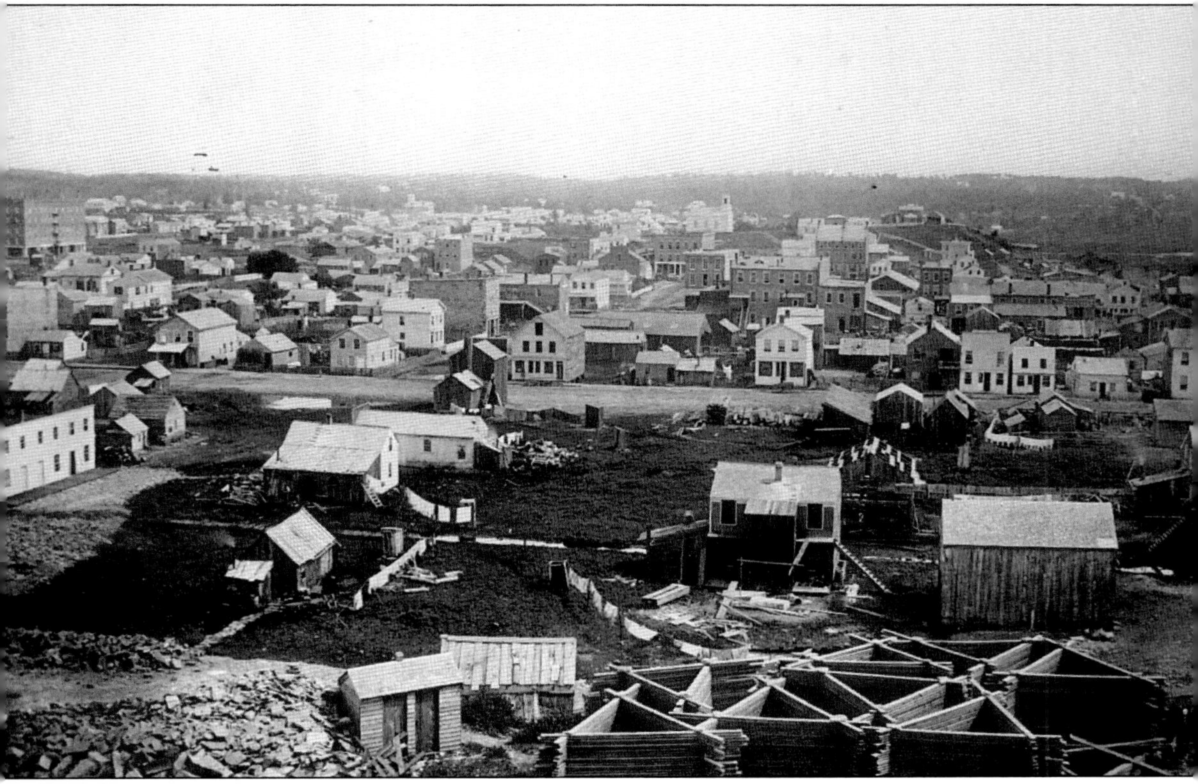

In the spring of 1857, B.F. Upton, a local photographer, climbed on to the roof the old courthouse, located at Fourth Street and Wabasha Street, and took some panoramic photographs of the skyline of St. Paul, Minnesota. His series of panoramic photographs are one of the few picture records of that era. They were taken in 1857, one year before Minnesota became a state. This shot was of Minnesota Street, left and horizontal through the middle. By the fall of 1857, economic disaster struck St. Paul with the collapse of the Ohio Life Insurance Company, and a national depression set in. (From the photo archives of the Minnesota Historical Society)

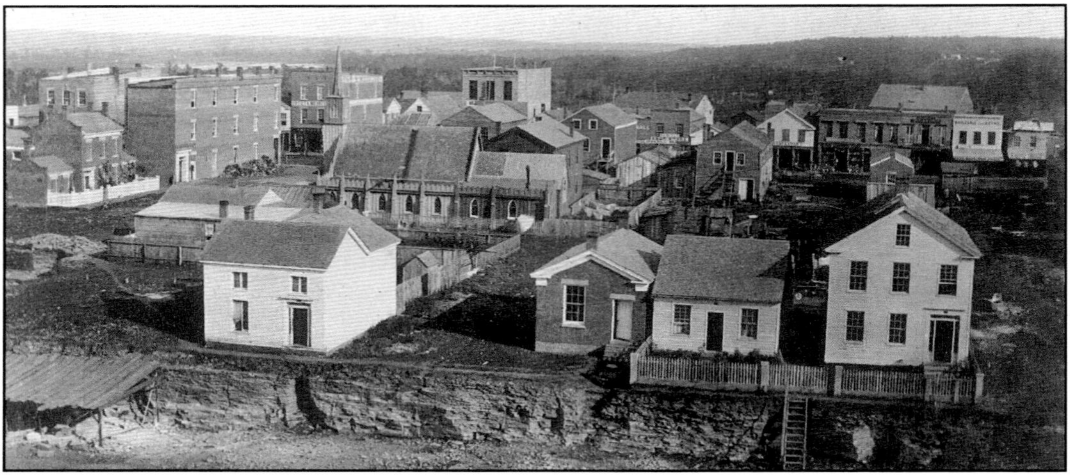

This is another photograph taken by B.F. Upton from the roof of the old courthouse. His panoramic shots of St. Paul were taken in 1857, one year before Minnesota became a state. (From the photo archives of the Minnesota Historical Society)

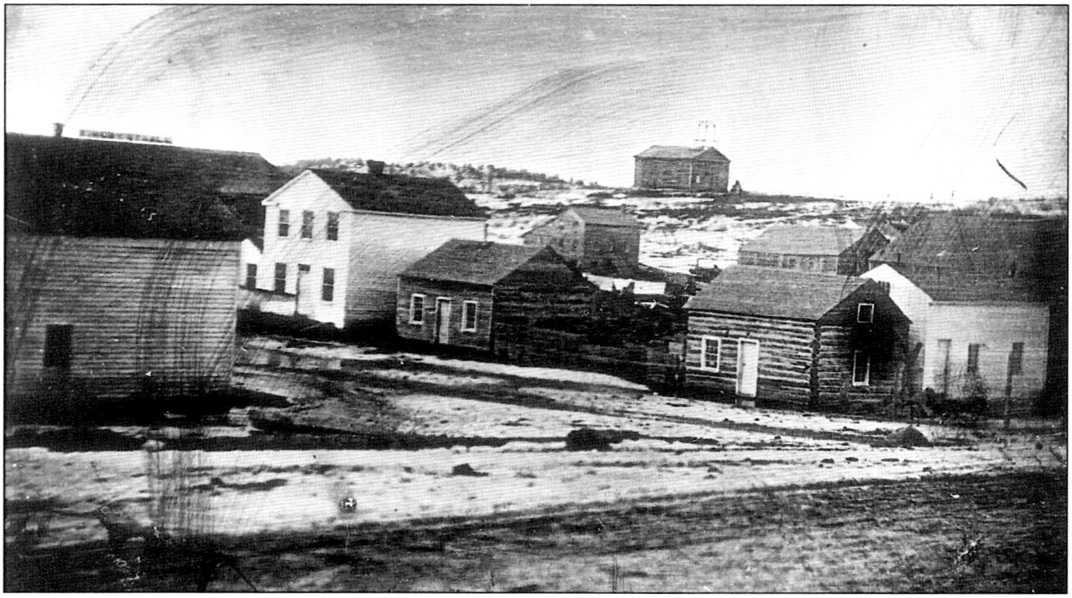

Photographer Joel Whitney, who had his photo studio in Charles Elfelt's building at Third Street (now Kellogg Boulevard) and Cedar, took this daguerreotype of early St. Paul in 1851. When this picture was taken there were still forests throughout the center of the city; there was a waterfall at Tenth and Cedar Street, a lake at Eighth Street and Robert Street, and a very deep ravine leading to the Mississippi River. Until 1870, so-called "Baptist Hill" at Third Street and Sibley Street provided early pioneer residents a place to watch for incoming steamboats. It was sliced into deep road cuts, and slowly hauled away to provide fill for the railroads as they expanded throughout the city. (From the photo archives of the Minnesota Historical Society)

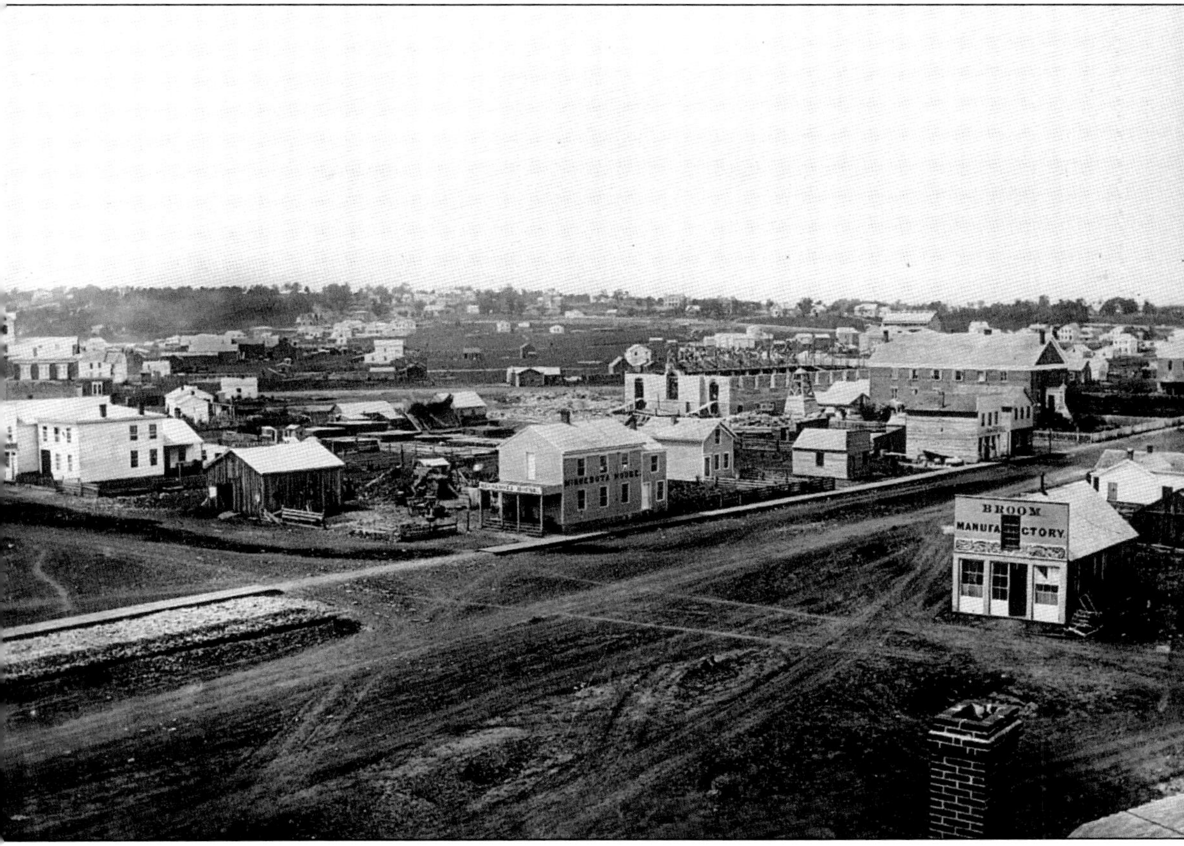

This is another shot taken by B.F. Upton of early St. Paul in 1857. It was taken from the roof of the old courthouse in 1857. (From the photo archives of the Minnesota Historical Society)

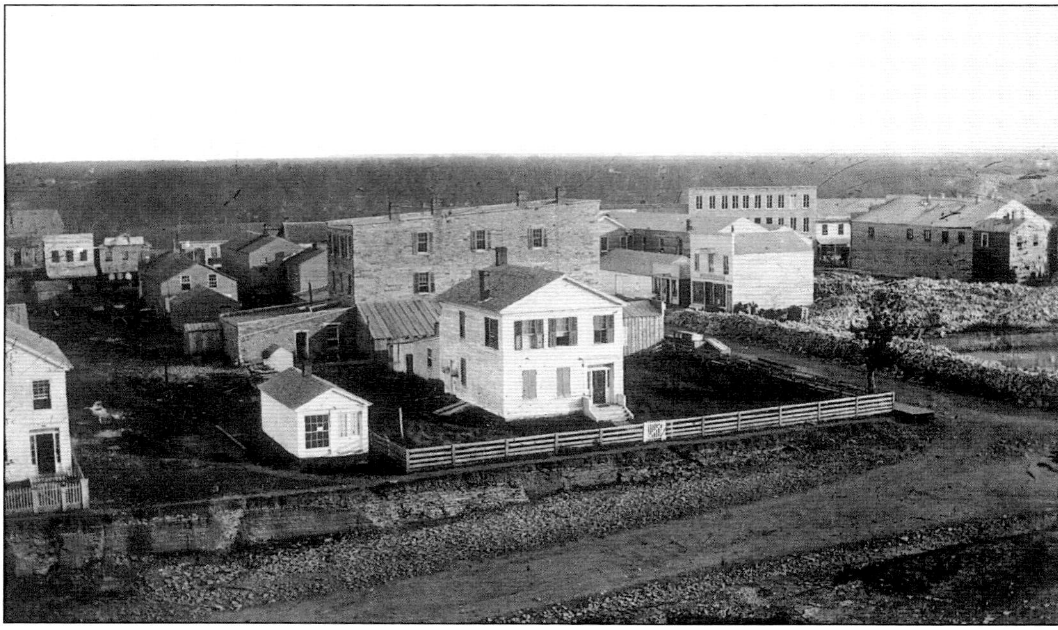

Another one of B.F. Upton's panoramic photographs taken from the roof of the old courthouse, taken in the spring of 1857, displays the corner of Fourth Street and Wabasha Street. By the fall of 1857, half the population had left the area. (From the photo archives of the Minnesota Historical Society)

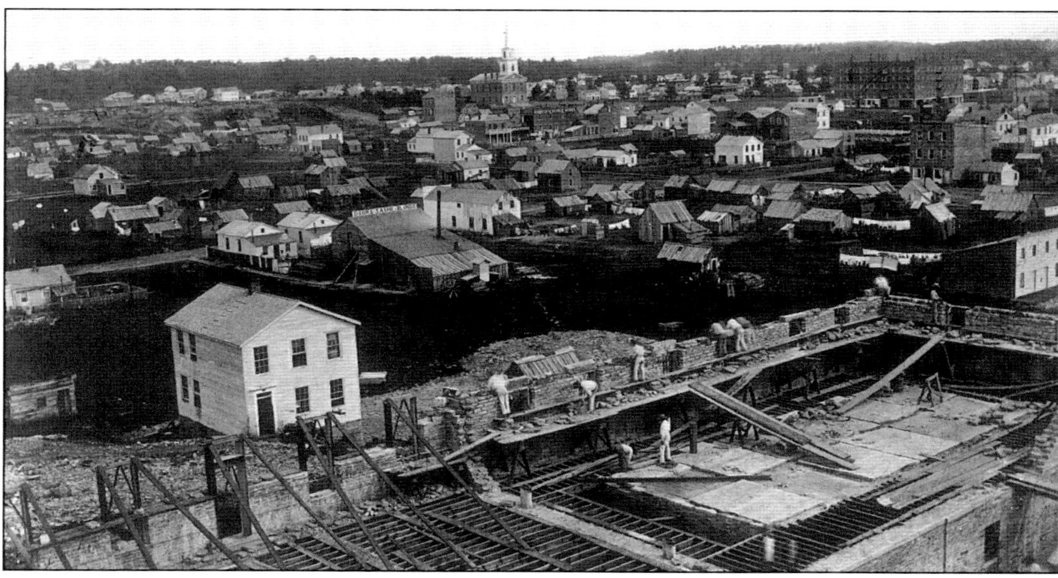

This is another panoramic shot taken by B.F. Upton in 1857. Construction stopped, and half of the population relocated due to the crash of the economy, fueled by the failure of the Ohio Life Insurance Company. (From the photo archives of the Minnesota Historical Society)

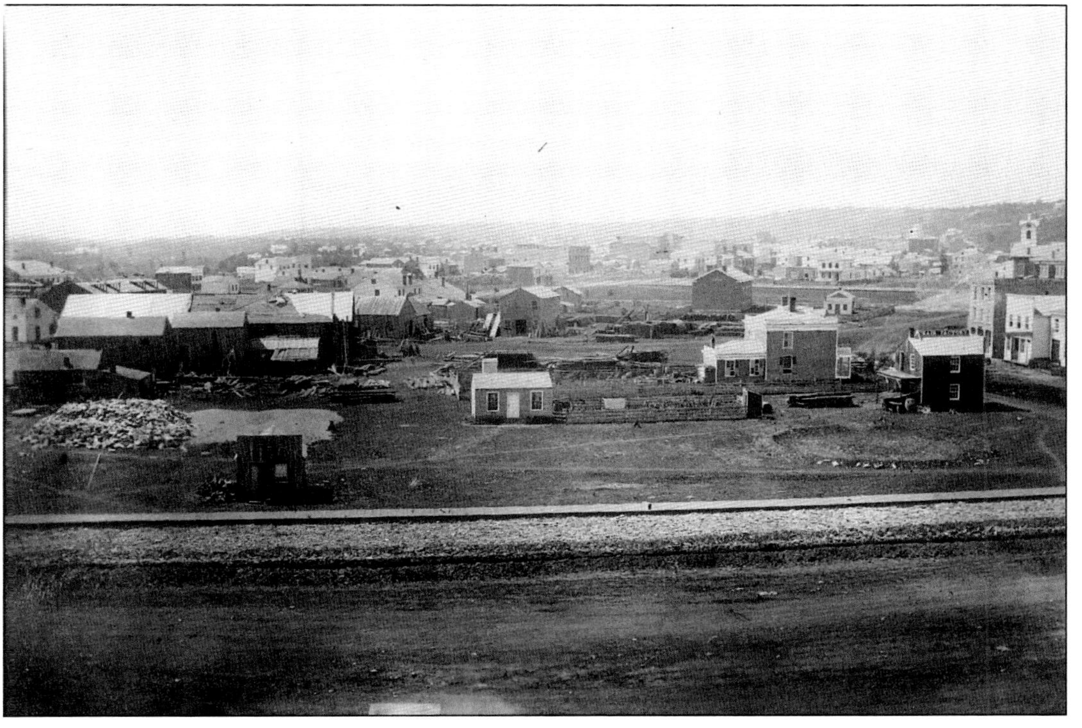

This is another one of B.F. Upton's panoramic shots taken from the roof of the old courthouse, taken in the spring of 1857. (From the photo archives of the Minnesota Historical Society)

Chapter 1
OUR ROOTS

The roots of the of the Jewish community of St. Paul were established in 1849 with the arrival of two American-born brothers from Pennsylvania, who stepped off the steamboat at the foot of what was then the "Upper Landing" at Eagle Street, just west of what is now the Municipal Grain Elevators on Shepard Road.

From these early pioneer roots, the community grew and spread, moving through Irvine Park along the Mississippi River front on Third Street (now Kellogg Boulevard), up Robert and Jackson Streets to Williams Hill (around the present State Capitol), through the Mt. Airy area, and up St. Anthony Hill (present site of the Cathedral and Kellogg Boulevard Hill) and even to the far reaches of the Dayton's Bluff Payne Avenue area on the near East Side.

After the Civil War, new settlers came with a wave of immigrants from Europe. Many who came during this period were of German descent, and these later arrivals of the Jewish faith felt a certain kinship for fellow Germans. These new German-born settlers were accepted as family by the early Jewish pioneers (1). Other descendants, not of German birth, were Jews from Poland, Russia, and Eastern Europe. They did not feel this same kinship, and developed a community of their own. They first settled on Robert Street, between 12th and 14th Streets, and the adjacent areas on Jackson and Minnesota. They later moved to the so-called West Side "flats," south of the Wabasha and Robert Street bridges and the St. Anthony Hill District(2).

This separation was by circumstance as well as by desire; the settlers of German descent used the German language exclusively in their prayers and in most of their social dialogue. Until 1878, German remained the language of prayer at Mt. Zion, and even then until

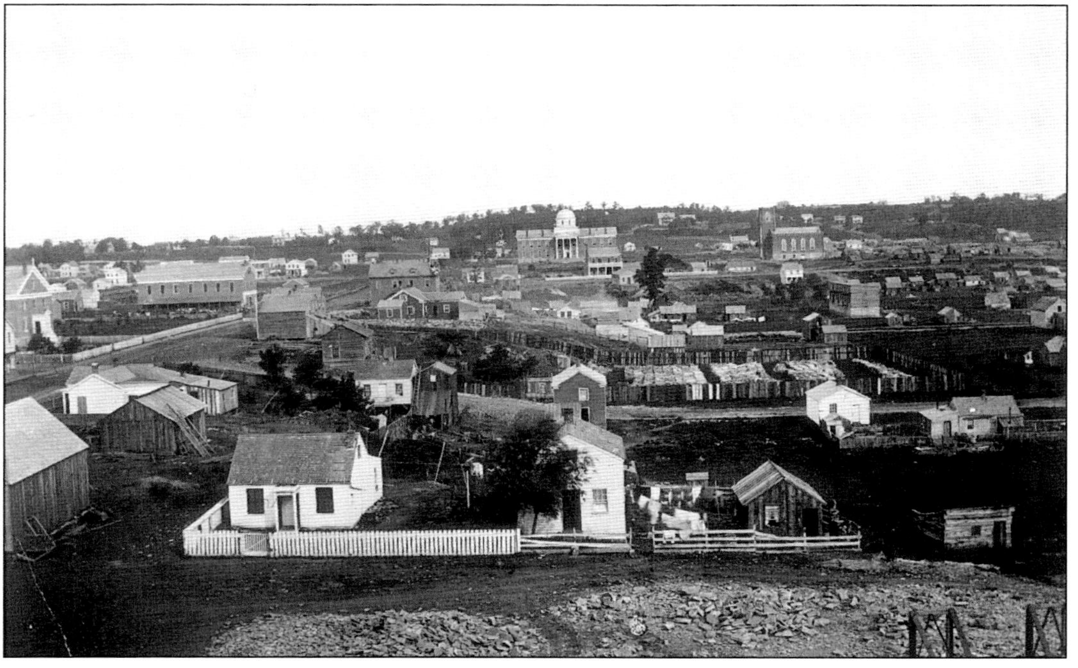

B.F. Upton's view of St. Paul in summer of 1857 shows the first State Capitol, located on a block bounded by Wabasha, Cedar, Exchange, and Tenth Streets. Many of the early pioneering Jewish families lived in proximity to this building.

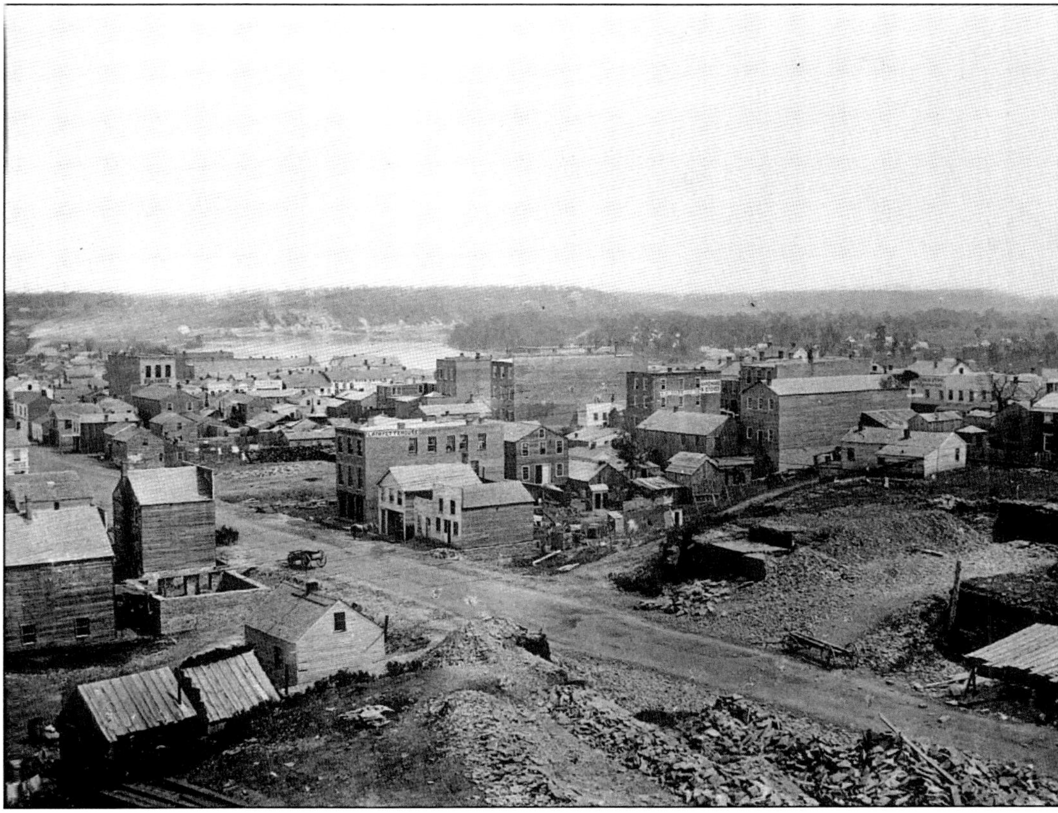

Pictured here is another of B.F. Upton's panoramic shots taken from the roof of the old courthouse in the spring of 1857. It shows the corner of Fourth Street looking down towards Robert Street, where a number of early Jewish businessmen had located. By the fall of 1857, the economy had collapsed as a result of the failure of the Ohio Life Insurance Company. Construction stopped, and half of the population left. (From the photo archives of the Minnesota Historical Society)

about the turn of the century, German and English were used alternately (3). Also, it was absolutely necessary to live within walking distance of a synagogue, as religious law only allowed walking on the Sabbath. Each of the groups that resulted from this separation thus clustered around their own place of worship. Though within blocks of each other, they were worlds apart.

In the early 1870s, several distinct Jewish communities developed, and two major synagogues. Mt. Zion, established in 1856, was established for the German Jews, whose members clustered around the first Temple at 10th and Minnesota, a simple frame wooden structure. The second was Sons of Jacob, established in 1874, which attracted the new arrivals from Eastern Europe, whose ancient prayers remained in Hebrew, and who lived, worked, and prayed in the close vicinity of Robert and 13th Streets. They met and prayed in a private home until 1876, and then established the beginnings of their first synagogue in a rented home at College and Wabasha. The development of these several communities was to decentralize the Jews of St. Paul as an ethnic, religious, and cultural group well into the 20th century.

In the wake of this movement of the early Jewish settlers through the topography of St. Paul, the Jews of St. Paul have left "ghost communities" of which no visible trace remains today. There are no remaining synagogue structures in the downtown area or around the Capitol. Even the West Side community has disappeared. By contrast, the Vienna Stadttempel, the foremost Jewish house of worship in Vienna, Austria, celebrated its 170th birthday as an intact religious building, and the Newport, Rhode Island Touro Synagogue celebrated its 235th birthday. The only reminder that there ever was a Jewish community in the Payne Avenue area on the near East Side of Dayton's Bluff is the fact that all Jewish cemeteries, except the Temple of Aaron Cemetery, are located in the Payne Avenue area. The families representing these various roots seemed endlessly restless, and this book will attempt to trace some of the families of these people of the Jewish faith who populated St. Paul. These were our roots.

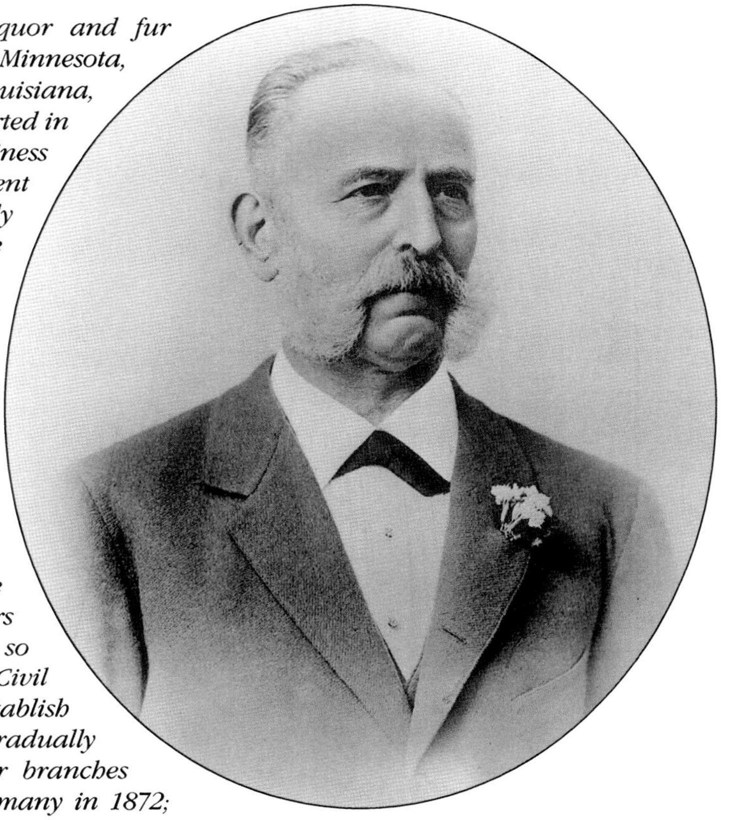

Joseph Ullmann, pioneer liquor and fur dealer, first came to St. Paul, Minnesota, in 1850 from New Orleans, Louisiana, and St. Louis Missouri. He started in the liquor and tobacco business as a commission man. Payment was often made in furs in early Minnesota, and gradually he devoted his business more and more to the collection and marketing of furs, hides, beeswax, ginseng, seneca root, mess pork, butter, wool, and tallow. By 1863, his firm was known as "Joseph Ullmann, Commission Merchant and Dealer in Hides, Wool, and Skins, Importer and Wholesale Dealer in Wines Liquors, Cigars and Cheeses." The firm grew so fast that in 1866, after the Civil War, he went to Chicago to establish a new headquarters. It gradually expanded abroad and other branches were created in Leipzig, Germany in 1872; London, England in 1882; and Paris, France in 1896. The firm's headquarters moved from Chicago to New York City. He was connected with Jewish religious life from the very beginning, when he joined the "Ahabath Achim," the splinter group from Mt. Zion, and became its treasurer. Later, the two splinter groups merged into Mt. Zion, and he remained a loyal supporter, even after he had removed to Germany. He lost one child, who is buried in Mt. Zion cemetery, but he had at least three other sons, Samuel, Charles, and Joseph Ullmann, Jr. He died in Germany in 1906. (From the photo archives of the Minnesota Historical Society)

Chapter 2
THE PIONEERS

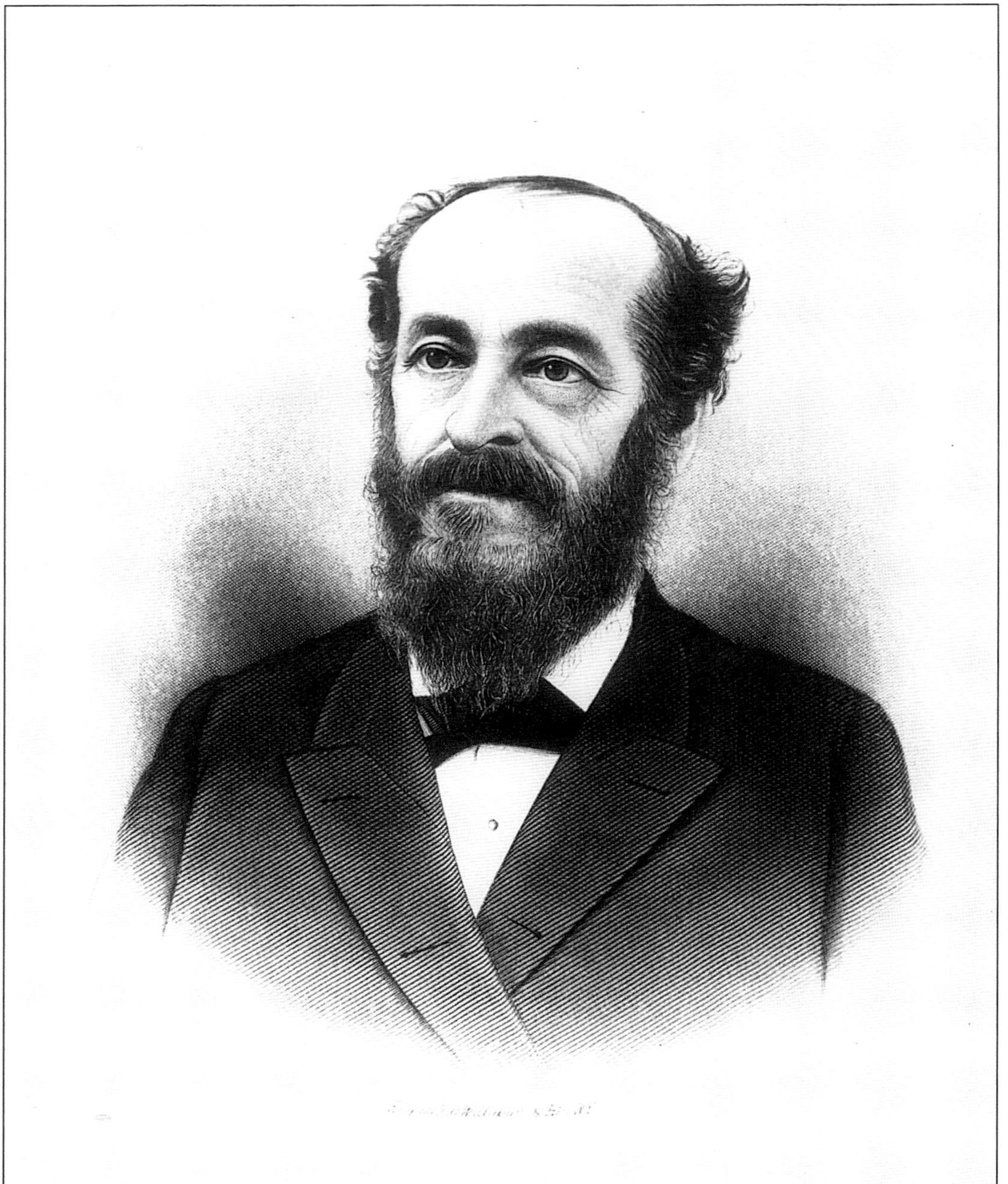

Abram Elfelt. (From the photo archives of American Jewish World, September and October, 1979)

The Elfelts were relatively wealthy merchants from Philadelphia. Simon Elfelt, the patriarch, and his parents had been settlers in San Domingo, but when the Negro Republic had been established there in 1801, they moved to Pennsylvania (4). One of Simon's daughters married into the Bloomingdale family, whose large department stores in Philadelphia and New York still flourish today. Simon appears to have died in 1835, leaving his widow, seven sons, and one daughter(5).

Edwin Elfelt, 12; Abram, 8; and Charles, 7; hadn't even heard of the Minnesota territory in their school geography lessons. In 1849, the Territory of Minnesota was created from the Louisiana Purchase, and the West beckoned. With capital from their family, Edwin and Charles Elfelt were the first Jews to establish permanent residence in St. Paul (6). The Elfelts settled in St. Paul even before it was incorporated, but today their images have all but disappeared. Few traces of the Elfelt family remain; a street named Elfelt on the east side of St. Paul, and several real estate subdivisions carrying the family name are all that are visible today.

Abram Elfelt came to St. Paul in 1850 to join his two brothers and became the dominant member of the family. He originated the first board of trade in 1864, and was an active member of the Minnesota

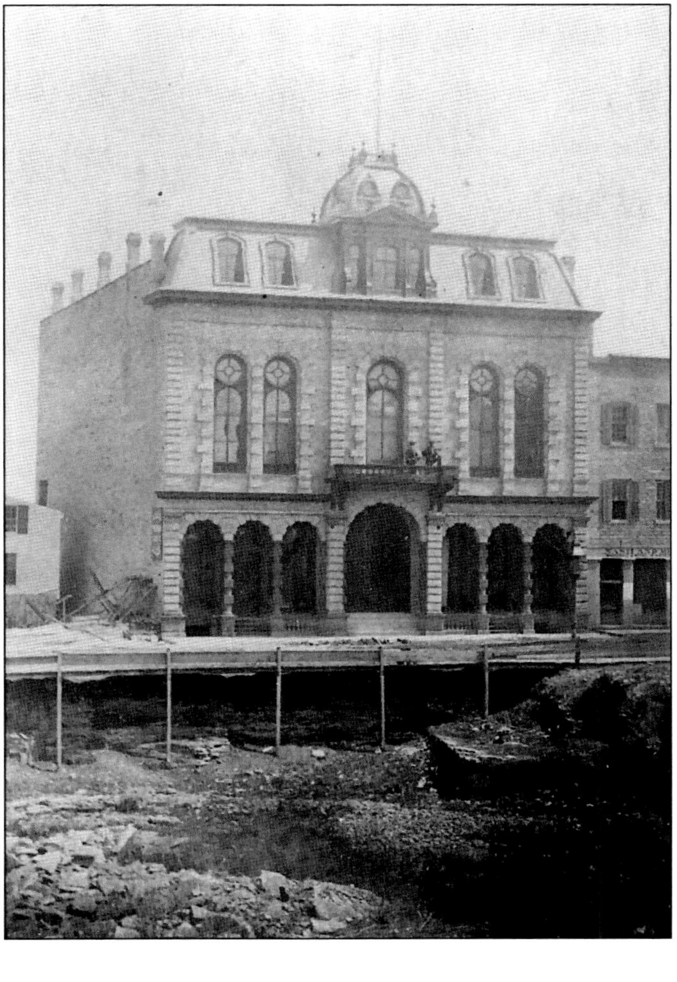

Pictured is St. Paul's first Grand Opera House, which succeeded the Mazourka Hall located above Elfelt's store building. Constructed in 1867, it was located on Wabasha between Third and Fourth streets. Photo by R.W. Ransom. (From the photo archives of the Minnesota Historical Society)

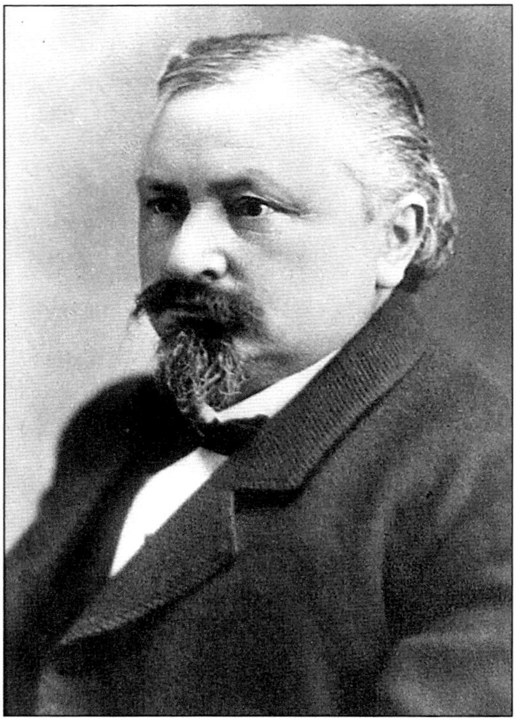

Isadore Rose. (From the photo archives of American Jewish World, September and October, 1979)

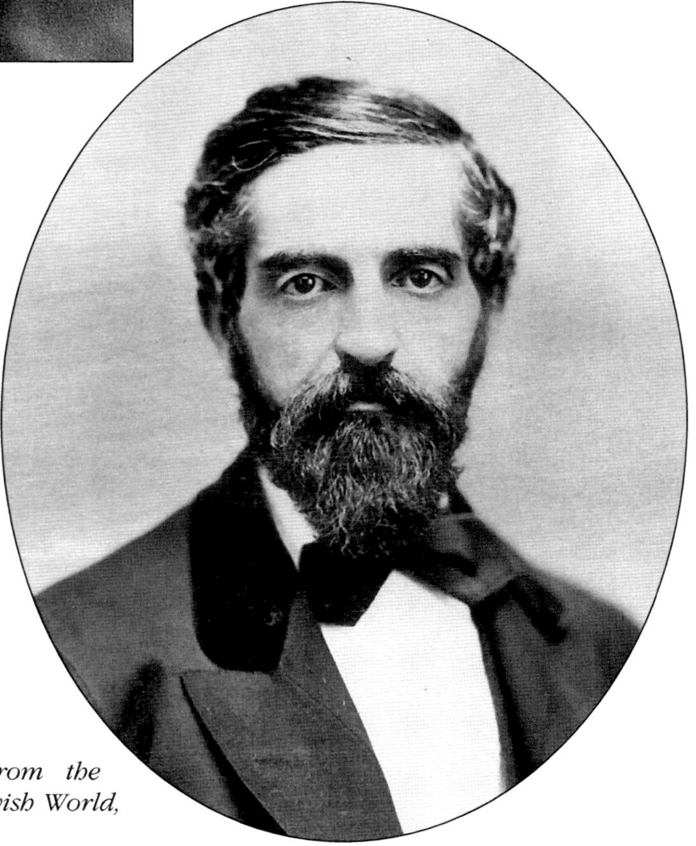

Judge Isaac N. Cardozo. (From the photo archives of American Jewish World, September and October, 1979)

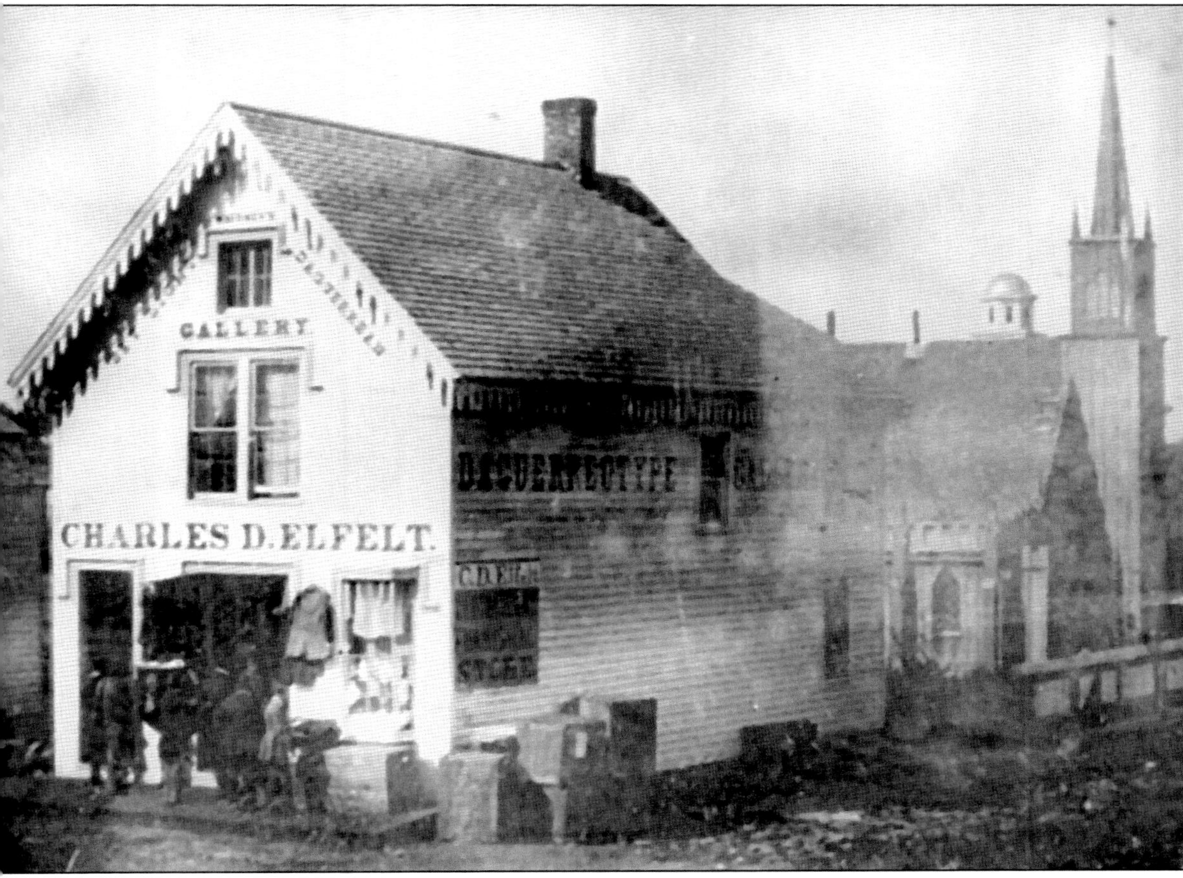

One of Elfelt's clothing stores at Third and Cedar Streets, as shown in 1855. Photographer Joel Whitney had his Joel Whitney's Daguerrean Gallery above Elfelt's store when he took this picture. In the background is the Christ Episcopal church. (From the photo archives of American Jewish World, September and October, 1979)

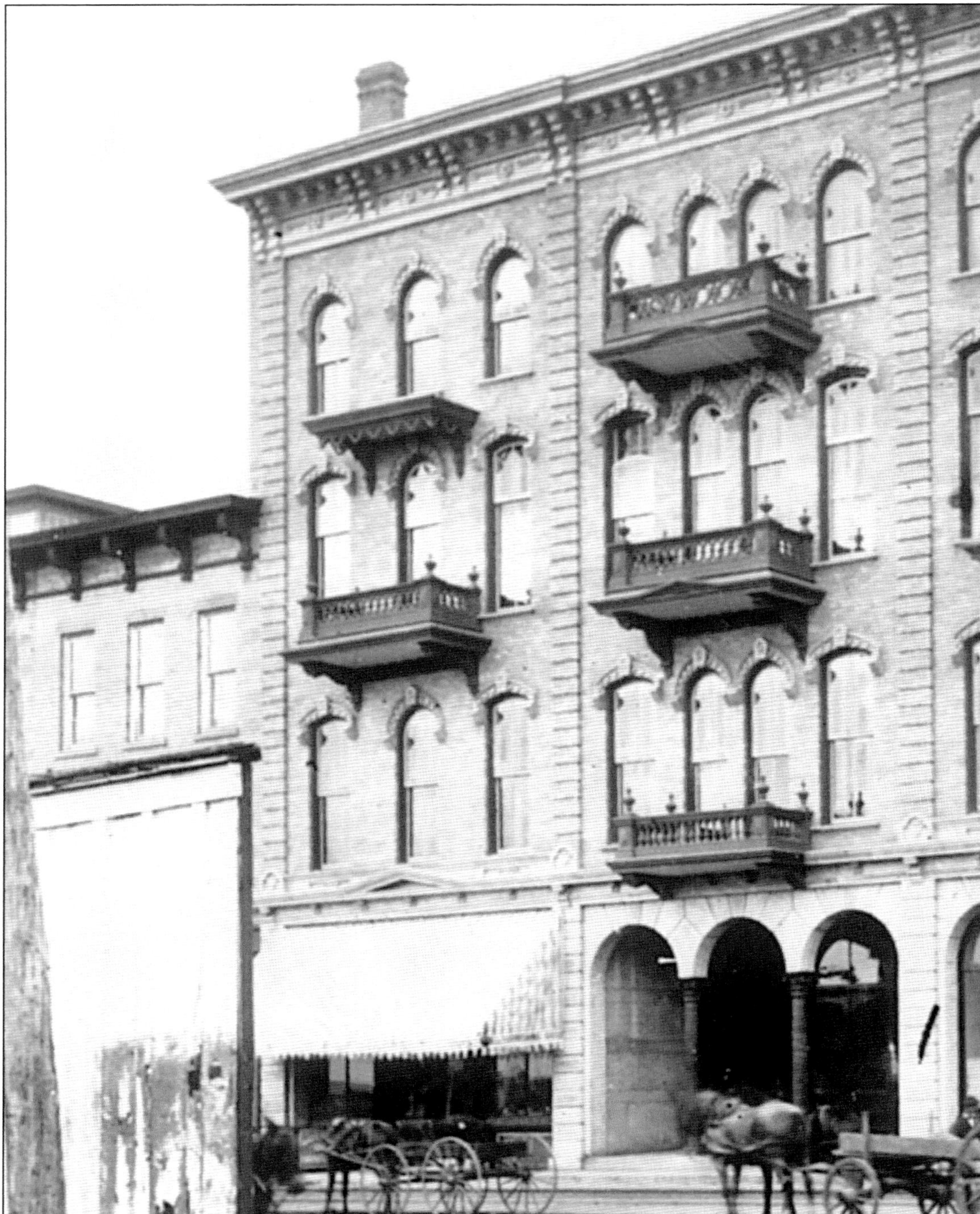

Charles D. Elfelt lived in the Metropolitan Hotel at Third Street (now Kellogg Boulevard) and Washington Street, opposite Rice Park, most of his life and died there in 1903. Photo by William

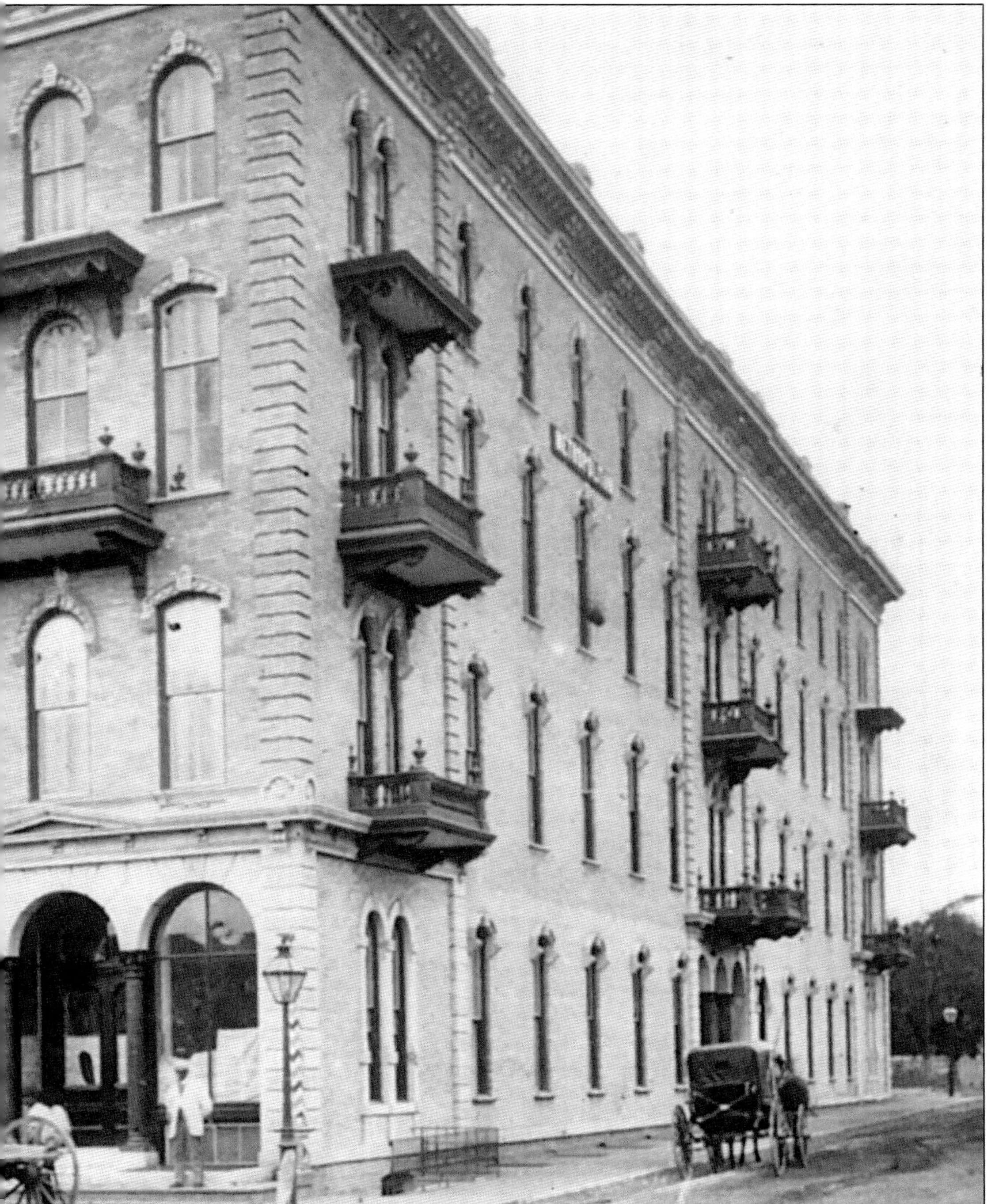

H. Illingworth. (From the photo archives of the Minnesota Historical Society)

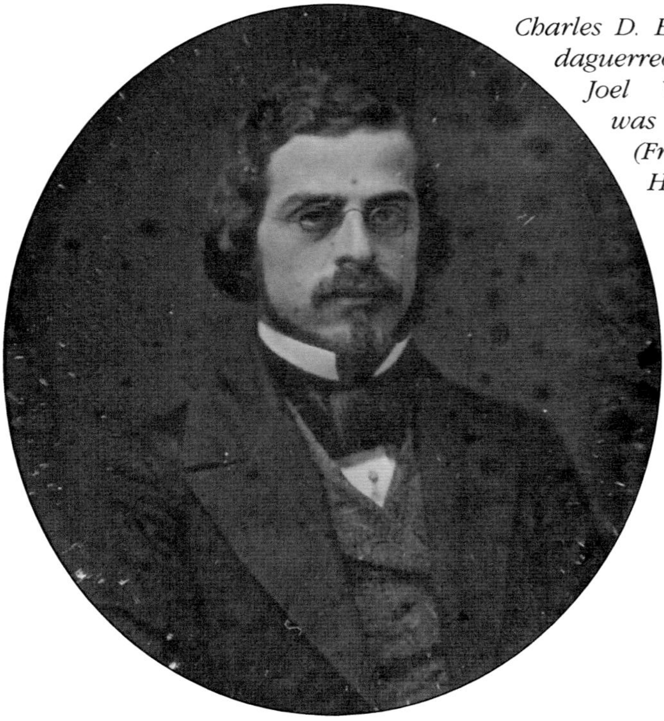

Charles D. Elfelt is seen here in 1850,in this daguerreotype by Joel Whitney, whose Joel Whitney's Daguerrean Gallery was above Charles Elfelt's store. (From photo archives of Minnesota Historical Society)

In 1852, pioneer artist Robert 0. Sweeny stood on old St. Anthony Street (now Kellogg Boulevard) and did an ink and pencil sketch of what he saw. On the Northwest corner of old St. Anthony Street (now Kellogg Boulevard) and Washington Street, he saw the American House, a three-story brick hotel built in 1849, one of the first hotels in St. Paul. Shortly after it was constructed, the Minnesota State Democratic party held its first convention there. In 1851, the Minnesota Legislature held its session here, prior to the construction of the first Minnesota Capitol building. Pioneer liquor and fur dealer Joseph Ulmann and his wife spent their first years living in the American House. On the opposite corner stood Mazourka Hall, above one of Elfelt's stores. Next door was the Jam Saloon. (From the photo archives of the Minnesota Historical Society)

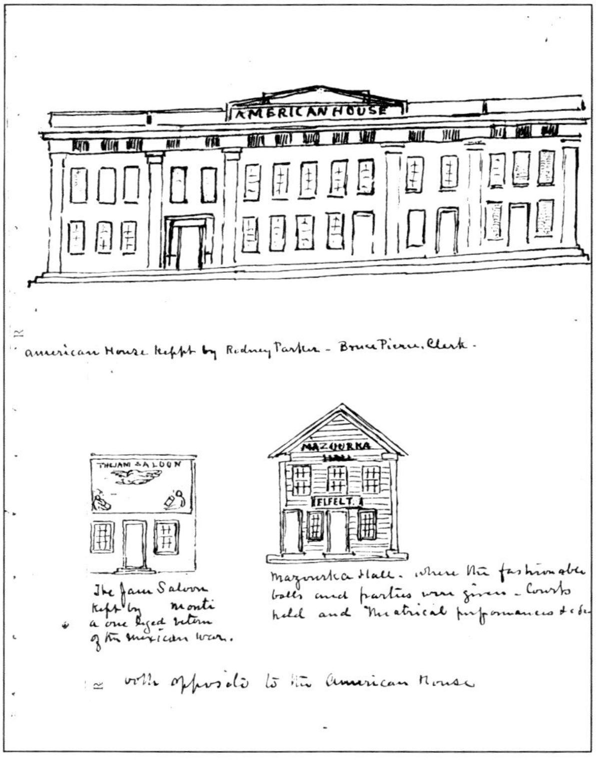

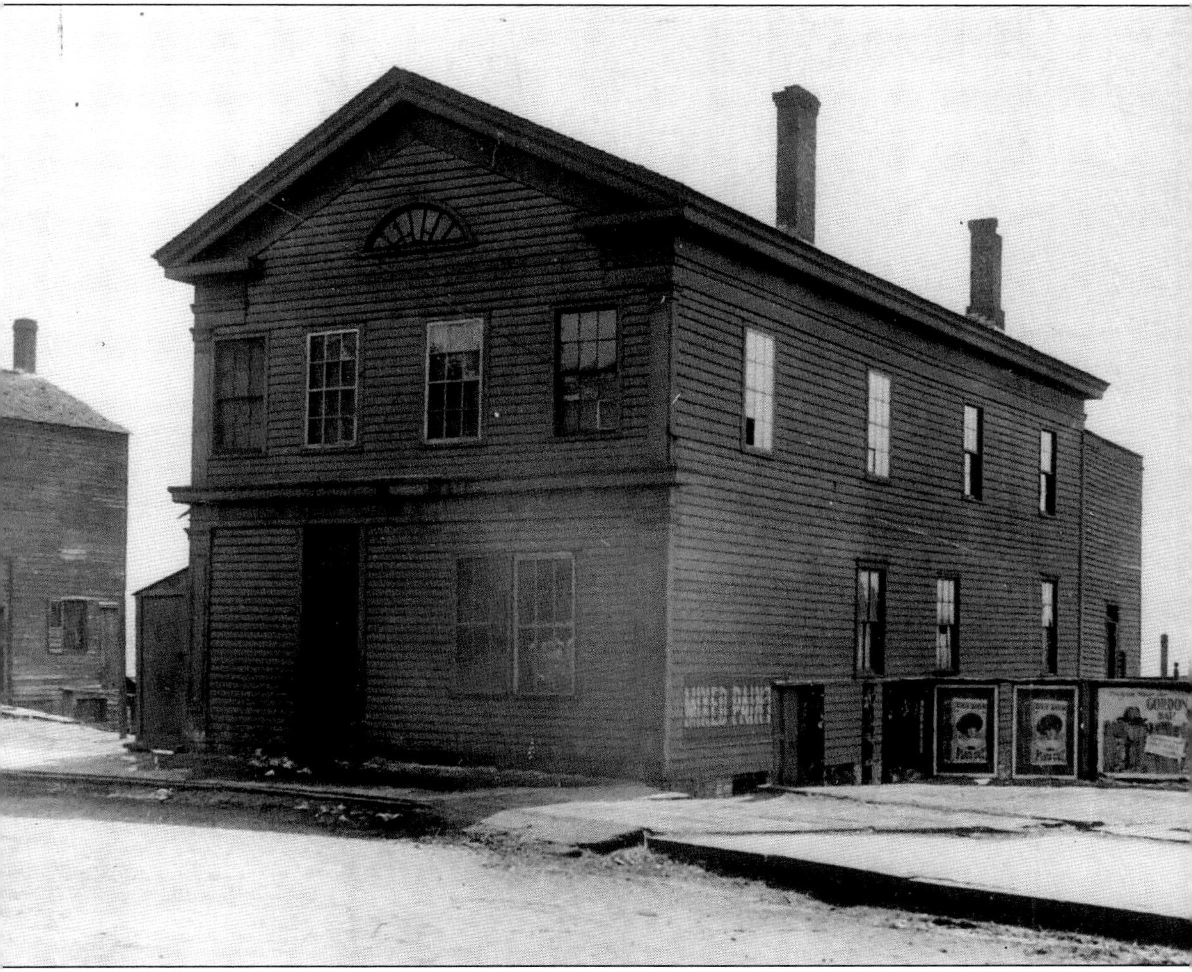

Another one of Elfelt's clothing stores was located at Third and Exchange Streets, as shown in 1852. Mazourka Hall was on the second floor. (From the photo archives of the Ramsey County Historical Society)

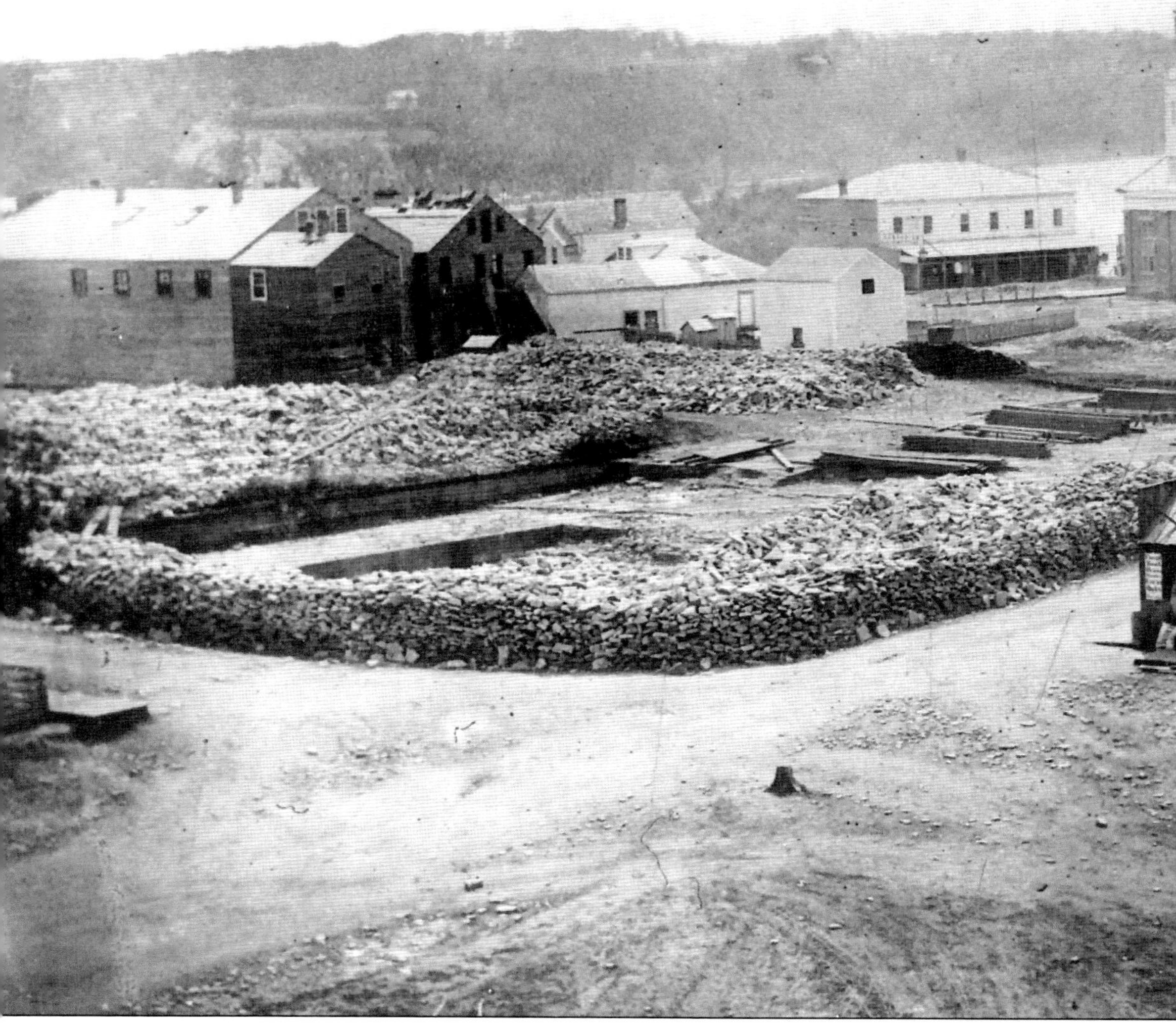

Another photographer, E. A. Bromley, climbed up to the steeple on the first Ramsey County Courthouse in 1857 to shoot this photo. Looking up the river, it shows the Presbyterian Church near which Aron Aaronheimer had his clothing store. In 1857, there was a building boom, and at least 32 Jewish families had settled in the small river town. In the fall of 1857, the

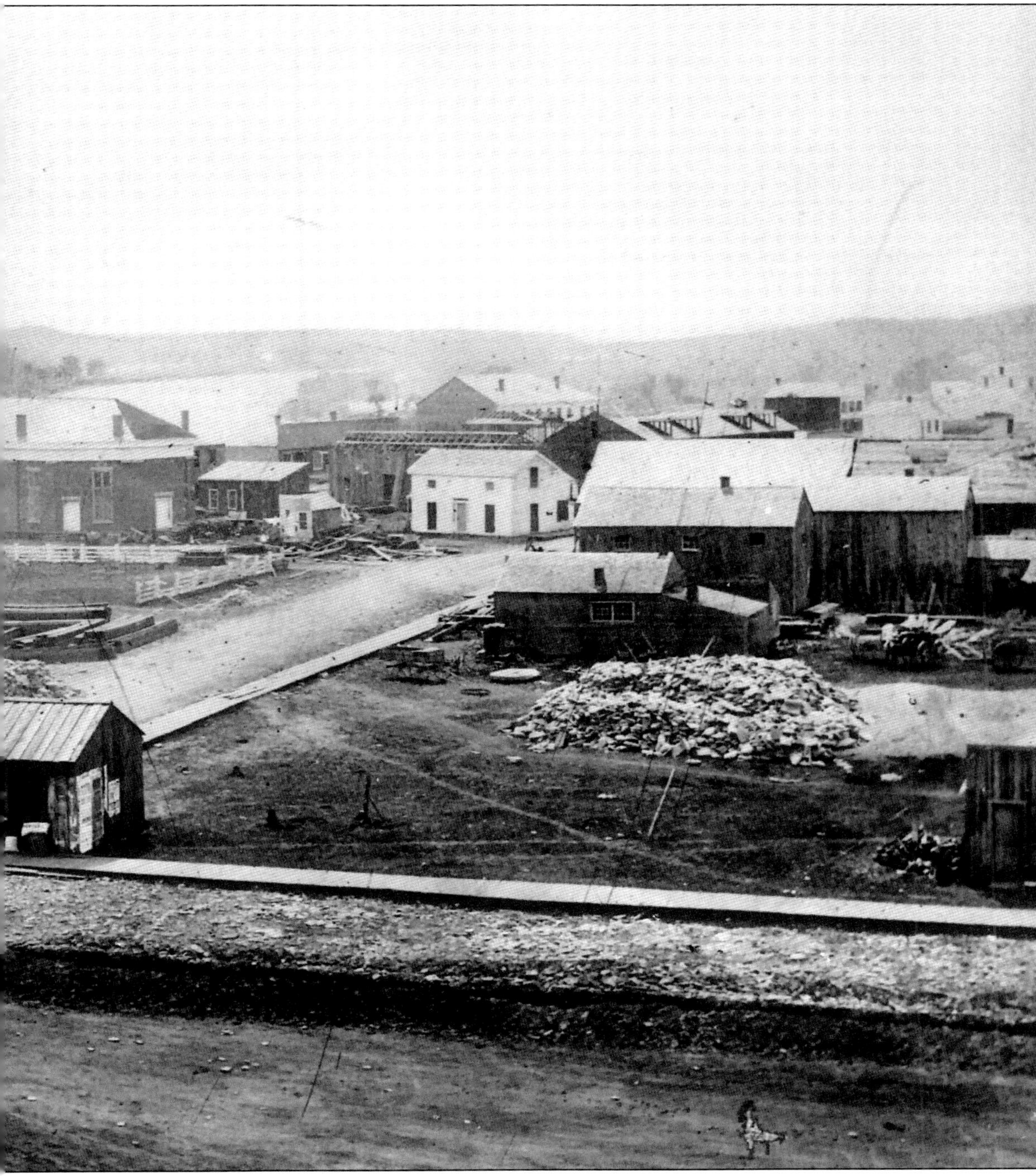

economy collapsed after the Ohio Life Insurance Company failed. The value of lots were worthless, all new construction ceased, and half of the estimated 10,000 residents of St. Paul, including the small Jewish community, left the city. (From the photo archives of the Minnesota Historical Society)

Historical Society. He was also involved in the completion of the Northern Pacific Railway (7). He was particularly active in real estate, and platted the area just west of what is the State Capitol, bounded by University Avenue on the north, St. Anthony (Interstate Freeway No. 94) on the south, Galtier on the east, and Western Avenue on the west (8). Many of the early Jewish settlers eventually moved into this area.

The Elfelts established a store at the foot of Eagle Street near the Upper-Levee (Upper Landing), and were among the earliest to specialize in dry goods. This signified a change from the early general store of the frontier village to the urban diversification of trade (9). In 1851, the Elfelts erected what became the largest building in the city; the upper portion comprising what became known as Mazourka Hall, or St. Paul's first unofficial auditorium. In that hall, the first theatrical representations and entertainment were given (10). The building was located at Third Street (now Kellogg Boulevard) and Exchange, near the present Public Library. Abram Elfelt later made the first contributions towards property purchased by the Minnesota Historical Society (11).

In 1874, there were six Elfelts in business in St. Paul, but by 1886, practically all had disappeared from the scene (12). Abram died in his 3-story, 15-room home at 32 Irvine Park in 1883 (13). His brother, Charles, who apparently never married, lived until 1903, leaving considerable real estate in Washington County, Minnesota. "One leather trunk, one watch, one watch chain, one pair of silk sleeve buttons, and one scarf" were left in his apartment in the old Metropolitan Hotel, which was opposite Rice Park and the present "old" Federal Court Building (14). Edwin Elfelt, the eldest of the Elfelt brothers, apparently moved to San Francisco, California, where he died (15).

There were others, like Henry Cali (or Cole) and his wife, Fannie. Cali was the first president of the Mt. Zion synagogue. In 1856, he was 36 years of age. Both he and his wife were born in Prussia, and had lived in New York and Illinois. He had a clothing store, but when the 1857 Depression hit, he packed up and left (15a).

Isaac Ansel and his son also owned a clothing store. On March 16, 1860, most of the buildings on Third Street (now Kellogg Boulevard) from Robert Street to Jackson Street in St. Paul were destroyed by fire. According to J. Fletcher Williams, at that time Secretary of the Minnesota Historical Society, in his classic *A History of St. Paul to 1875*, he wrote that "… the fire started in the clothing store of a well known character named Isaac Ansell" (15b).

Joseph Ullmann and his wife Amelia were in the liquor business. He was also an early affiliate and benefactor of Mt. Zion Synagogue, the first Jewish place of worship in the city of St. Paul and the state of Minnesota. He retired back to Germany, but was a financial backer of Mt. Zion until he died. He had started in the liquor business, but later went into the fur business with Isadore Rose, a boarder in his home (15c). His wife, Amelia, kept a diary that is now with the Minnesota Historical Society's documents collection (15d). L. Phillips had served as recorder for Mt. Zion. S. Adler, Solomon Becker, S.E. Beckert, S. Ettlinger, M.L. Saloman, W. Schreiber, S. Josephs, M. Rice, and S. Jacoby are just a few more early settlers. In the spring of 1857, there were at least 32 pioneer Jewish families in St. Paul. In the summer of 1857,the Ohio Life Insurance and Trust Company collapsed and precipitated a national depression. Many of the families left shortly thereafter for parts unknown.

Among the early pioneers were also early religious functionaries with the Mt. Zion synagogue. Between 1871, when Mt. Zion was formally organized, and 1878, Leopold Winterer, J. Burgheim, Isaac N. Cohen, and Judah Wechsler all served as rabbis. In minor religious roles were E. Marcuson, teacher and cantor, H. Cahn, A. Applebaum, and A. Braun, who served as *schocets*, (butchers who supervised the slaying of kosher meat and poultry) (15e).

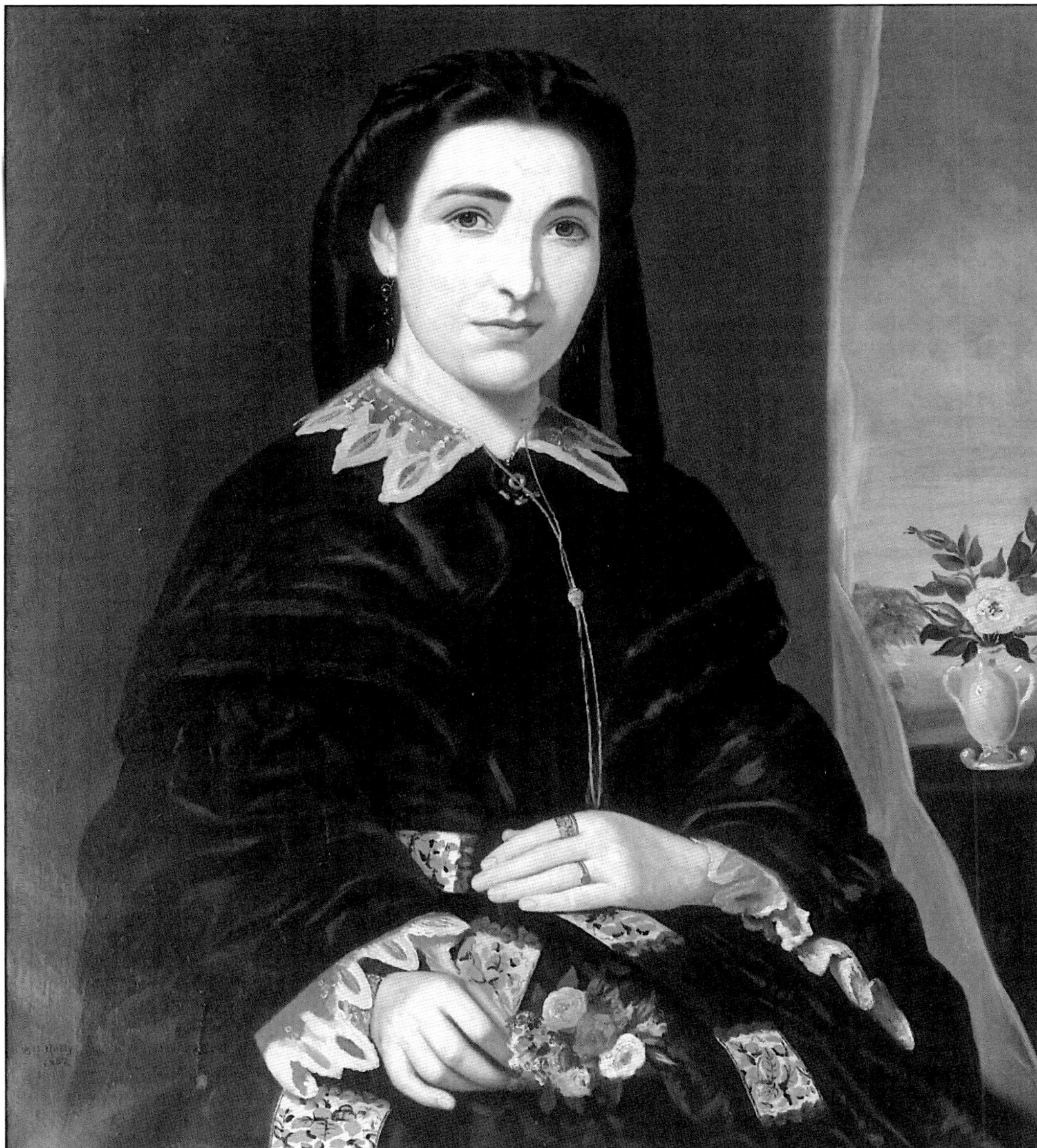

Mrs. Joseph Ullmann, as shown in a portrait by famous pioneer painter Thomas Cantwell Healy, done in 1857. She kept a diary, written solely in German, detailing pioneer life in early St. Paul, Minnesota. It did not detail Jewish life, but rather dealt with the problems of everyday living, including clothing, food, and so on. After she and her husband, Joseph Ullmann, returned to Germany, they remained as loyal followers of the Mt. Zion congregation, and in 1887, she and her husband sent a Torah (the Holy Scriptures) from Leipzig, Germany as a gift to the Mt. Zion congregation. Her diary is part of the Minnesota Historical Society's collections, and has been translated into English. (From the photo archives of the Minnesota Historical Society)

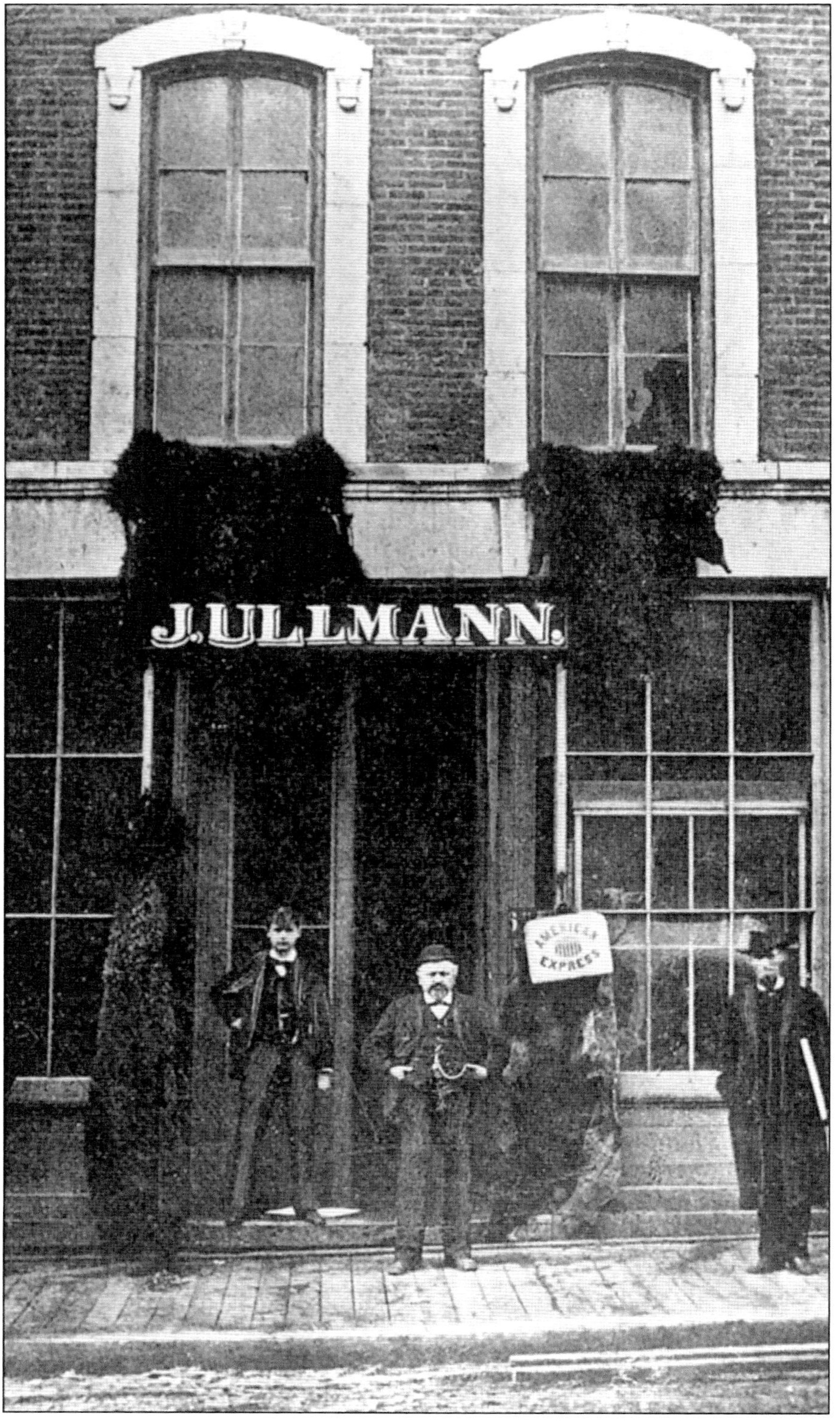

When Mr. and Mrs. Joseph Ullmann retired back to Germany, Isadore Rose took over the operation of the Ullmann fur business. This photo shows Mr. Rose (second from right) in front of the Ullmann store on Jackson Street, right down the block from the Bergman fur operation. (From the photo archives of the Minnesota Historical Society)

Mysteries remain about some of the other pioneer families; like whatever happened to the Arneheimer (or Aaronheimer) family who had a store on old St. Anthony Street; or the Ferdinand Beckers, who were some of the founders of the Ahabith Achim Synagogue, which eventually merged into Mt. Zion congregation? Or Morris Appel, who had a clothing store on Robert Street between Sixth and Seventh, and was an active Mason(16)? All were the earliest of pioneer residents of St. Paul. What happened to them? Where did they go?

Gundelfinger, Hurshler, Hirsberg, Koritowsky, Lowitz, and Schuster, all pioneer Jewish families, appeared briefly on the scene, helped organize Minnesota's first Jewish congregation, which eventually became the Mt. Zion synagogue, and then disappeared. Rabbi Gunther Plaut, former Rabbi of Mt. Zion, in his *The Jews of Minnesota*, speculates that the depression of 1857 was a factor contributing to the fact that many of the early pioneer Jewish families, as well as non-Jewish families, moved to greener pastures (17).

Some pioneer families established roots in St. Paul that remain today. One of the first were the descendants of the brothers Isadore and Emmanuel Rose, and their cousin Benjamin Rose.

Isadore and Emmanuel Rose were born in Speyer, Germany, as sons of Albert H. Rose.

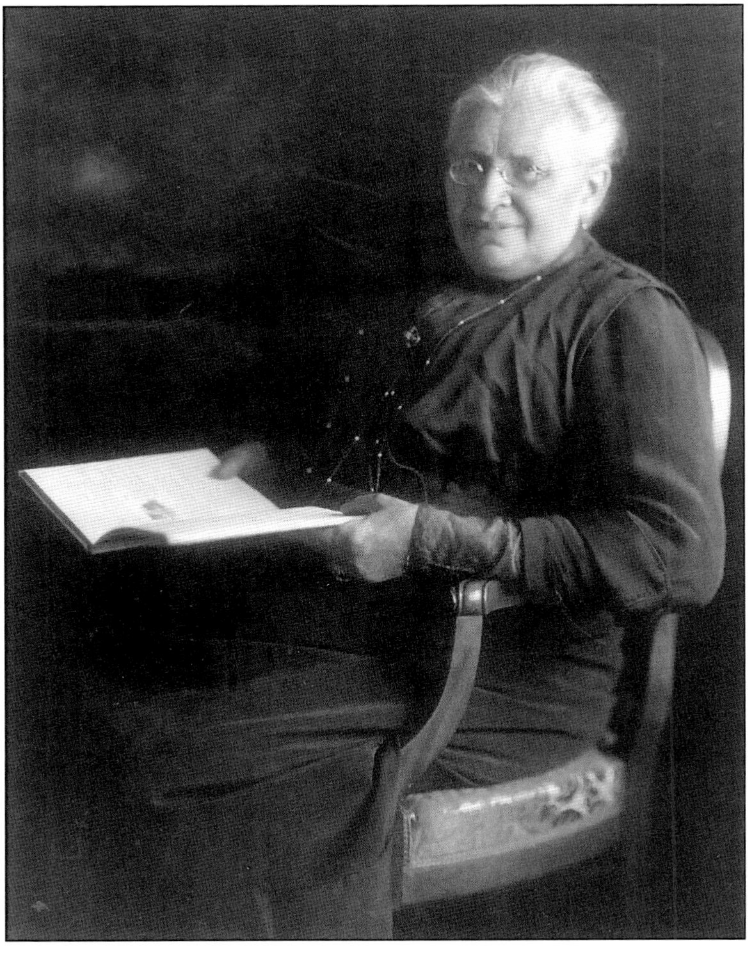

This photo of Mrs. Isadore Rose was taken by Golling. (From the photo archives of the Minnesota Historical Society)

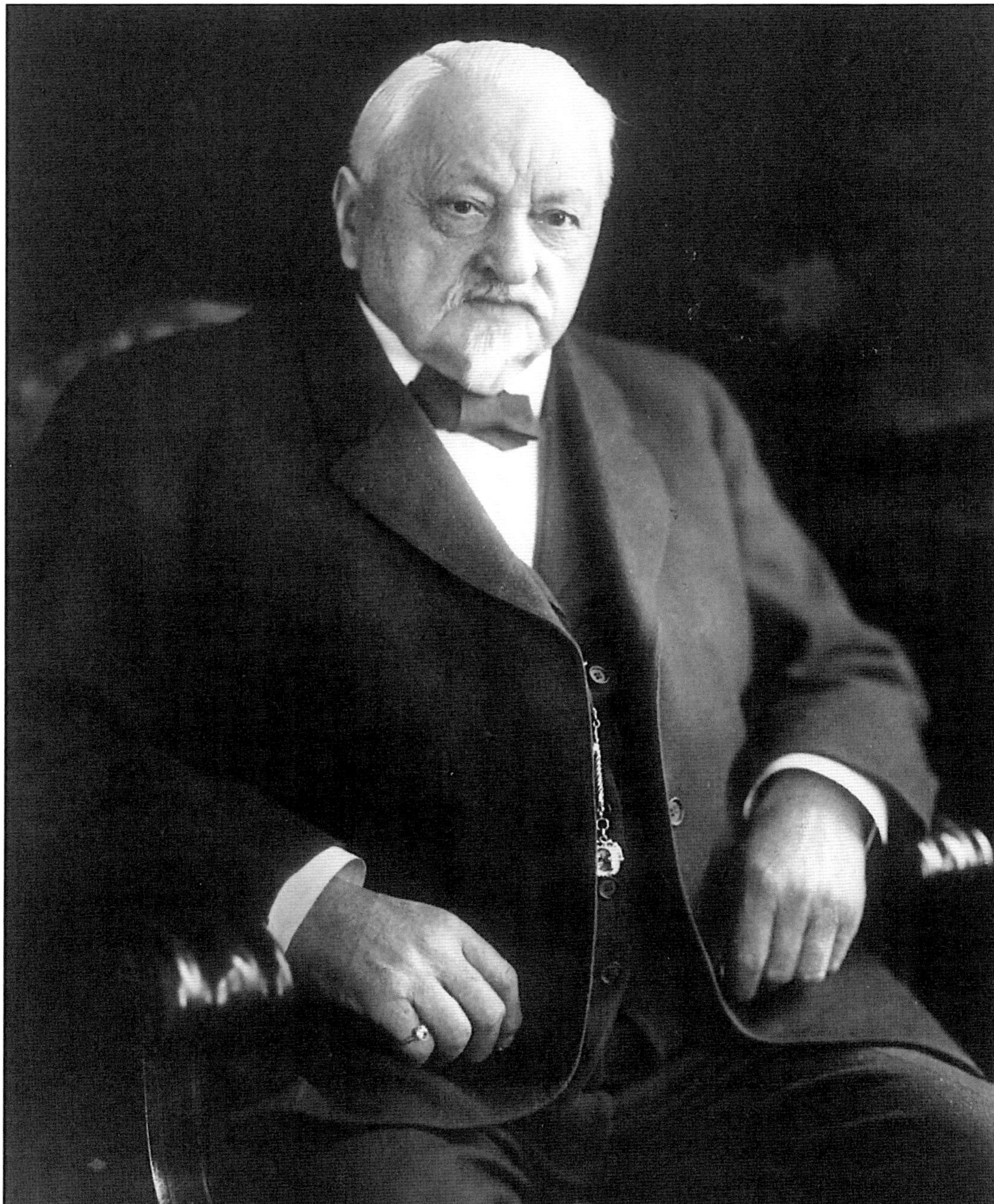

This photo of Isadore Rose was also taken by Golling. (From the photo archives of the Minnesota Historical Society)

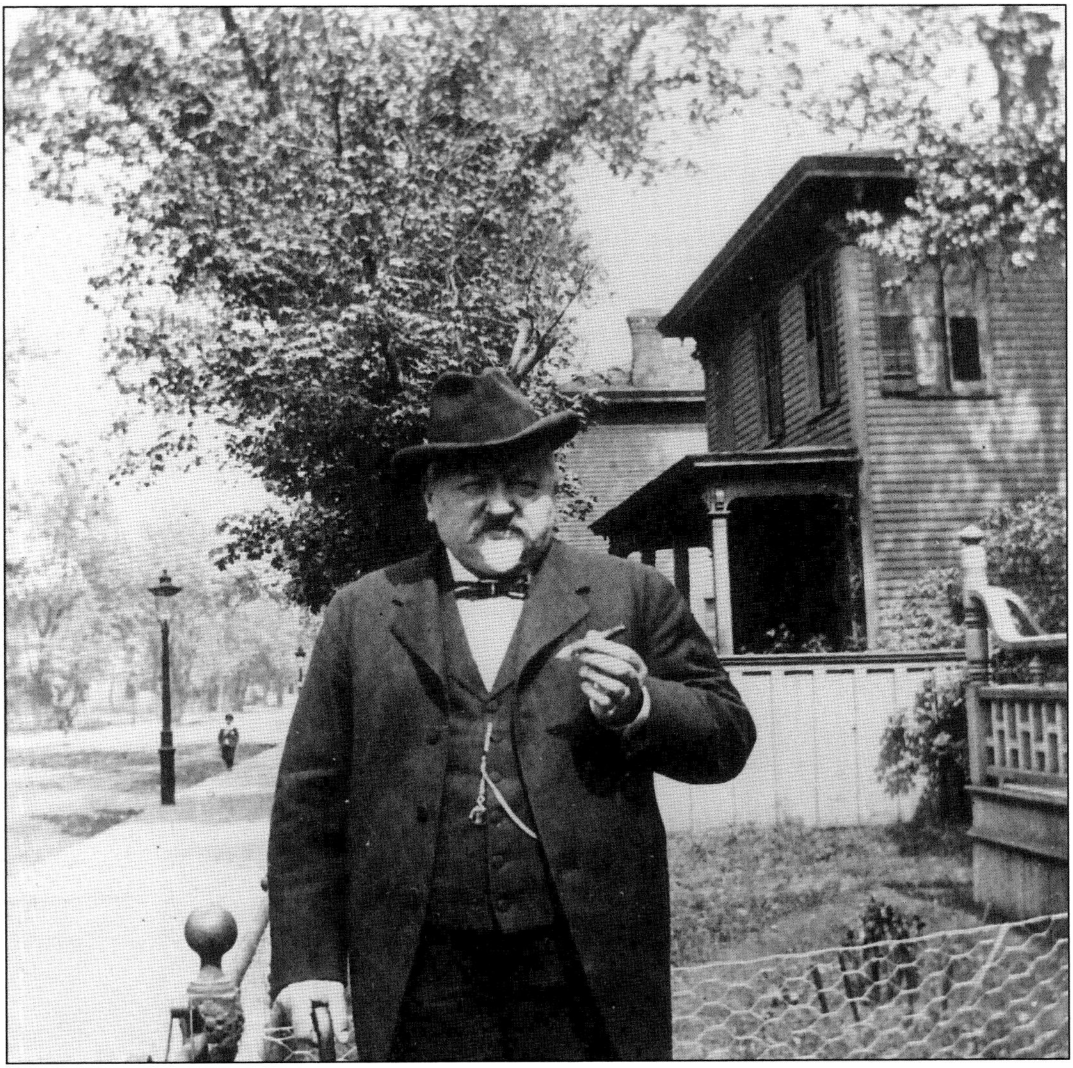

Isadore Rose is shown in front of his home on Sibley and Ninth Streets. Many of the early wealthy families lived in the same area of "Lowertown," including James J. Hill. Shortly after this picture was taken, the railroads bought all of the Lowertown neighborhood, and Mr. Rose relocated to Summit Avenue. (From the photo archives of the Minnesota Historical Society)

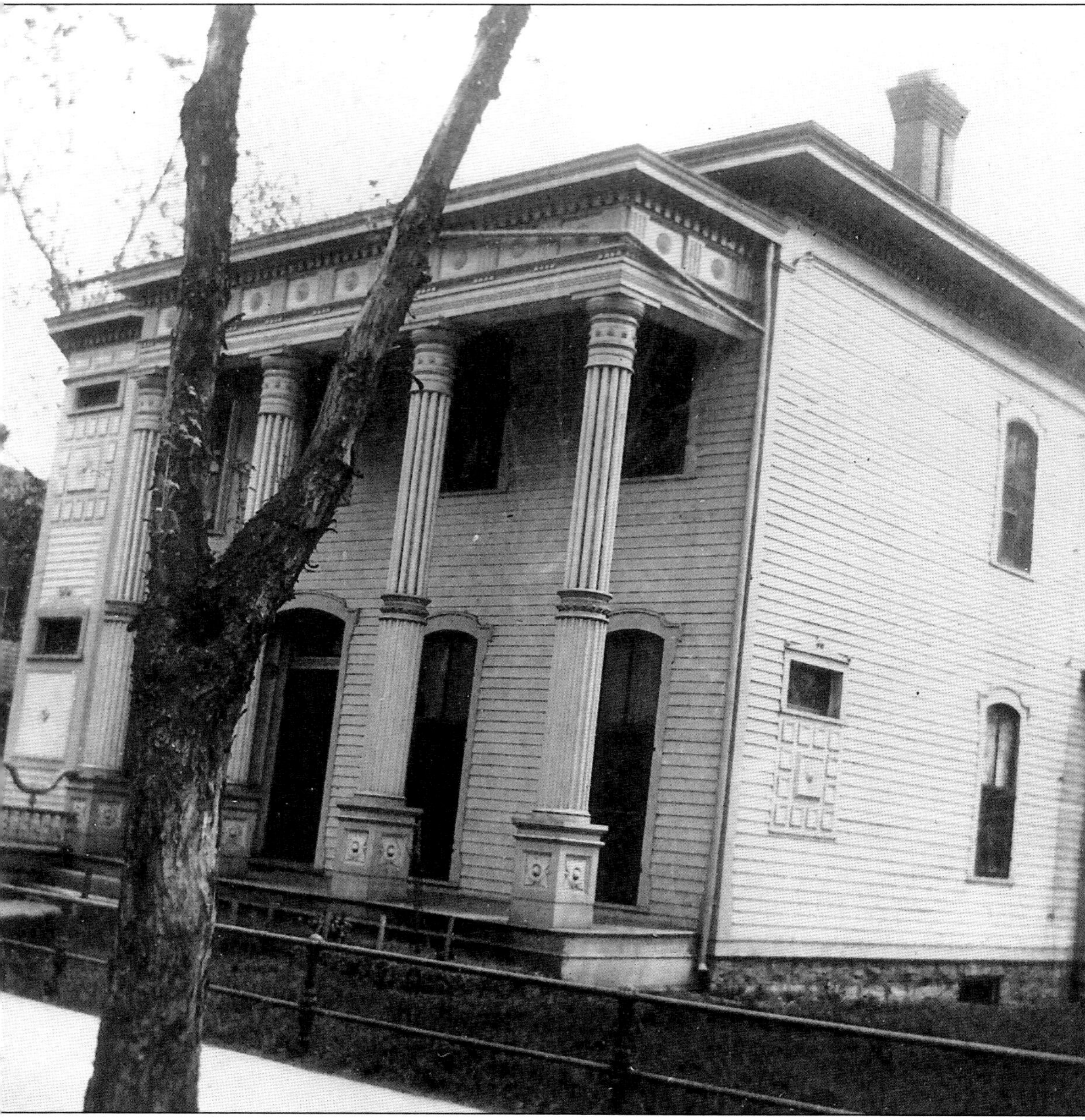

Isadore Rose and his family lived in this house at 220 East Ninth (at Sibley Street) in the "Lowertown" area for many years until the railroads came along and bought all of the homes and tore them down for railroad purposes. (From the photo archives of the Minnesota Historical Society)

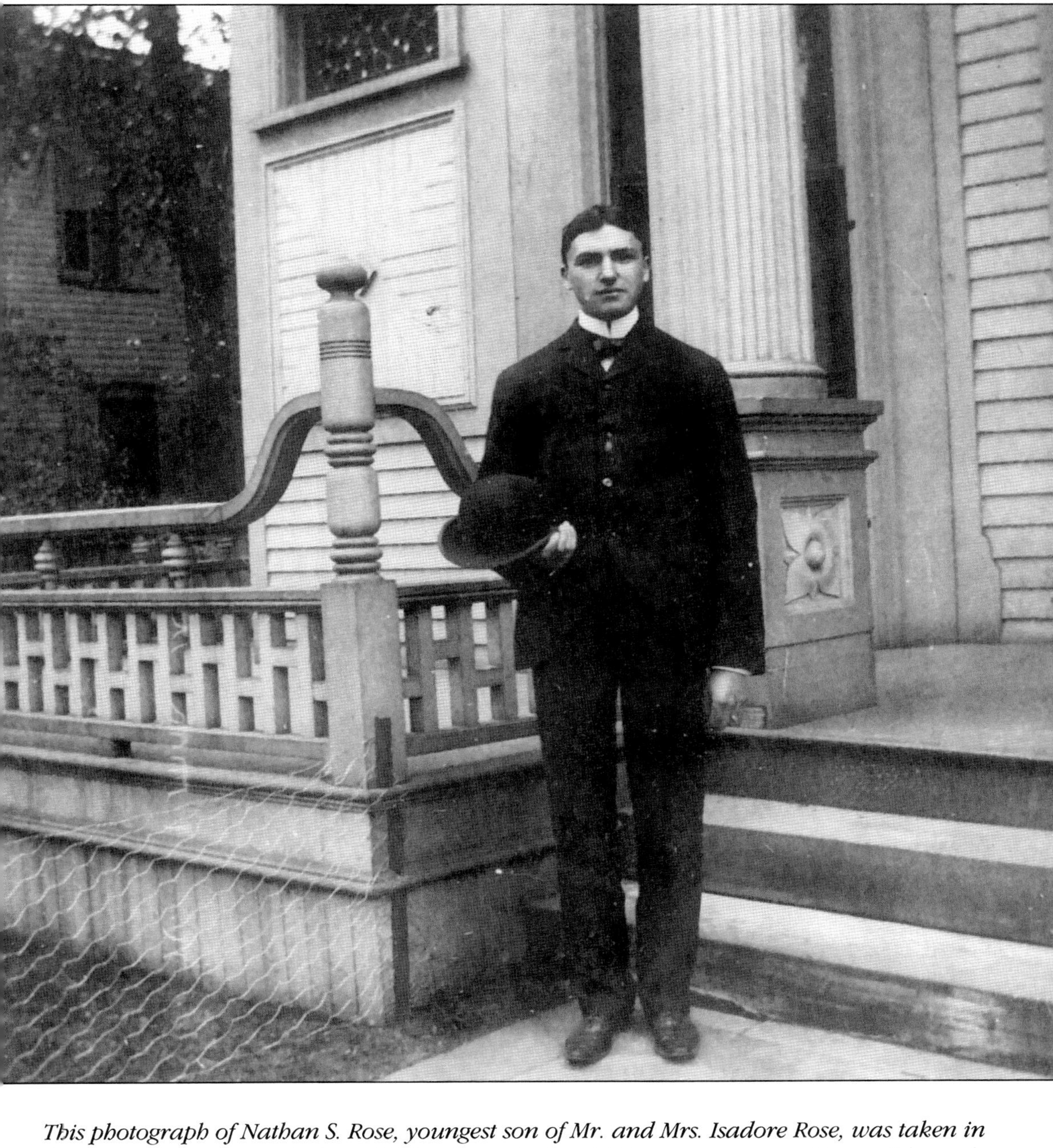

This photograph of Nathan S. Rose, youngest son of Mr. and Mrs. Isadore Rose, was taken in front of their home on Ninth and Sibley Streets in the old "Lowertown" area. Many of the early Jewish families of means lived in the "Lowertown" area, alongside their wealthiest neighbor, James J. Hill. The railroads came in and bought up most of the neighborhood for railroad purposes, and all of these handsome homes were torn down. (From the photo archives of the Minnesota Historical Society)

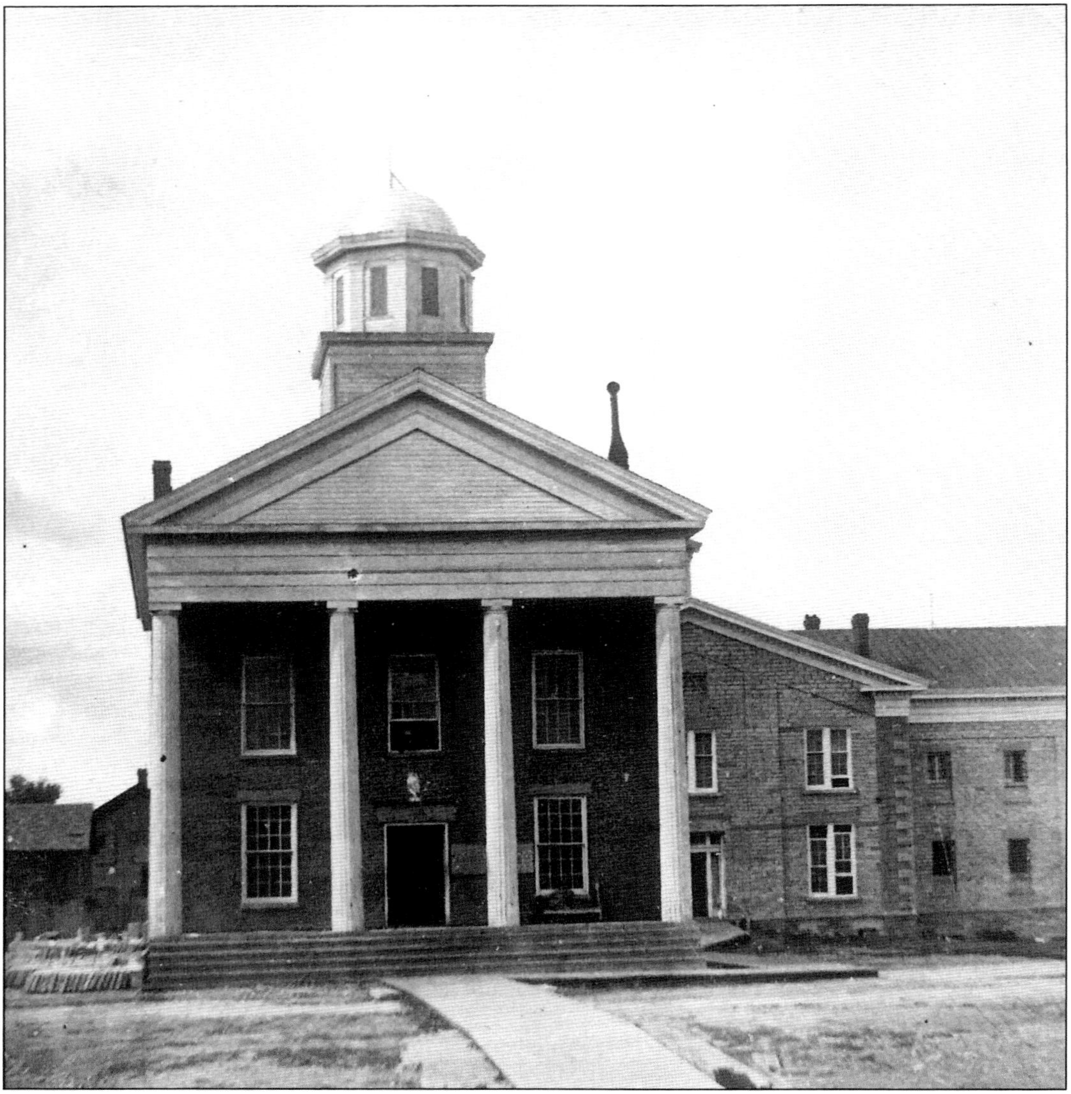

Seen here is the first Ramsey County Courthouse at Fourth Street and Wabasha Street. Constructed in the 1850s, it was designed by Dr. David Day, an amateur architect, who received the handsome sum of $10 for his design. It was small, provincial, and very cheaply built. The photo was taken by McLeish and Pasel in 1873. At the time it was constructed, Ramsey County was much larger than it is today. In the spring and summer of 1857, B.F. Upton, a pioneer photographer, climbed onto the cupola of the building and took a series of photos showing a panoramic view of the city. Later, E.A. Bromley also climbed onto the roof and took pictures. Joseph Ullmann, pioneer Jewish liquor and fur dealer, spent a great deal of time visiting the courthouse, as he was involved in frequent litigation dealing with his businesses. Note the plywood sidewalk to the entrance. (From photo archives of the Minnesota Historical Society)

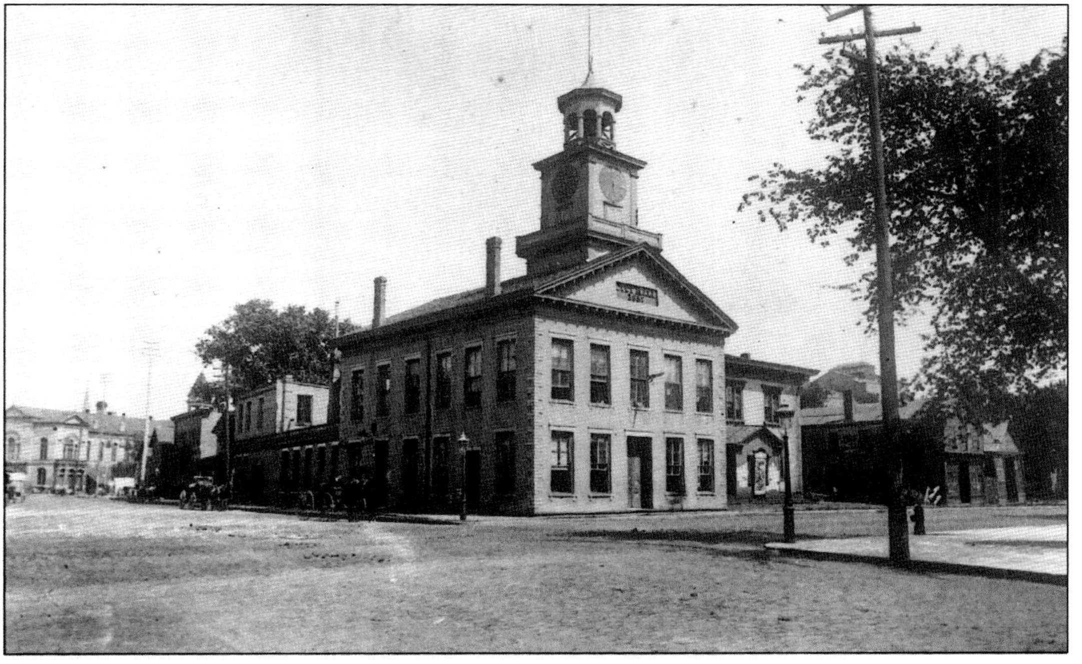

The first St. Paul City Hall, constructed in the 1850s, is shown c. 1890, with Market Hall at far left. (From the photo archives of the Ramsey County Historical Society)

At the age of 18, Isadore came to America and settled in New Orleans, Louisiana. He came to St. Paul four years later in 1854, and boarded with Joseph Ullmann, a prominent young pioneer fur and liquor merchant. Isadore married in 1865, and had three sons: Albert N.(Napoleon), Isaac E., and Nathan S. Rose, all who went to work with their father in Ullmann's business. Isadore Rose eventually managed and gained a share of Ullmann's business when Mr. Ullmann returned to Germany (18).

Benjamin Rose also boarded with Joseph Ullmann, but he chose to go into the clothing business with Hirsch Heimann, one of the older St. Paul pioneer clothing merchants. Benjamin married one of Hirsch Heimann's daughters, and had three sons and a daughter: Hyman, Leopold, Simon, and Carrie. He died young, leaving his widow, Eva, and their 4 children ages 12–18 (19). He was one of the first leaders of Mt. Zion congregation, was an active Mason in Ancient Landmark Lodge No. 5, and an early president of Minnesota Lodge of B'nai B'rith, a Jewish fraternal and service group (20).

Little is known of Emmanuel, except that he too went to work with Joseph Ullmann after arriving in St. Paul. Isadore outlived both Benjamin and Emmanuel, and established family homes at 9th and Sibley, 513 Summit and 701 Summit, where he died in 1915 at the age of 82, in a city whose growth paralleled his own (21). Their descendants have remained active in the civic life of St. Paul and the Mt. Zion synagogue.

Jacob Newman was another early pioneer, but he was older than most of the other men in town. He was a clothing merchant and a partner with Abraham Greenwald, who later disappeared from the scene. Their store was on old St. Anthony, opposite the Market, in 1856 (22). He later became a clothing tailor. Both Newman and his wife, Fannie, were from Germany, and she was considerably younger than he. They had two children, a daughter

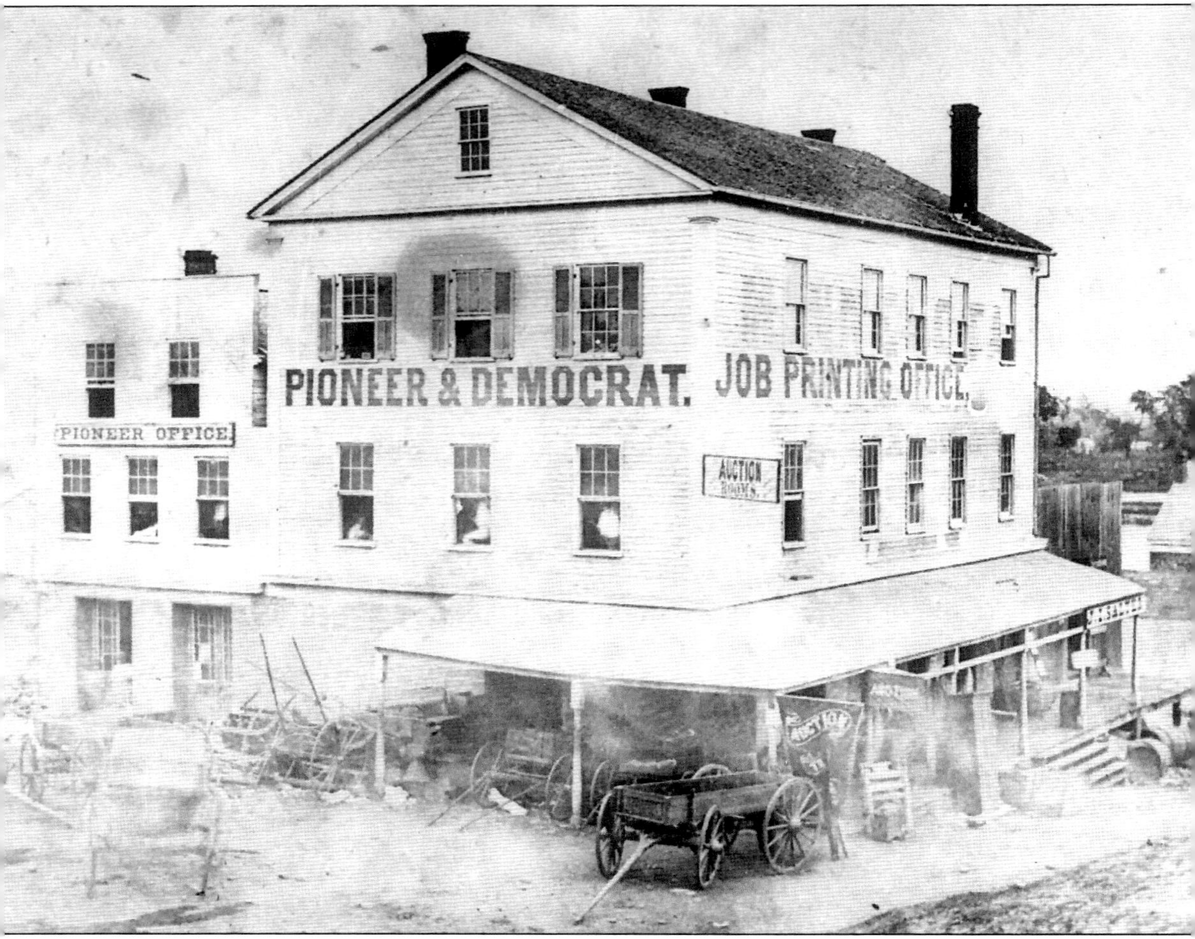

This Pioneer and Democrat *newspaper office was constructed in 1854, located at the corner of Third Street (now Kellogg Boulevard) and Jackson Street. Around the corner was the original Isaac Ansel and Son clothing store. On March 16, 1860, most of the buildings on Third Street (now Kellogg Boulevard) from Robert Street to Jackson Street were destroyed by fire. (From the photo archives of the Ramsey County Historical Society)*

Josephine—who had been born in the State of Virginia and later married Max Frankel (23)—and Simon, who was born in St. Paul (24). They lived on Robert Street, between 6th and 7th, and the Apples, the Frankels, and the Aaron Meyer families at one time lived with them (25). Jacob Newman is one of the few that remained with Mt. Zion after the early split in the spring of 1857. Both factions had bills introduced in the Territorial Legislature to provide for their incorporation, one as Mt. Zion and the other as Ahabeth Achim. The Mt. Zion bill was signed into law by Governor Willis A. Gorman on February 26, 1857, (26) even though the Ahabeth Achim group had at one time triple the membership of the old Mt. Zion group. The split was eventually healed, and the two groups became one Mt. Zion, the first Jewish congregation in Minnesota (27). Jacob Newman moved to Philadelphia, and eventually died there in 1907.

Hirsch Heimann, a Prussian by birth, was another of the Mr. Zion holdouts among the pioneer families, and one of the earliest of pioneer clothing merchants. In 1857 he was in his mid 40s, and like Jacob Newman, one of the older men in town. He and his wife Teresa, with three of their children, had come to America before 1845. They had spent some time in New York where the last four children were born (28). In the 1850 census, only five of the children are listed, as the older ones—Morris, Augusta, and Louisa—had moved away. His clothing store was on

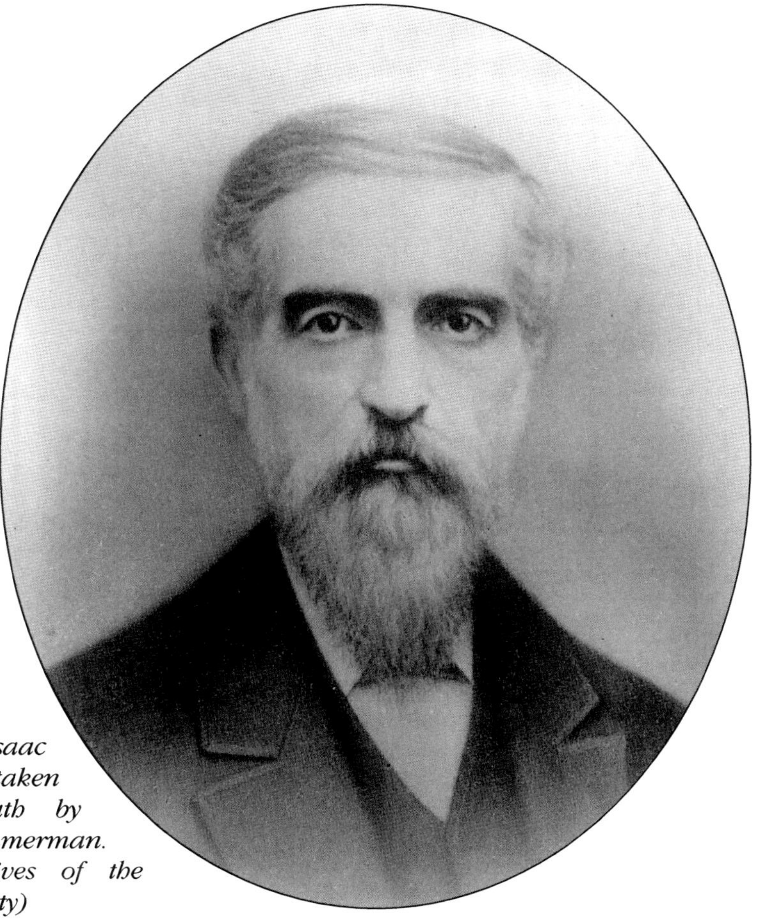

This portrait of Judge Isaac Nunez Cardozo was taken shortly before his death by photographer C.A. Zimmerman. (From the photo archives of the Minnesota Historical Society)

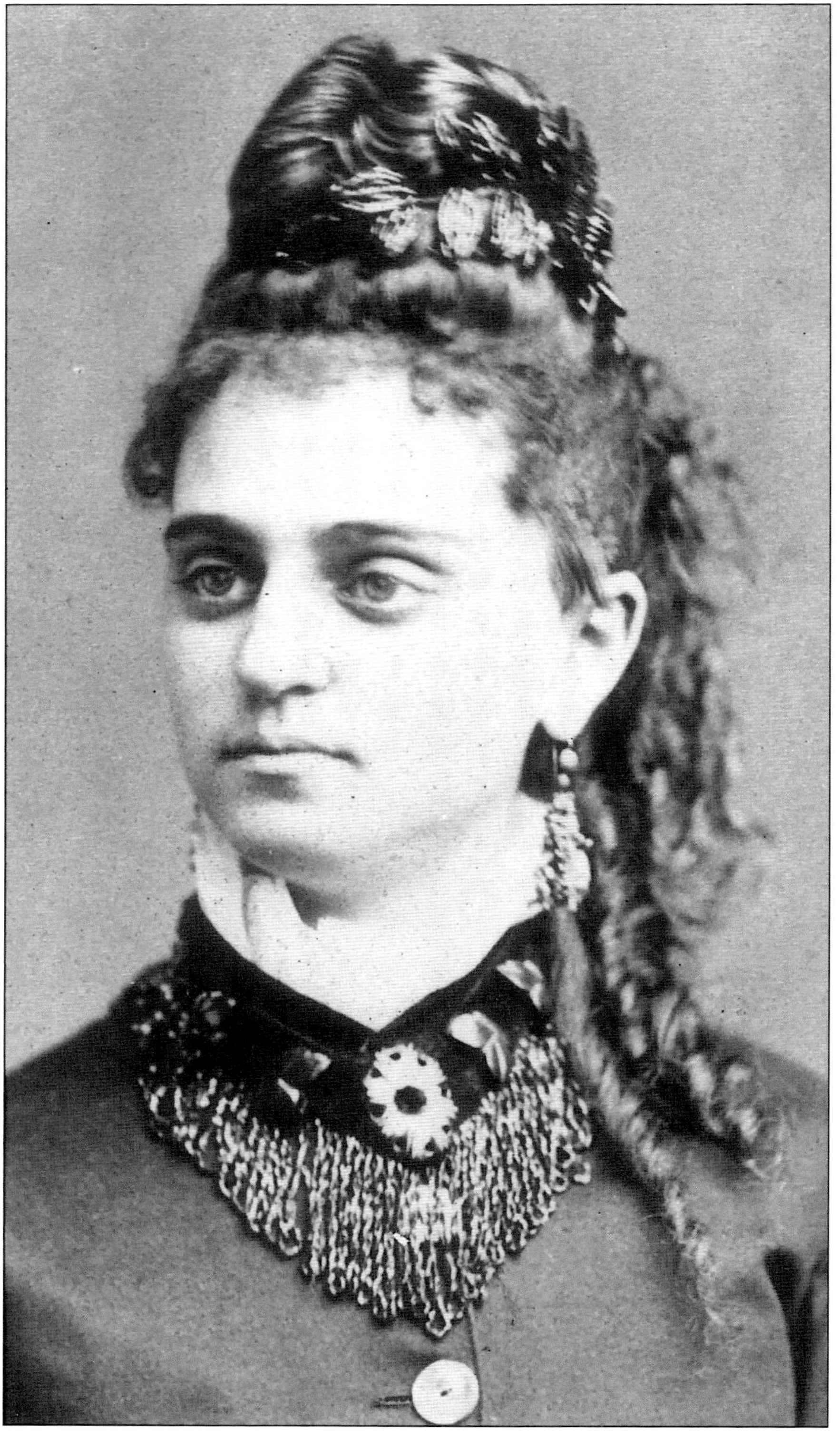

Seen here is Ellen Cardozo, daughter of Isaac N. Cardozo. This photo was taken by C.A. Zimmerman. (From the photo archives of the Minnesota Historical Society)

Minnesota Street, between 6th and 7th. He died suddenly on September 9, 1869, and the goods from his store were sold as part of the probate for $2935.32 (29).

Isaac Nunez Cardozo, namesake and direct descendant of one of America's most important and distinguished Jewish families, arrived in St. Paul in 1857. His father was married to the granddaughter of Rabbi Gershom Seixas, Revolutionary War patriot who took his pulpit to Philadelphia from New York during the Revolutionary Wars rather than serve under British rule, when the British occupied New York. Rabbi Seixas was one of the clergymen to officiate at President George Washington's first inaugural (30). Isaac N. Cardozo was also the uncle of Justice Benjamin Nathan Cardozo of the United States Supreme Court (31). His wife was descended from both the Seixas and Judah families (32). Both husband and wife were what Stephen Birmingham, in his book *The Grandees*, referred to as the "elite," tracing their origins back to medieval Spain and Portugal (33).

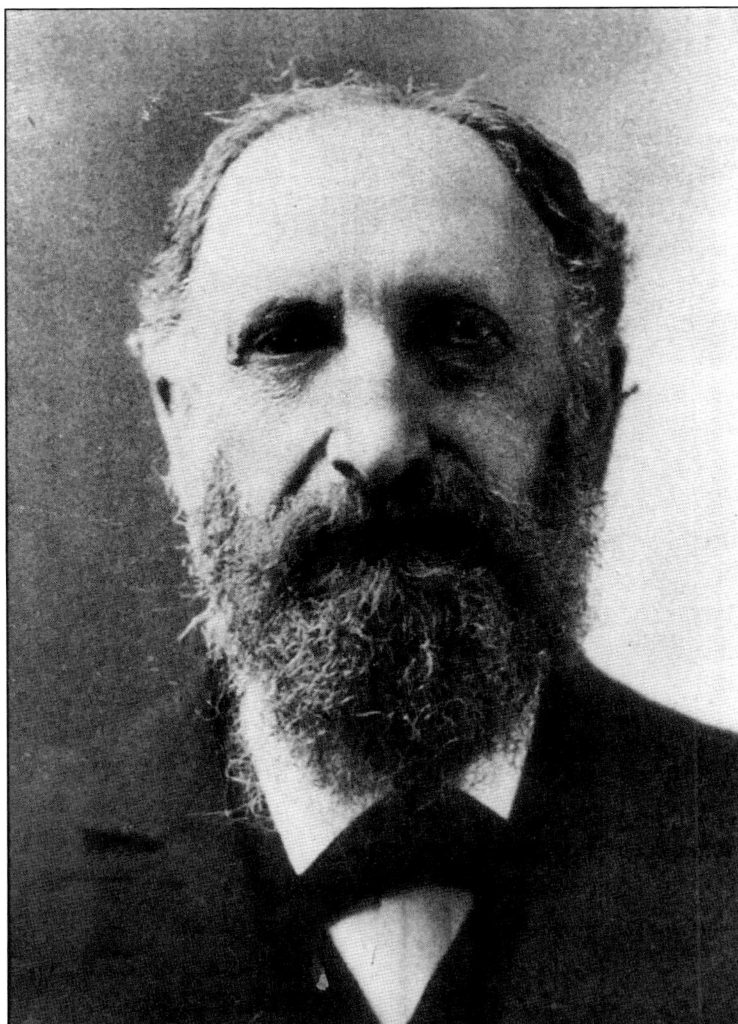

When this picture of Joseph Bergfeld was published in 1904 in the Golden Anniversary Book of Ancient Landmark Lodge No. 5, A.F.A.M., *Mr. Bergfeld was the third oldest living initiate. He was the first Jewish Mason, having been initiated on September 7, 1854, into Ancient Landmark Lodge No. 5. Others soon joined him: M. Levy in 1855, Julius Mendelsohn in 1858, Morris Appel in 1866, and Benjamin Rose in 1867. In 1870, he received the 32nd degree Scottish Rite, becoming the first Jew to do so. (From the photo archives of the American Jewish World, September and October, 1979)*

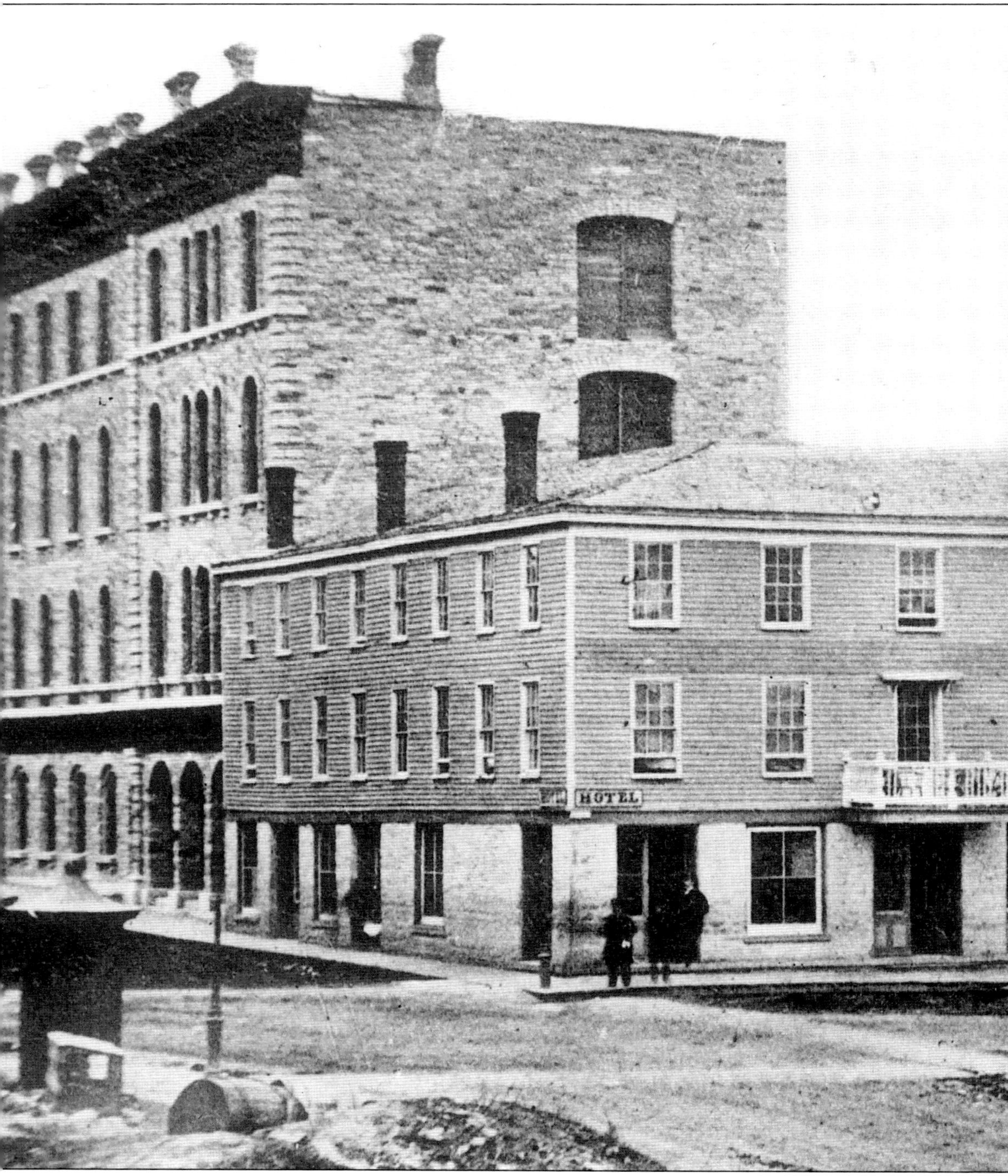

The first hotel in the city of St. Paul opened in 1847. The St. Paul House-Merchants Hotel, shown in 1867, was located on the northeast corner of Third Street (now Kellogg Boulevard) and Jackson Streets. Many of the early Jewish peddlers and traveling salesmen stayed here, unless

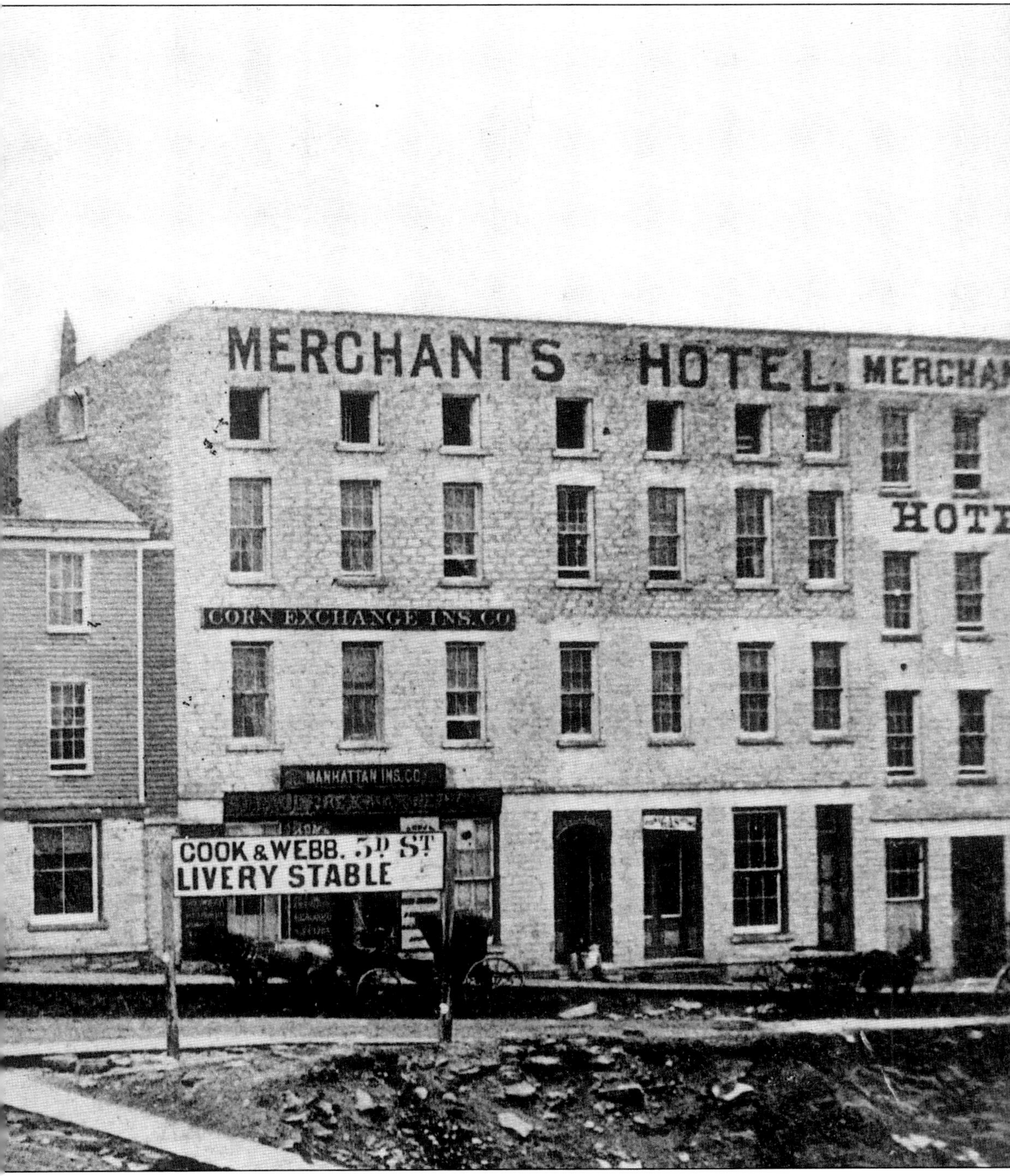

they lived in the American House or over their place of business. A number of the early Jewish businesses were located within walking distance of the hotel. (From the photo archives of the Minnesota Historical Society)

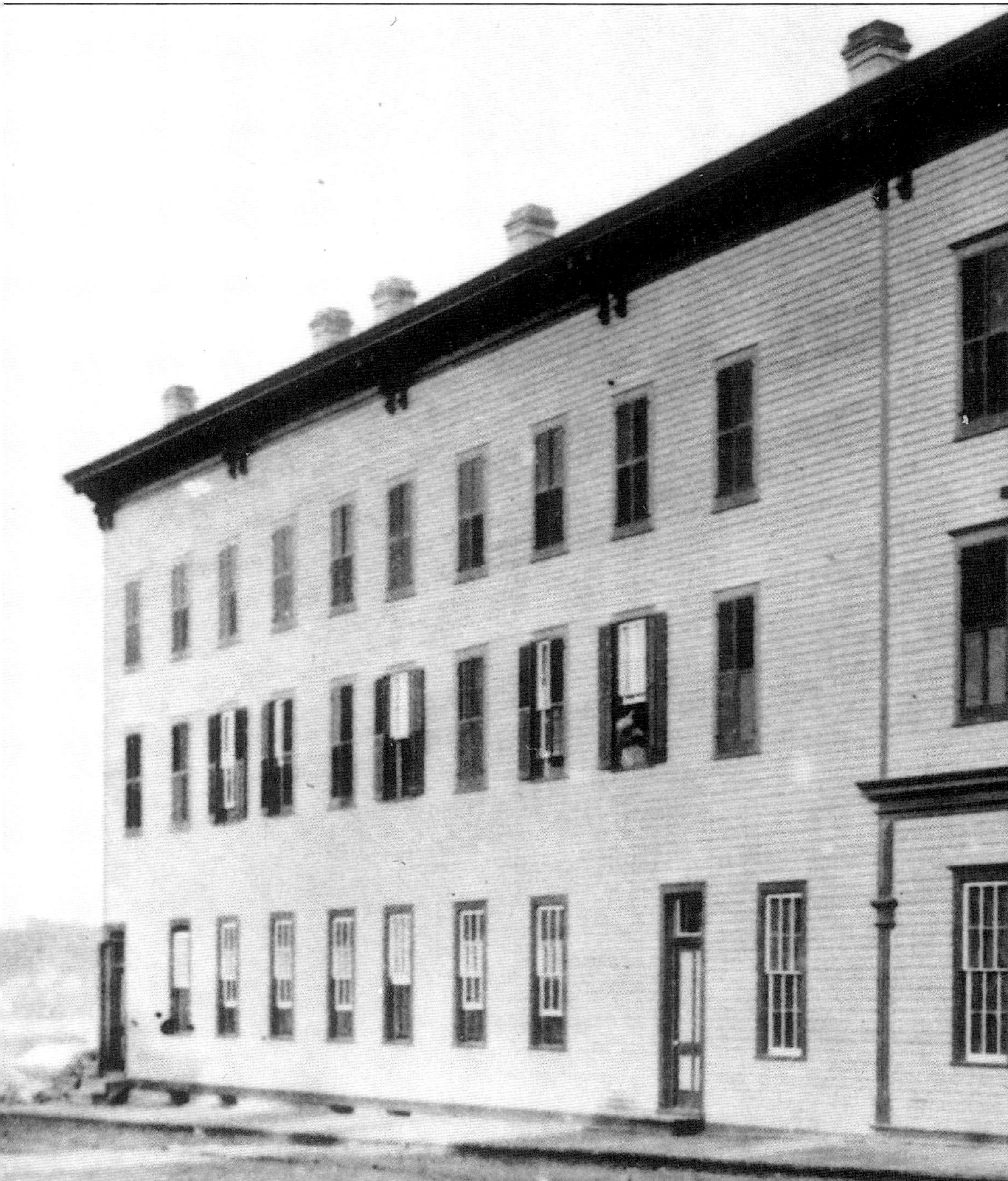

The Sherman House, constructed in 1865, was located at Fourth Street and Sibley Street. It was one of many pensioner hotels, in which early Jewish peddlers and traveling salesmen stayed. Its billiard hall, advertised on the first floor window, was one of six when this picture

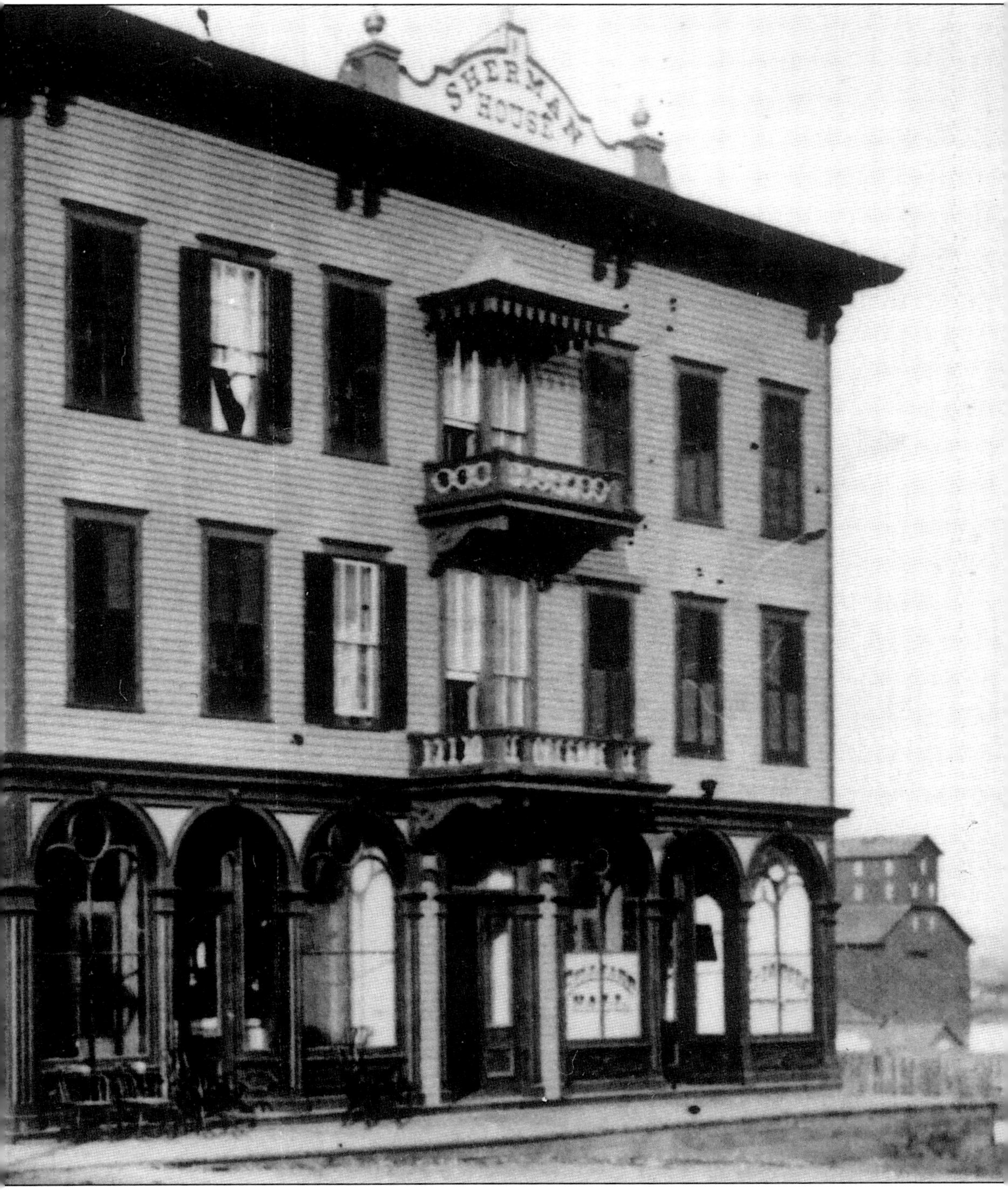

was taken in 1873, by William Illingworth. (From the photo archives of the Ramsey County Historical Society)

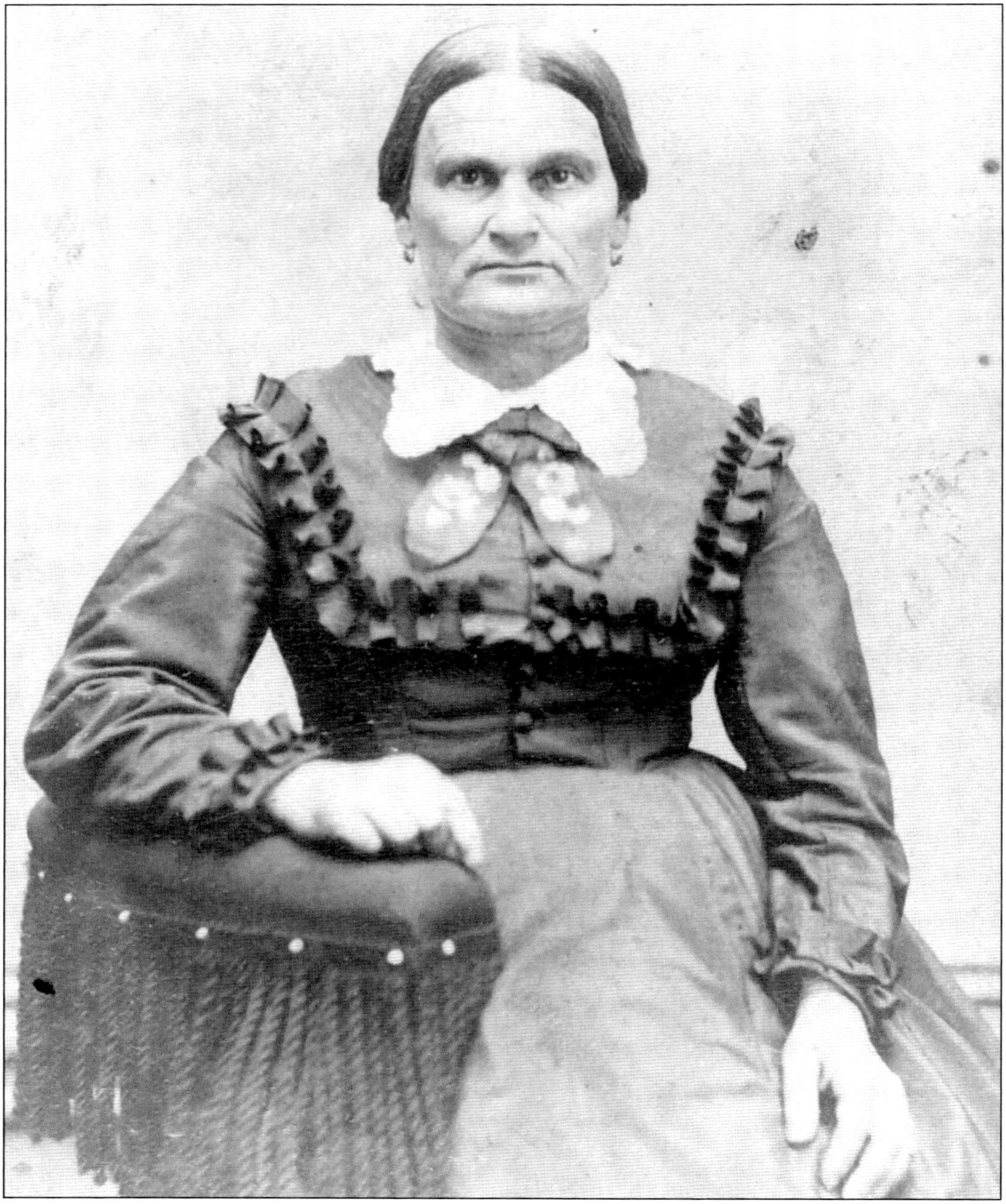

Kalmon Lion and his wife Dina (formerly Lederer) were among the very early pioneers. Kalmon was Minnesota's first religious functionary. He had been born and educated in Koblenz, Germany, had come to the United States in 1851, and settled in Cleveland, Ohio, where he had been in charge of a small Jewish congregation. In 1856, he had answered the call of the early organizers of Mt. Zion as Cantor and shochet, *(the synagogue's ritual director in the slaughter of meat and poultry). During the time when the group split into two*

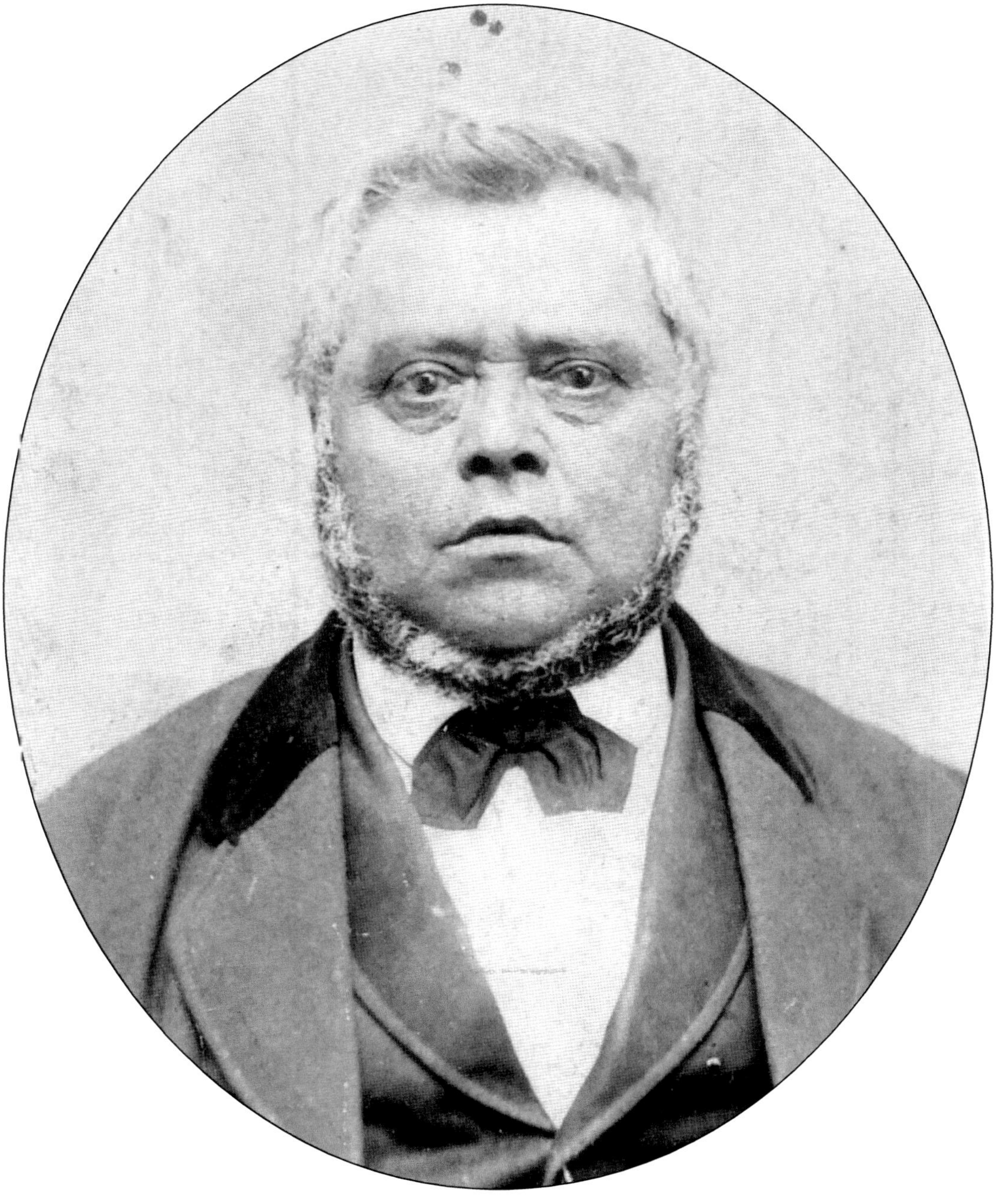

warring factions, Lion sided with the Ahabath Achim faction, and then he left, answering a call in Plattsburgh, New York. Thereafter, the Lion family returned to St. Paul. In 1872, their daughter Fanny married Daniel Goodman from Philadelphia in the first Jewish marriage in the State of Minnesota. The ceremony was conducted by Mt. Zion's first rabbi, Rabbi Leopold Wintner. Daniel Goodman died in 1878. (From the photo archives of the Minnesota Historical Society)

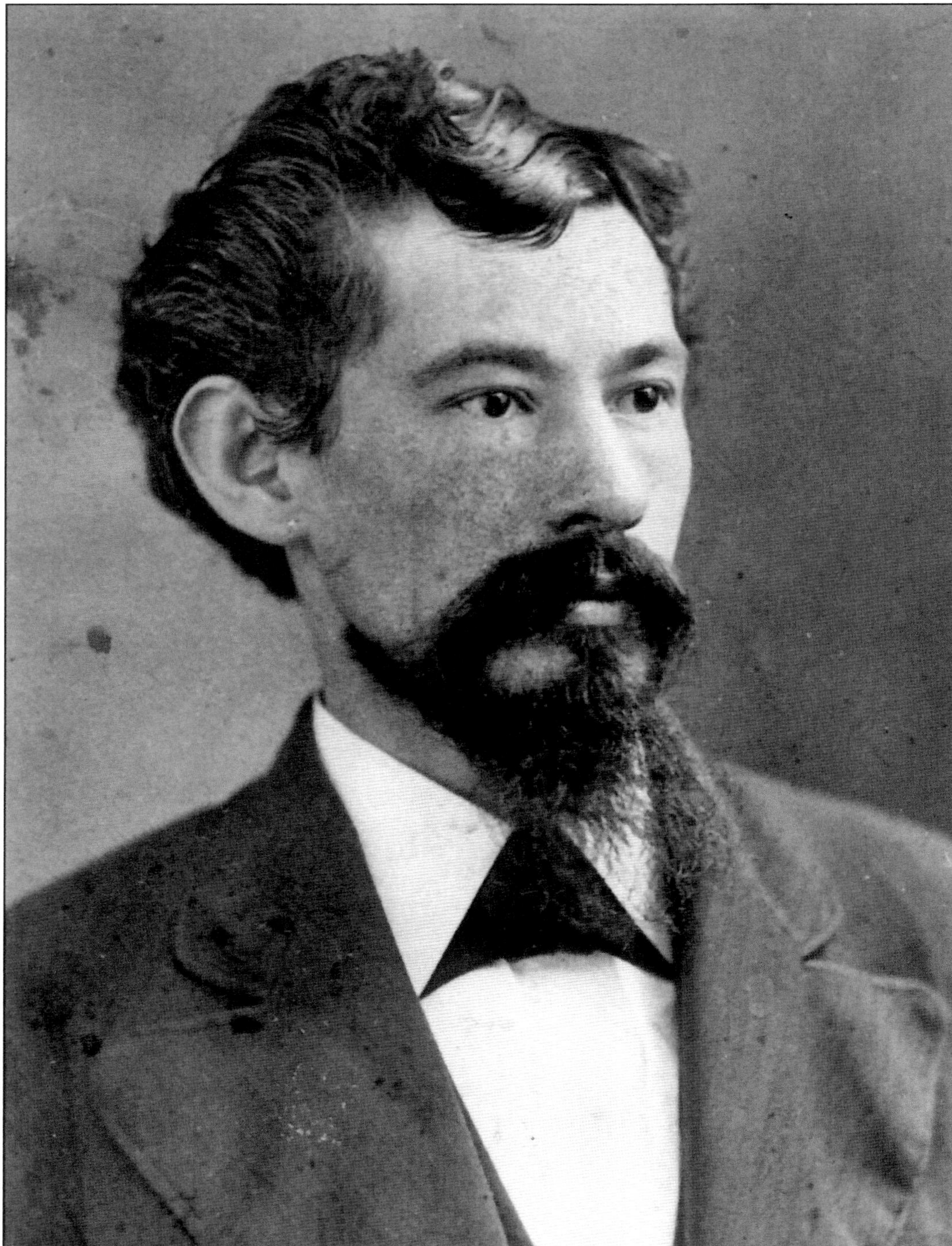

This photo of Daniel Goodman was taken by Northrup's Photographic Gallery. (From the photo archives of the Minnesota Historical Society)

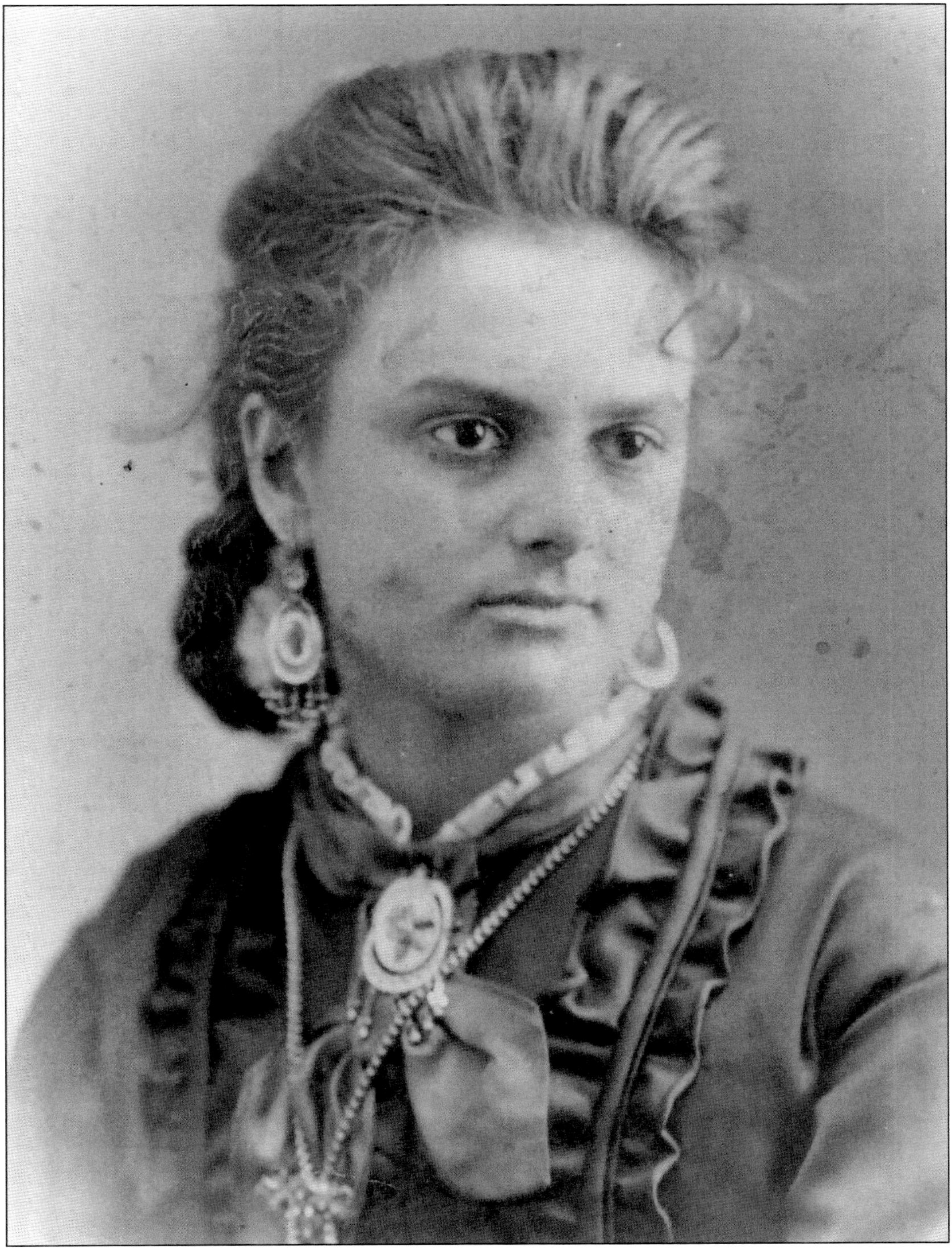

Fanny Lion Goodman was Daniel Goodman's wife. This photo was taken by Flower and Hawkins. (From the photo archives of the Minnesota Historical Society)

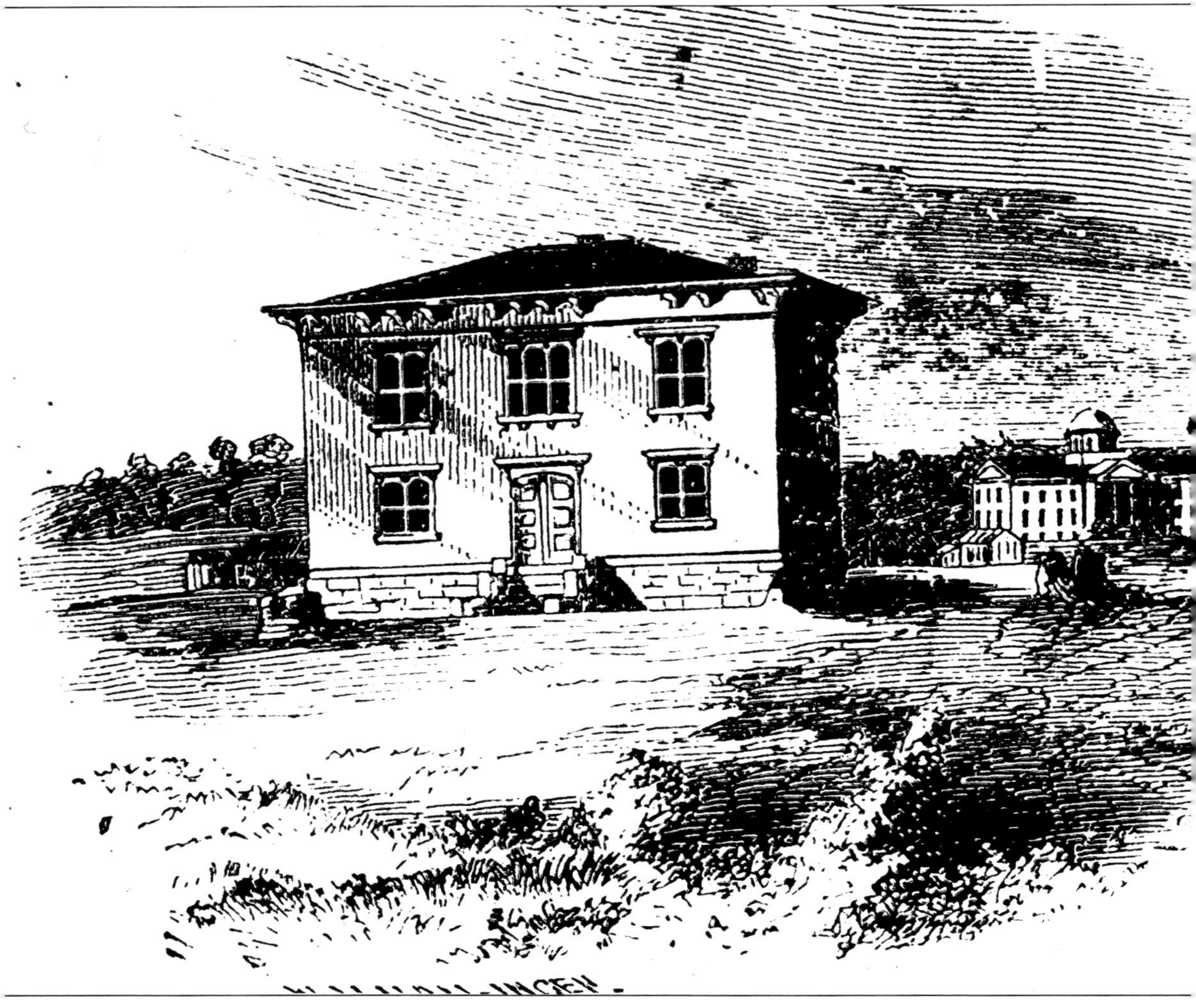

The Baldwin School was the first school building in St. Paul, erected in 1853. It was used as such until 1857, when the St. Paul school system was organized. It then became a temporary post office, and then was leased for public offices by the city. In the background of this sketch by an anonymous artist stands the first St. Paul post office constructed in 1857. (From photo archives of the Ramsey County Historical Society)

This "nobility" of Jewery, the Sephardic Jews from Spain and Portugal, were not only the bankers and financial advisers to the royal courts of Spain and Portugal, they were also Spain's scientists, physicians, jurists, philosophers, and poets. The Sultan of Turkey, when he heard that Ferdinand and Isabella had in 1492 ordered all of the Spanish and Portuguese Jews expelled, commented, "The King of Spain must have lost his mind. He is expelling his best subjects." These Sephardic Jews wandered until 1654, when a tiny band came to America aboard the *St. Charles*, the Jewish *Mayflower* (34). The Seixas family directly descended from this small band of Jewish pilgrims (35).

Isaac N. Cardozo, born in Richmond, Virginia, was an active Democrat, and while living in St. Paul, was appointed the first United States Commissioner serving the Circuit and United States District Courts from St. Paul. He had been admitted to the bar in Philadelphia, moved to New York, joined the 1849 Gold Rush to California, and then settled in St. Paul (36). In 1858 he had been appointed to one of the highest Federal Judicial jobs in Minnesota.

He was often referred to by his compatriots as "Judge" Cardozo, and he was the first president of Minnesota Lodge of the B'nai B'rith, which organized in 1871. He was also among the founders of Mt. Zion. For many years, he and his wife, Rachel, lived at Chestnut and West 7th (old Fort Street). When he died in 1887, his family—including three daughters, Eva, Rebecca, and Nellie—lived at 249 Marshall (old Nelson) (37). He died without a will, leaving a $2,000 insurance policy and $300 in cash (38). The St. Paul Pioneer Press, printing his obituary on November 10, 1887, said that "Judge Cardozo was considered an able man in his office, distinguished, and well-read and social, though eccentric in some particulars…" (39).

Isaac Cardozo's widow and three daughters remained with his wife's sister, Mrs. Zipporah Seixas, widow of Benjamin S. Sexias, who had been living with them since the death of Mr. Sexias in 1866. For a time, Mrs. Cardozo, her sisters, her three daughters, and her nephew, Harry C. Seixas, lived at 363 Dayton in close proximity to the old Aberdeen Hotel. After Mrs. Zipporah Seixas died, they lived at 699 Laurel, where Mrs. Cardozo died at the age of 80. The Cardozo maiden daughters, being proper Sephardic ladies and unable to find suitable matches, remained unmarried. They moved next door to 697 Laurel, and then to 934 Ashland(40).

Joseph Bergfeld was born in Germany in 1827. He came to the United States in 1849, landing in New Orleans, where he remained but a short time. From there he went up the Mississippi River to St. Louis, Missouri, where he was employed in dry goods for three years. In 1853, at the age of 26, he came to St. Paul and was employed in the stove and tinware business. In 1856, he became the first Jew to be a member of Ancient Landmark Lodge No. 5 of the A.F. and A.M. (Masons). In that year he also embarked into business for himself, opening a store on Robert Street, between 3rd and 4th Streets. In 1863, he moved to California, but returned to St. Paul in 1866, following the end of the Civil War. He worked as a traveling agent from the Chicago men's furnishing house of Kuh and Loeb until 1870. From that time until he died, he engaged in various lines of business, including real estate and insurance. He served as Grand Master and Grand Patriarch of the Ancient Landmark Lodge No. 5 A.F. and A.M., and was vice president of a reorganized Mt. Zion congregation (41). He was also active in the Odd Fellows organization and served as the head of various lodges of that group. For many years he lived at 270 E. Ninth Street, in the "Lowertown" area. He had two sons, Nathan and Charles, late in life. He died a very old man, active in business and Mt. Zion affairs. His son Nathan moved to Chicago (42).

One of the earliest of pioneers, Marks Marks, was in the clothing business, as were many of the early Jewish settlers. He left us a puzzling mystery that even today remains unsolved. On November 12, 1856, "fearing imminent death," Mr. Marks, while in the hospital, dictated his last will and testament. In that will he left his father, his wife Babette, four sons, and two daughters the residual of his estate "according to the laws of Pennsylvania." In 1857, he died, and Aron Arenheimer (or Aaronheimer), his business partner in the clothing business, was appointed the Executor of his will. Upon opening the will, the Court discovered that part of the residual of Mr. Marks' estate was left to "my *lost* children and my present and *actual* wife." Its meaning then, as now, remains a mystery (43).

Kalmon Lion (or Leon) was the first religious functionary to settle in Minnesota who was of the Jewish faith. He was born and educated in Koblenz, Germany, and came to the United States in 1851, settling in Cleveland, Ohio, where he was in charge of a small congregation. His wife, Dina, and his infant son, Nathan, joined him in Cleveland. In 1857, they came to Mt. Zion when he answered Mt. Zion's call (44). During a tumultuous period of Mt. Zion's existence, the Lion family temporarily moved to Plattsburgh, New York. They moved back to St. Paul again, and in 1872 their youngest daughter Fanny married Daniel Goodman (45). Kalmon Lion did not return to his religious functions, but entered into a business partnership with his new son-in-law, and a partnership of Lion and Goodman was organized into the clothing business. Daniel and Fanny had three children—Frances, Laura, and Norman. Suddenly on March 29, 1878, Daniel Goodman died without a will, leaving Fanny a widow with three small babies, ages two–five (46). Thereafter Kalmon Lion and his son Nathan organized the business into another clothing operation known as Lion and Son (47). Kalmon died in the spring of 1884, leaving his estate to his son, Nathan, and two daughters, Fannie Goodman and Rosa Miller, and the children of Sarah Sternberg (48). Kalmon's granddaughter, Frances, married Julius Heilbron in 1892, and his great granddaughter, Bertha Heilbron, was for many years the editor of *Minnesota History*, and published a number of articles (49). Fanny Goodman, Kalmon's widowed daughter, remarried in 1888 to Levi Herz.

Abraham Blum had come to St. Paul from German-speaking Alsace-Lorraine with his wife and five children. He became one of the dissidents from the original Mt. Zion in the spring of 1857, but with Kalmon Lion, Judge Isaac N. Cardozo and Morris Appel, he helped to heal the breech in 1862, and rejoined Mt. Zion. Abraham Blum had four sons—Aaron, Isaac, Charles, and Herman— and they all lived on John Street between 8th and 9th. The elder Blum died in the early 1870s, and apparently the family left for other places, as nothing further is heard from them again in the St. Paul area (50).

David Lowitz was one of the "loyalists" at Mt. Zion, but his presence there, though apparently short-lived, was auspicious in that his second daughter was one of the first Jewish children born in Minnesota, in 1857. His first daughter had been born in the east, and his wife was a New York native. David Lowitz had been preceded here by an older brother, Elias. Both the Lowitzs were Prussians. David manufactured cigars, and Elias handled the retail outlet. Elias Lowitz was also the second president of Mt. Zion Synagogue, and proudly listed himself in the census as "naturalized" (51). David later went into furs and hides and lived with Aaron Lovenstein. Both David Lowitz and his brother Elias disappeared from the local scene after 1868 (52).

Henry Marks and Morris Marks were brothers who came to St. Paul from New York and both were in the clothing business, but as business competitors in 1856 when their presence is noted in the St. Paul Business Directory for that year (53). Julius Mendelsohn, also a Mt. Zion founder and an active Mason, was Morris Marks' brother-in-law. Morris Marks died in 1863. When his widow remarried and returned to her native New York with her new husband, "Uncle Julius," a Prussian, petitioned the Court

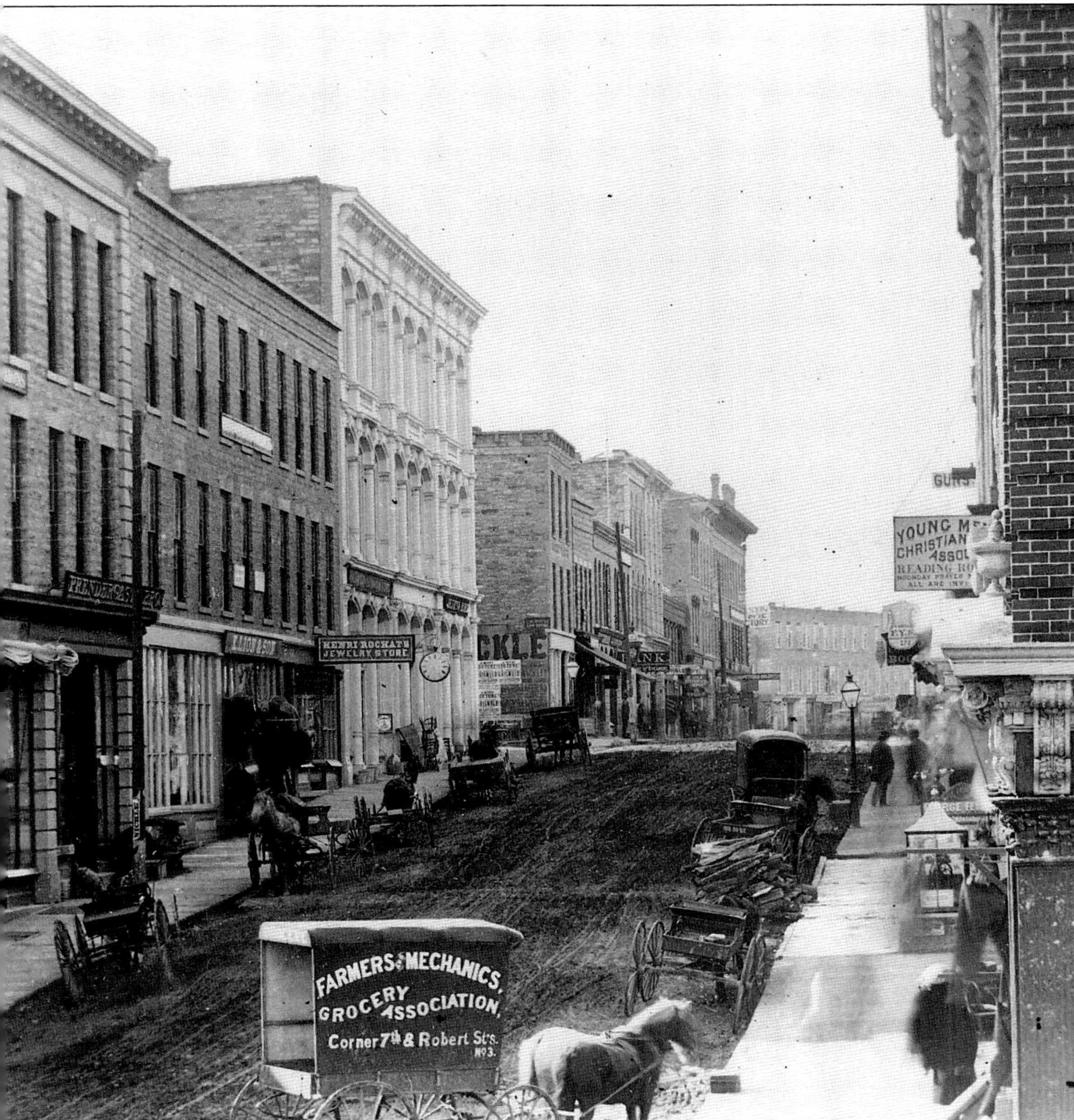

Kalmon Lion and Son's Gent's Furnishings store is shown on Third Street (now Kellogg Boulevard) west of Minnesota Street, on the south (left) side of the street, at 165 Third Street. It was between Prendergast Bros. Stoves and Tinware, at 161 Third Street, and Henri Rochat, watchmaker and jeweler, at 167 Third Street. This photo was by William H. Illingworth, who took many pictures of early downtown St. Paul. All of the buildings on the south side of the street were eventually torn down when Kellogg Boulevard was built. (From the photo archives of the Minnesota Historical Society)

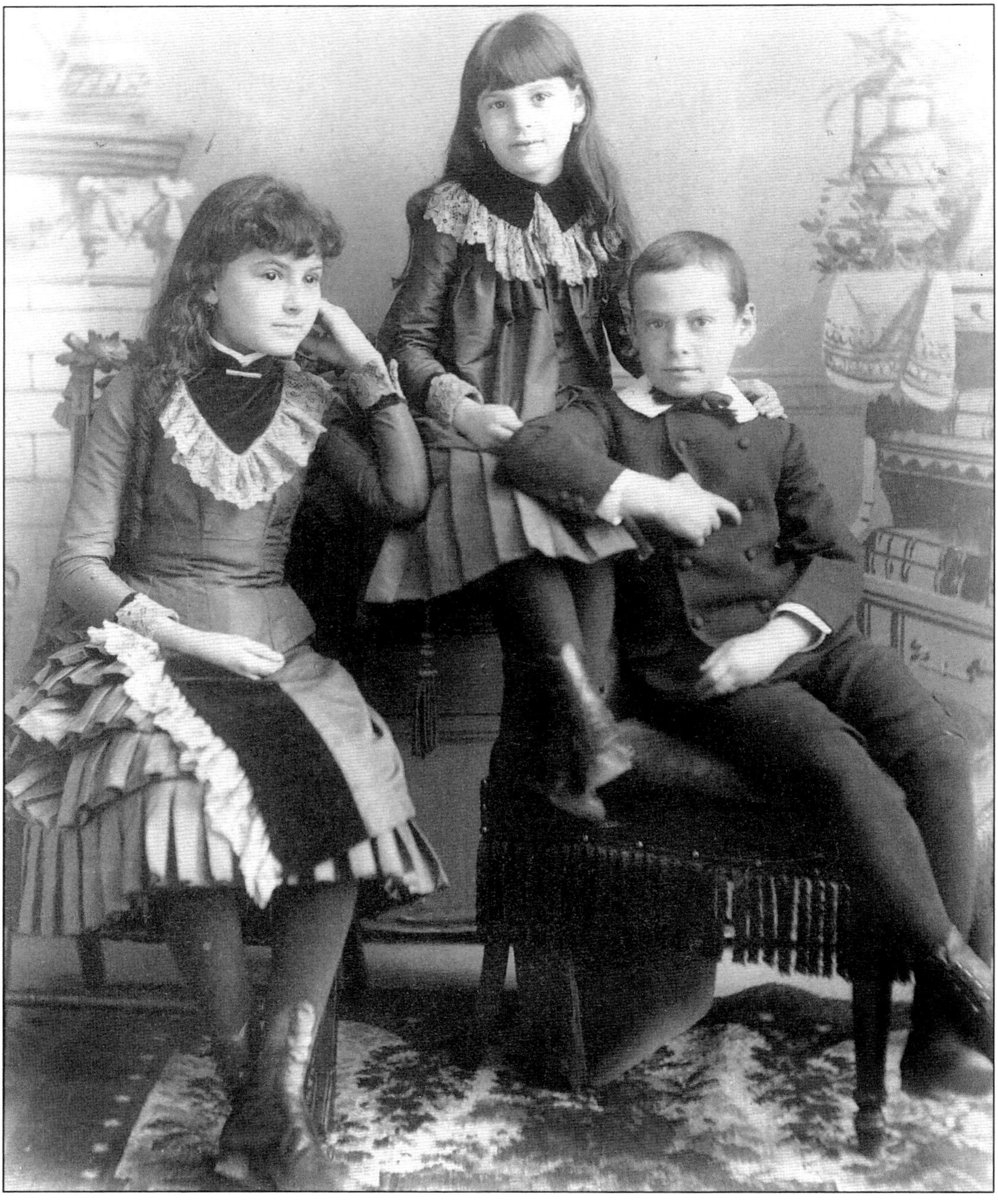

Kalman and Dina Lion's grandchildren, the children of Daniel and Fanny Goodman, are seen here. They are Frances, Laura, and Norman. Daniel Goodman died when the children were ages two–five, in 1878. Here they are shown six years later in a photo by the Schlattman Brothers. The Minnesota Historical Society incorrectly identifies them as Norman Goodman's children. Four years later, Fanny Goodman remarried to Levi Hertz. (From the photo archives of the Minnesota Historical Society)

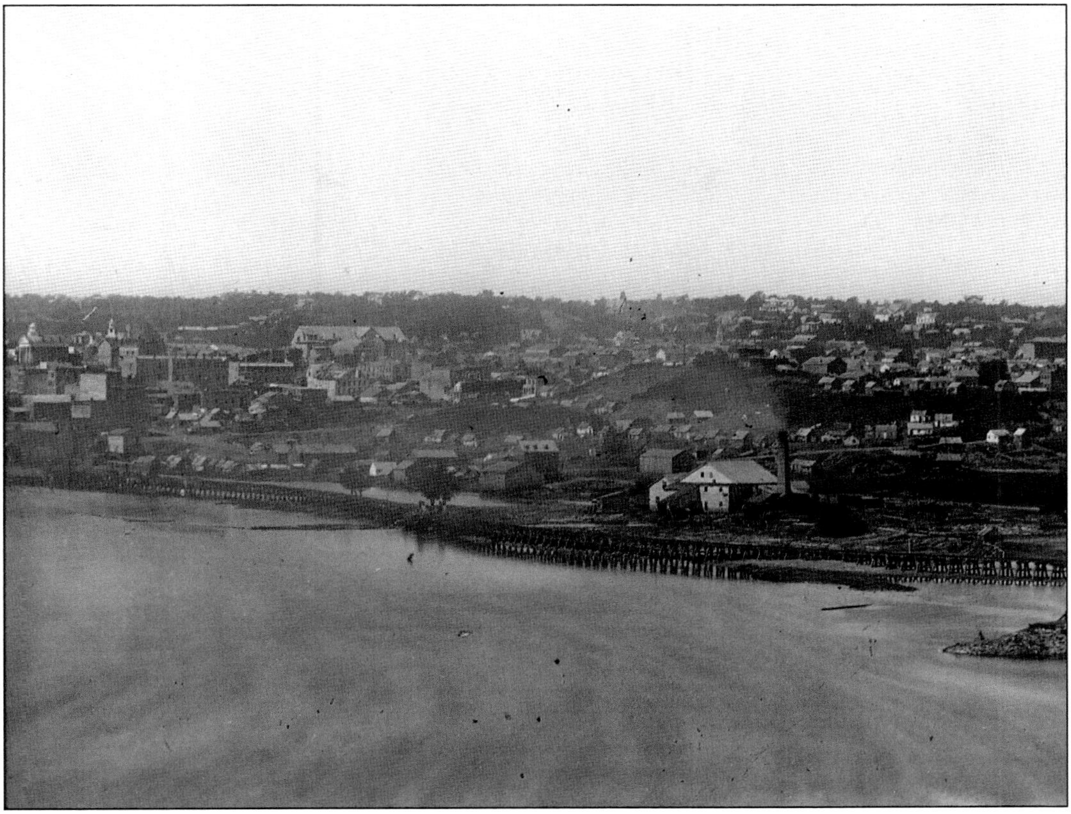

St. Paul's commercial district along the Mississippi River, in 1866, as seen from Dayton's Bluff. The rich and affluent wasted no time in heading for the highest ground in early St. Paul. Dayton's Bluff was one of those areas, located on the East Side of St. Paul. (From the photo archives of the Minnesota Historical Society)

and became the guardian for the two Marks children: six-year-old Elizabeth, and three-year-old Henry (54).

Julius Mendelsohn also served as President of Mt. Zion synagogue from 1859 to 1869, struggling to hold it together during the chaotic period of the Civil War (55). Louis Mendelsohn was a merchant tailor during this period and may have been Julius' son or brother. Both, however, disappeared from the scene with the Marks children after 1869. They apparently moved back to New York, where Julius Mendelsohn died in 1881 (56). In 1907, H.D. Frankel wrote that Morris Marks' brother Henry went on to form the Hart, Schaffner, and Marx Firm of Chicago (57). This cannot be verified.

Nathan Bernhaem (later spelled Bernheim and Bernheimer) arrived in St. Paul in 1863, at the age of 38 with a wife, Caroline, and a son, Emmanuel. For approximately 20 years he was in second hand goods, including copper and rags. He went into the livestock business with his son Emmanuel, in which he remained the rest of his life. The Bernheim family lived at 126 West Sixth Street until the turn of the century. Nathan, or Nathaniel as he called himself later in life, had two other children, Louis and Pauline. Nothing is heard of Louis Bernheim after the family moved to 695 Inglehart at the turn of the century.

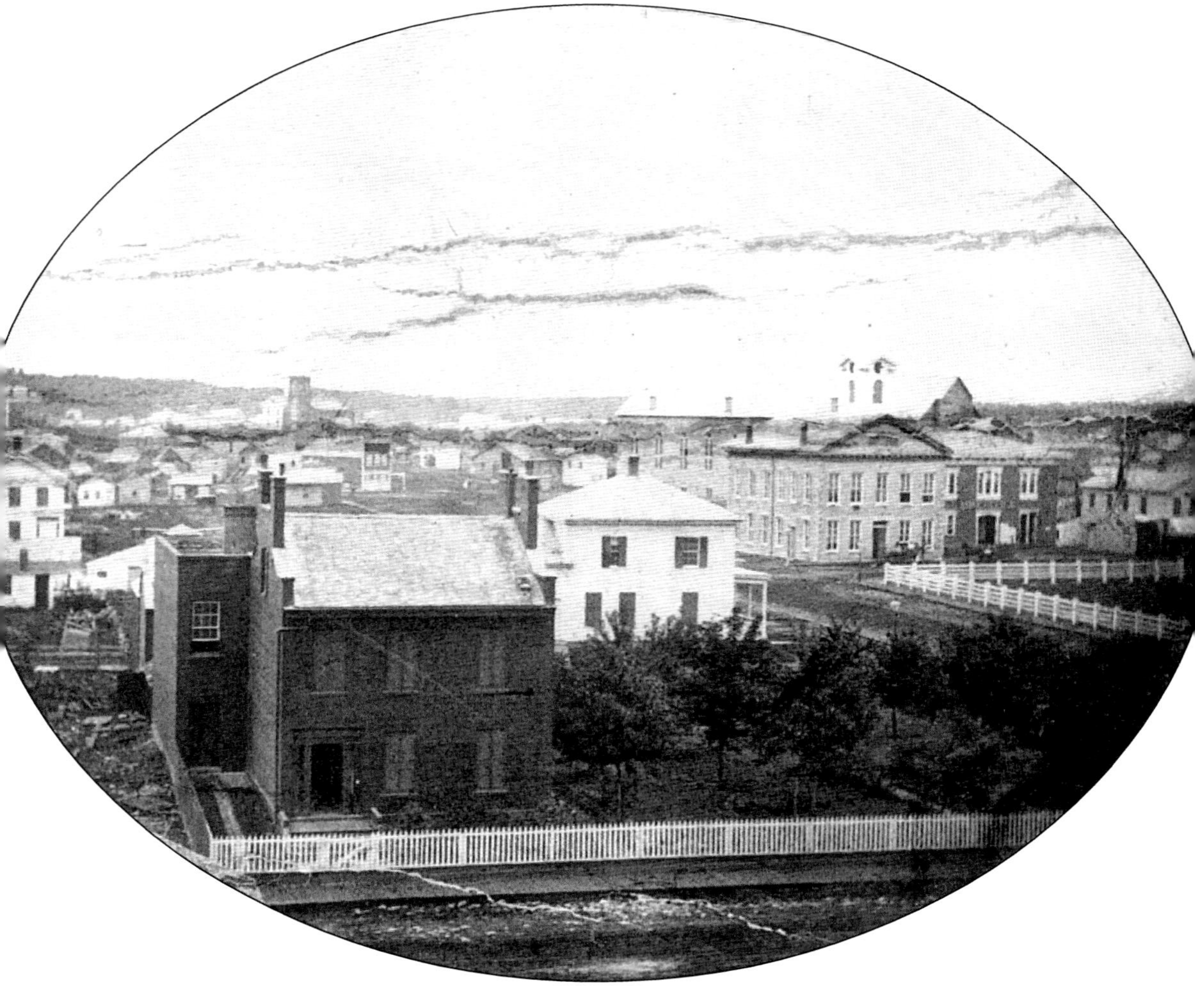

This picture of early St. Paul was taken right before the Civil War in 1859. The economy had collapsed as a result of the failure of the Ohio Life Insurance Company, and religious and community life was in a state of chaos. Life was hard. There were no public utilities, except gas for lighting, which began in 1856, to a limited number of affluent individuals. Gas for street lighting did not begin until 1867, no city water system until 1869, no city sewers until 1873, and until 1873, city streets were unpaved. (From the photo archives of the Minnesota Historical Society)

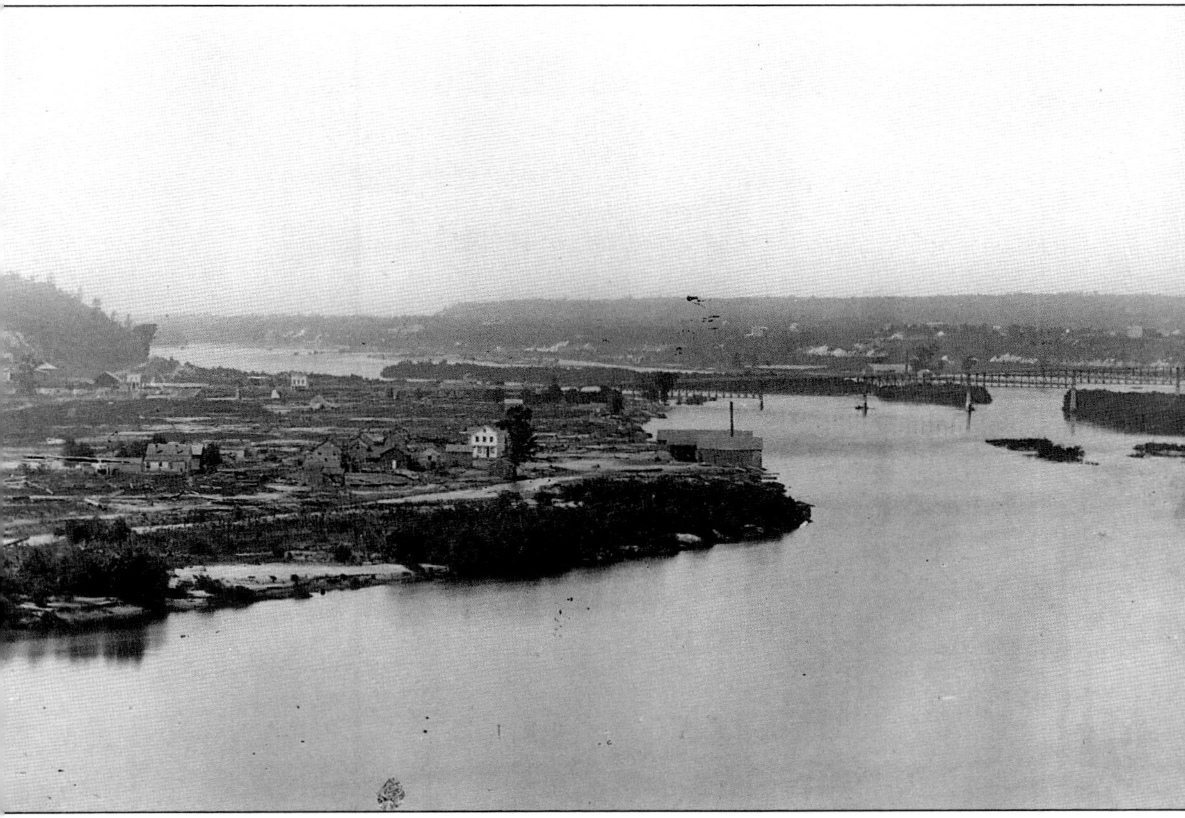

This photo of the St. Paul river frontage on the Mississippi River, taken in 1865, shows St. Paul as a pioneer river town, which it remained until the arrival of the railroads. After the railroads arrived, it became a major railroad center. (From the photo archives of the Minnesota Historical Society)

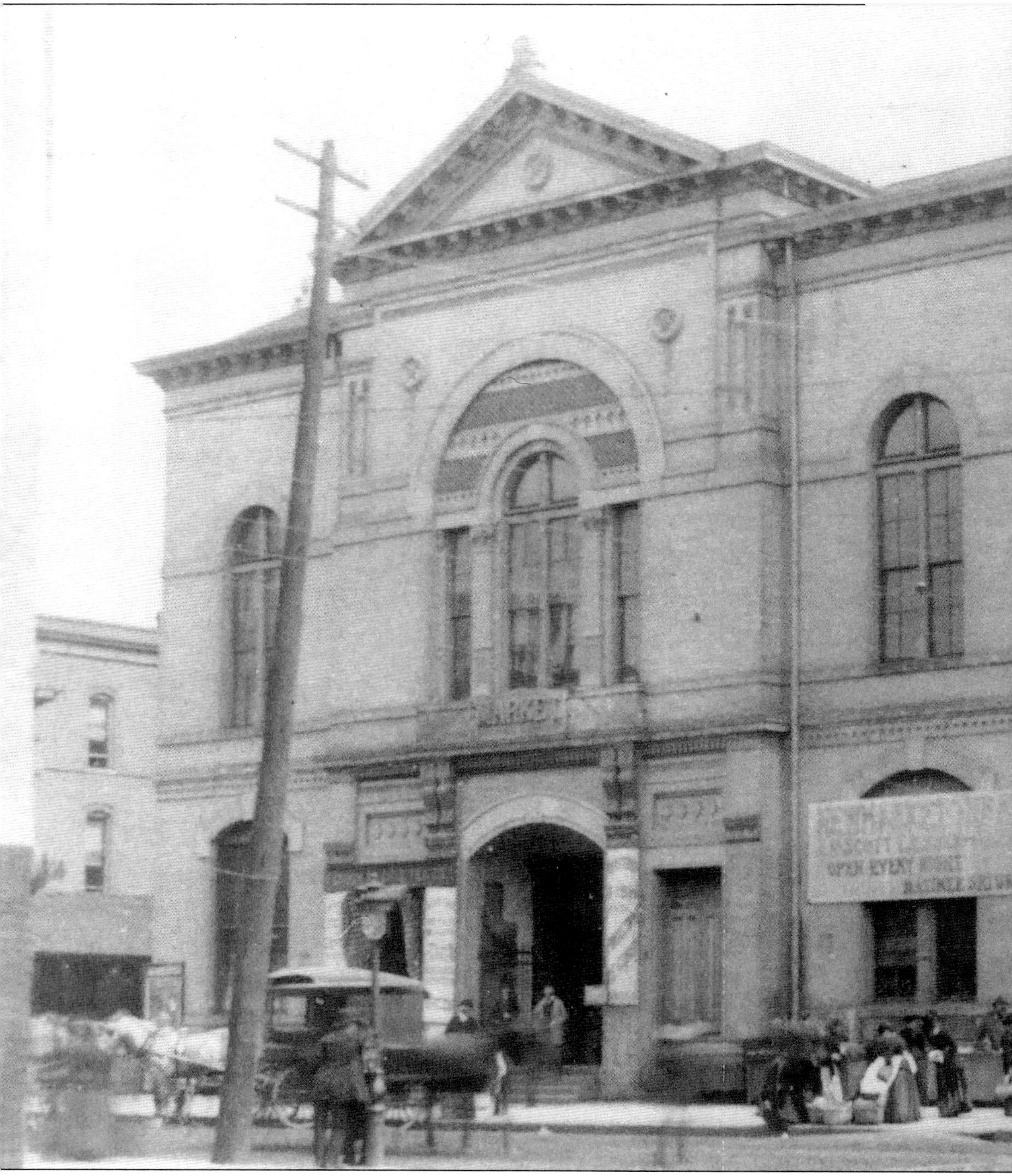

Pictured here is Market Hall, located on Seventh Street, between Wabasha Street and St. Peter Street. For a period after the State Capitol burned in 1881, the seat of state government was in this building. This was the first block-long public building in the Twin Cities. It occupied

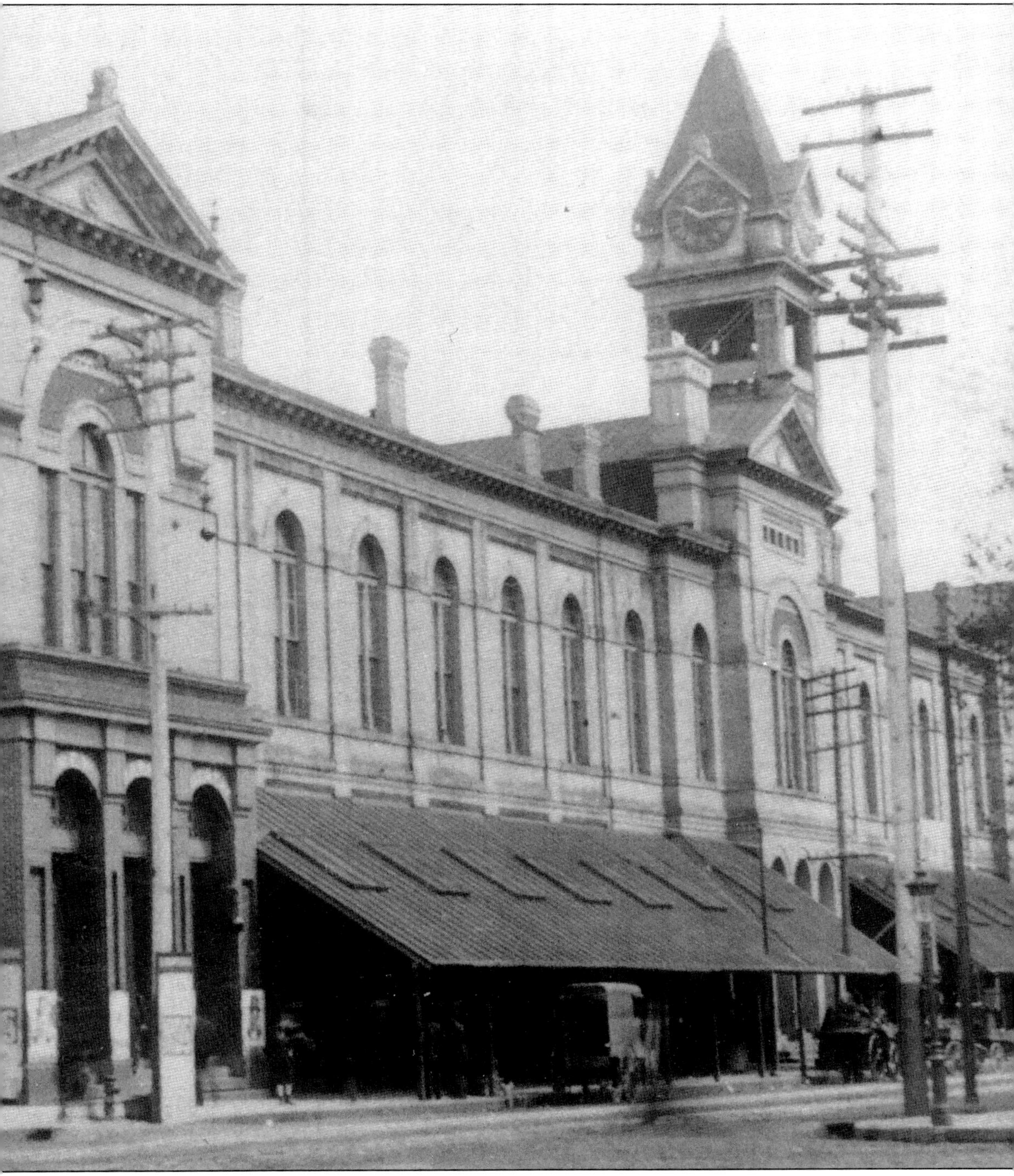

the site of the first city market. The St. Paul Public Library occupied the upper floor until the building burned down in 1915. Much of the early entertaining by the leading Jewish families was held in the Market Hall. (From photo archives of the Ramsey County Historical Society)

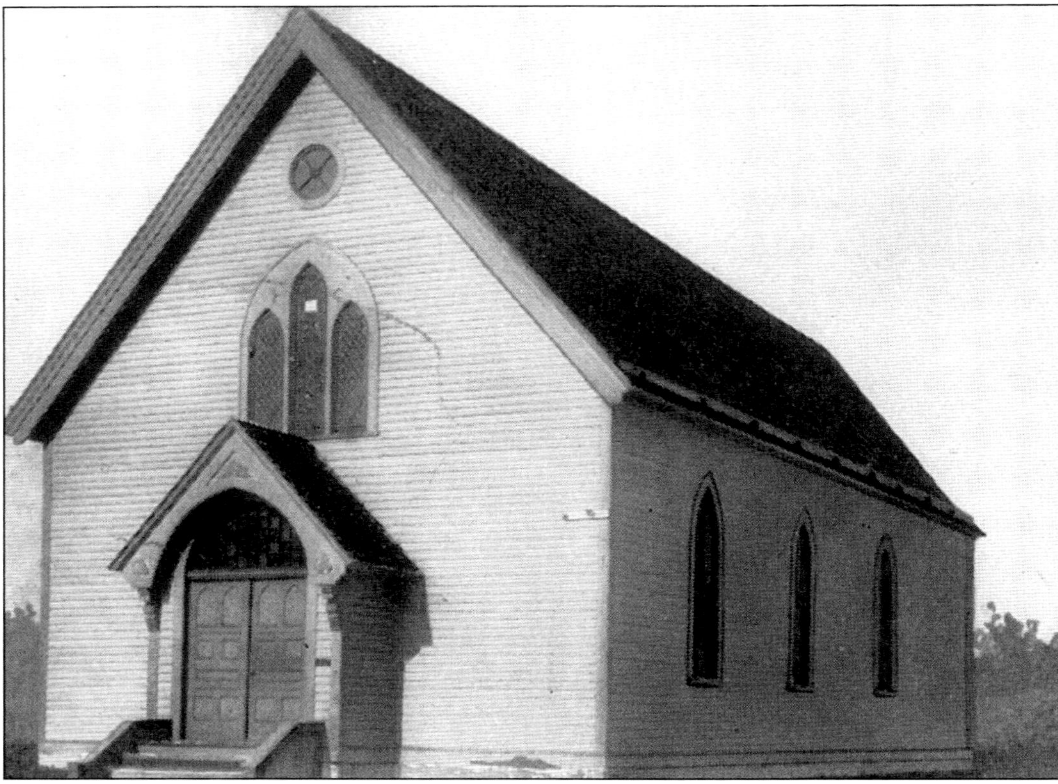

In 1870 the tiny Mt. Zion congregation voted to erect a temple and hold services every Friday evening and Saturday morning. A building committee was appointed, and a lot at Tenth Street and Minnesota Street was purchased for $1,500. The building committee, consisting of Solomon Bergman, Isadore Rose, and Joseph Abeles, were given the power to spend another $1500 to construct a simple frame building. The new building was dedicated and its first services were held in 1871. (From the photo archives of the American Jewish World, September and October, 1979)

Pauline worked for a time in the Ramsey County assessor's office and never married (58). Nathan Bernhein died in 1908 at the age of 83, and his widow, who was 20 years his junior, lived at 218 Rondo with her brother David Mayer until her death in 1915. There were no surviving children (59). Nathan Bernheim was one of a group of men who in the late 1860s assumed leadership roles in Mt. Zion synagogue and the Jewish community.

Edwin L. Fryer was 22 when he joined the 6th Minnesota Regiment in the Union Army in August of 1862. He was also Mrs. Abram Elfelt's brother, and when Edwin L. Fryer was wounded and discharged from the Union Army in December of 1864, he returned to St. Paul and went to work for the Elfelt family business (60). However, he did this only for a short period of time and later became a cashier for Averill, Russell, and Carpenter, a prominent pioneer stationery house, and worked for them for many years. His mother Anna, widow of William Fryer, lived with the Elfelts in Irvine Park until her death. For many years, Edwin L. Fryer lived at 126 Kent, a house which is still standing. He had at least one daughter, Edith, who was a school teacher. In 1912 he was living at 874 Linwood (61).

There were others of the Jewish faith who served in the Civil War on both sides. Some served in the 6th Minnesota Regiment on the Union side, others served the Union or Confederate armies elsewhere and settled in St. Paul after the Civil War. Joseph Rosenfield was another who served in the 6th Minnesota Regiment. His father and mother had died within one year of each other, and young Rosenfield was only 17 when he petitioned the Ramsey County Probate Court in St. Paul for permission to join the 6th Regiment of the Union army as a drummer boy (62). There is no record he ever returned to St. Paul.

Charles Hostetter, who was born in Germany, served in the 2nd Louisiana Regiment on the Confederate side. He was wounded 5 times and discharged in 1864 (63). He came to St. Paul with his brother Abram after the war ended. Benjamin H. Plechner was 27 when he enlisted in 1861 as a sergeant in the 6th Engineers Regiment of the New York State militia. He too came to St. Paul after the Civil War ended (64). Both men were active in Mt. Zion congregation, Hostetter serving as Trustee in 1879, and Plechner serving many offices, including president, in 1875. In 1874, Plechner also served as president of the Minnesota Lodge of B'nai B'rith, the Jewish fraternal and service organization (65). There were three other Jews who served in the Civil War who settled in St. Paul after the Civil War ended, and who are buried in Mt. Zion Cemetery as veterans of that war. They are Michael Harris, Bernard Neumann, and Joseph H. Smith (66). There are no service records available for them.

In 1864, Levi and Aaron Lovenstein arrived in St. Paul. Aaron was a clerk in the cattle business and lived with David Lowitz, another pioneer settler and dealer in hides and furs. Levi lived on Fort Street (West 7th) and was a clerk for Joseph Ullmann, also a fur and hide dealer (67). Levi became a charter member of the Minnesota Lodge of the B'nai B'rith when it was organized in 1871, and later became its president in 1878 (68). Levi was also active in Mt. Zion synagogue affairs. He had two sons, Morris and Louis, and a daughter, Lillie. The Lovensteins also lost two infants, Tessie in 1882, and Sidney in 1883 (69). Levi lived to be a very old man and helped the Minnesota Lodge of B'nai B'rith to celebrate its 50th birthday in 1922 (70). B'nai B'rith leaders from all over the country came to St. Paul and attended this Golden Anniversary celebration to pay their respects to Mr. Lovenstein. Levi lived in the Mt. Airy area for many years on De Bow Street, and at the turn of the century was living at 282 E. Eighth Street in the "Lowertown" area (71). Mrs. Ann Lovenstein, Levi and Aaron's mother, lived with Aaron until her death.

The Civil War ended the pioneering era of the St. Paul Jewish community. The community had, in a short period of 15 years, established its roots. Several of the pioneer families were still on the scene at the close of the Civil War. Other had just arrived or were yet to arrive who were to have a profound effect on the growth and development of the religious and cultural life of St. Paul's small Jewish community.

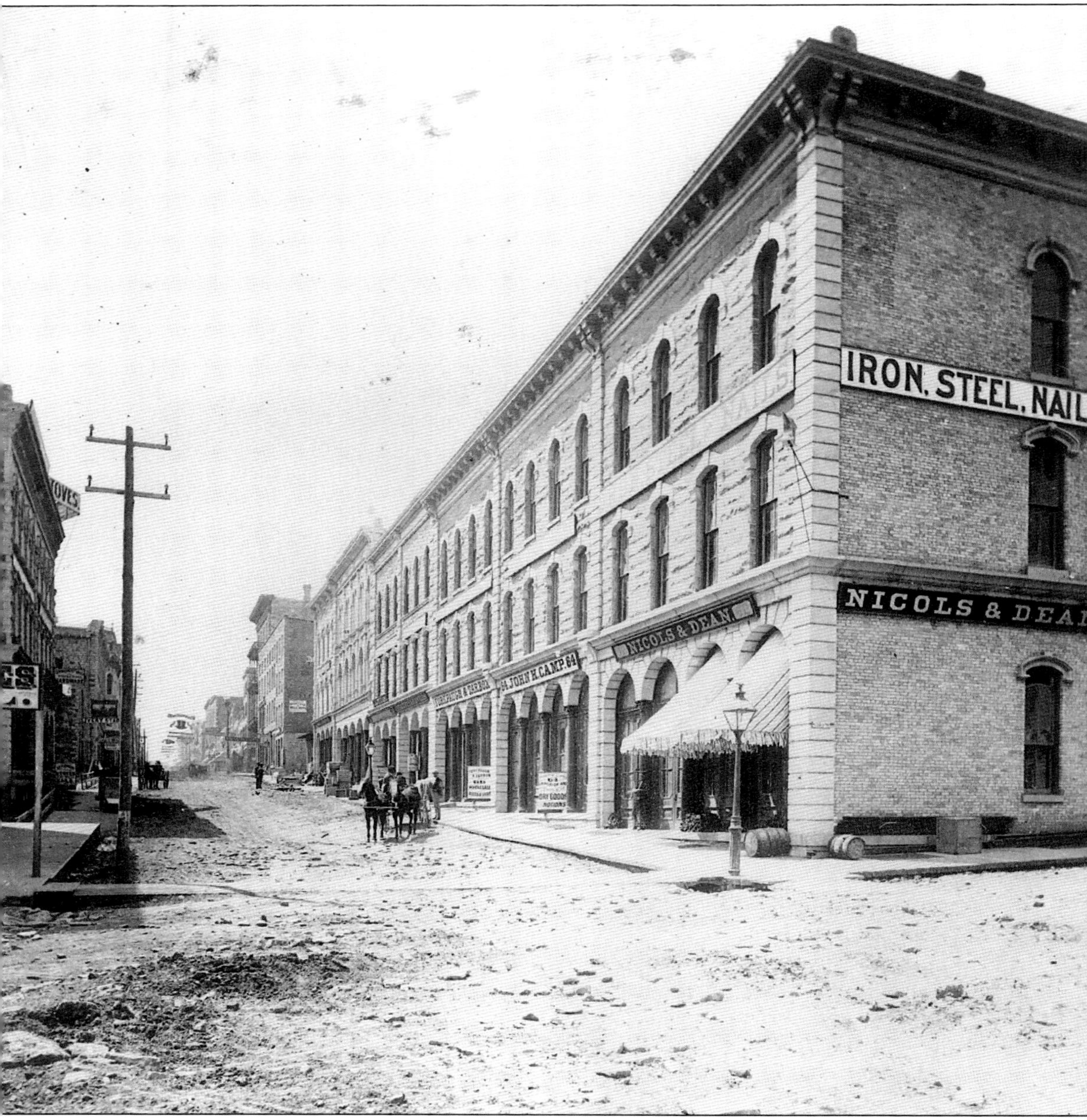

Third Street (now Kellogg Boulevard) looking west from Sibley Street, about 1870. All of the buildings on the South (left) side of the street were torn down when Kellogg Boulevard was built. This picture was taken by William Illingworth, pioneer photographer of early downtown St. Paul. This part of the "Lowertown" wholesale district along East Third Street and East Fourth Street was the heart of the St. Paul commercial district in the 1860s and 1870s. In the Northeast corner of the "Lowertown" area, many of the wealthiest Jewish families, together with their famous neighbor, James J. Hill, built large handsome frame homes. (From the photo archives of the Minnesota Historical Society)

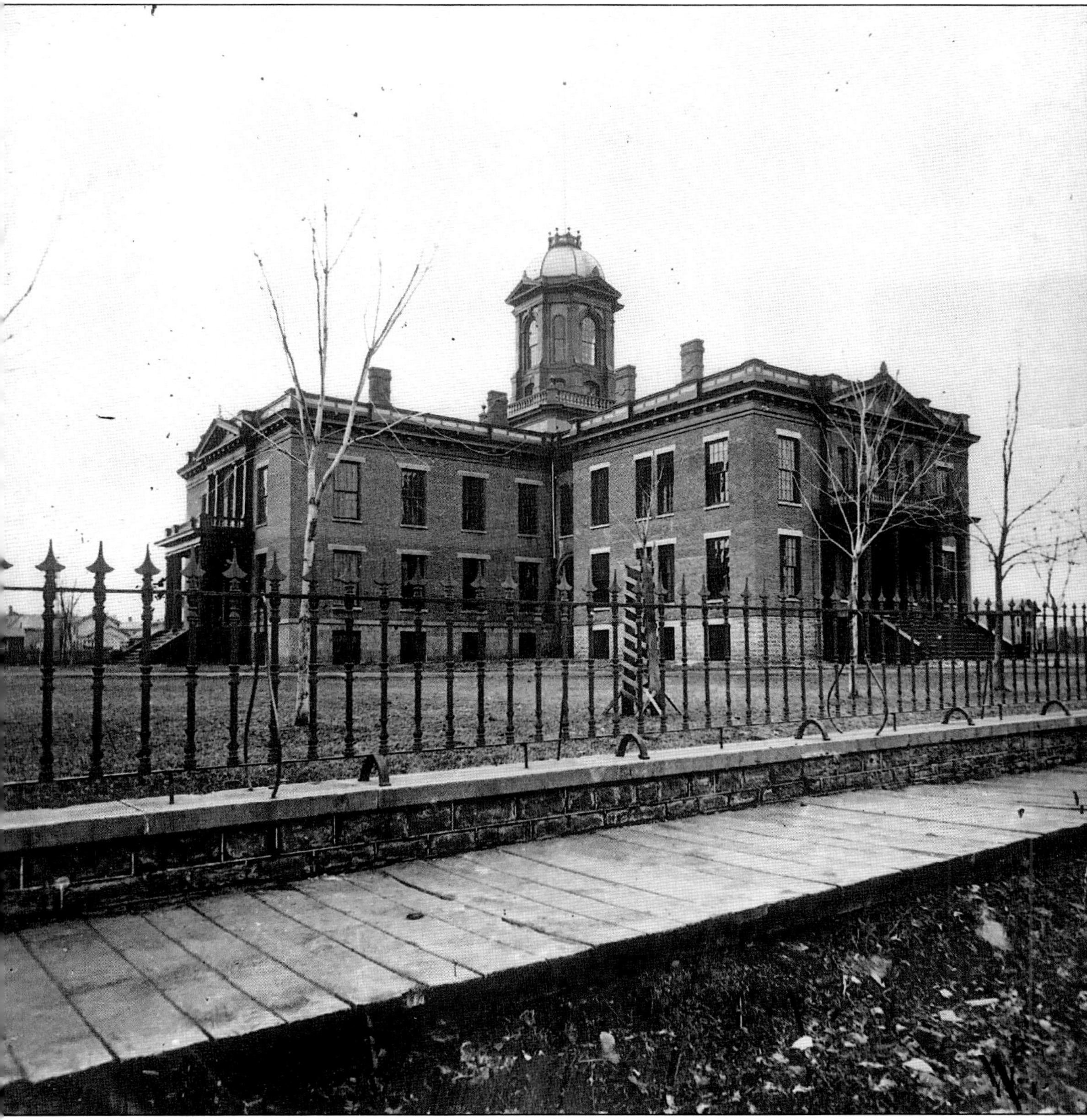

The first State Capitol building, completed in 1853, was a simple Greek Revival style building. Minnesota's first capitol block, located on a block bounded by Wabasha, Cedar, Exchange, and Tenth Streets, is shown after first remodeling in 1872. Much of the early Jewish community clustered around this area. The first Jewish synagogue, Mt. Zion, was constructed on Tenth and Minnesota in 1871, just a block away. (From the photo archives of the Minnesota Historical Society)

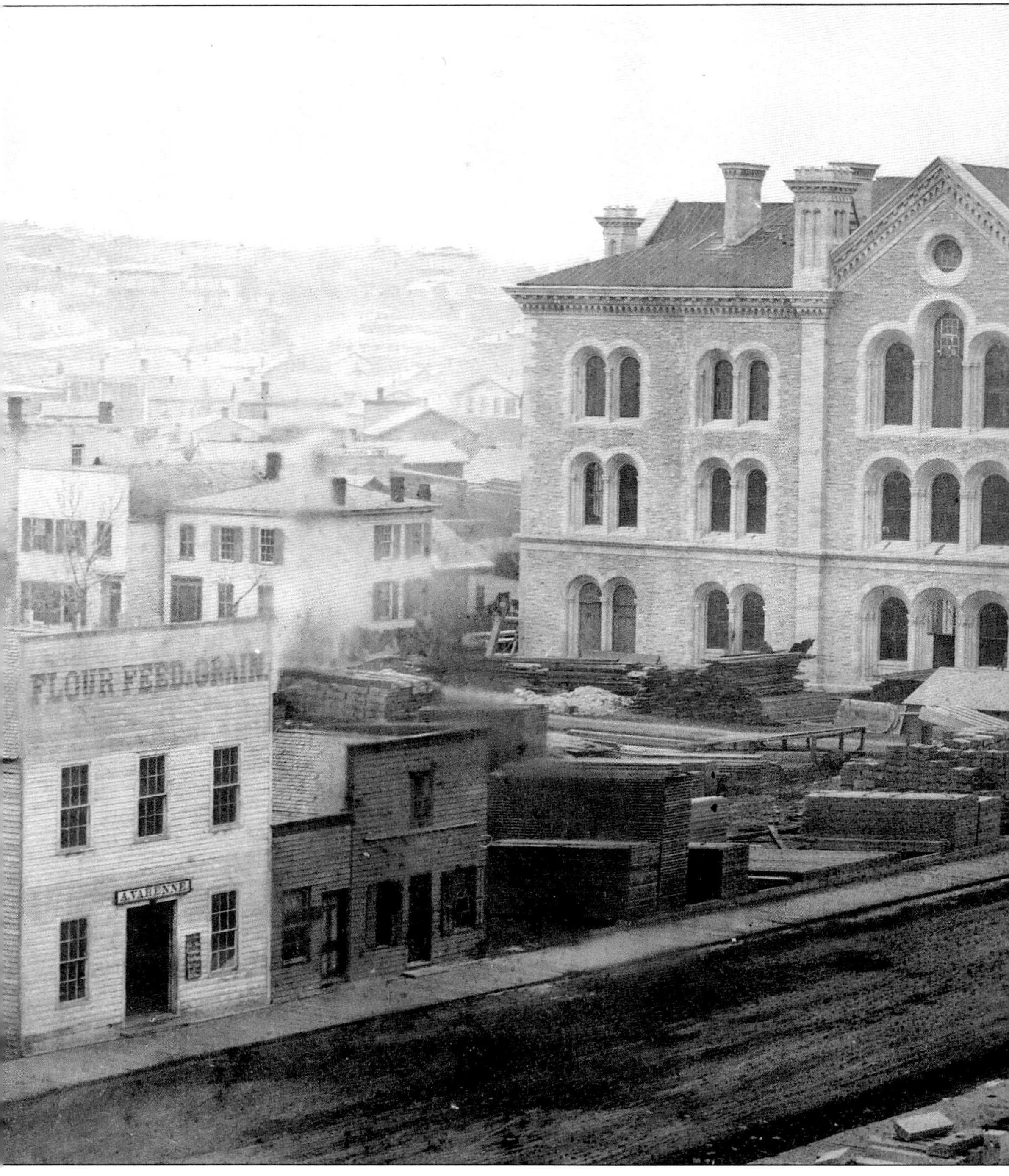

United States Customs house, built to hold the U.S. Post Office, federal courtrooms, and offices of other federal agencies. It was the first downtown federal building in the Twin Cities, and is shown in 1873 shortly after its completion. It was located at the northwest

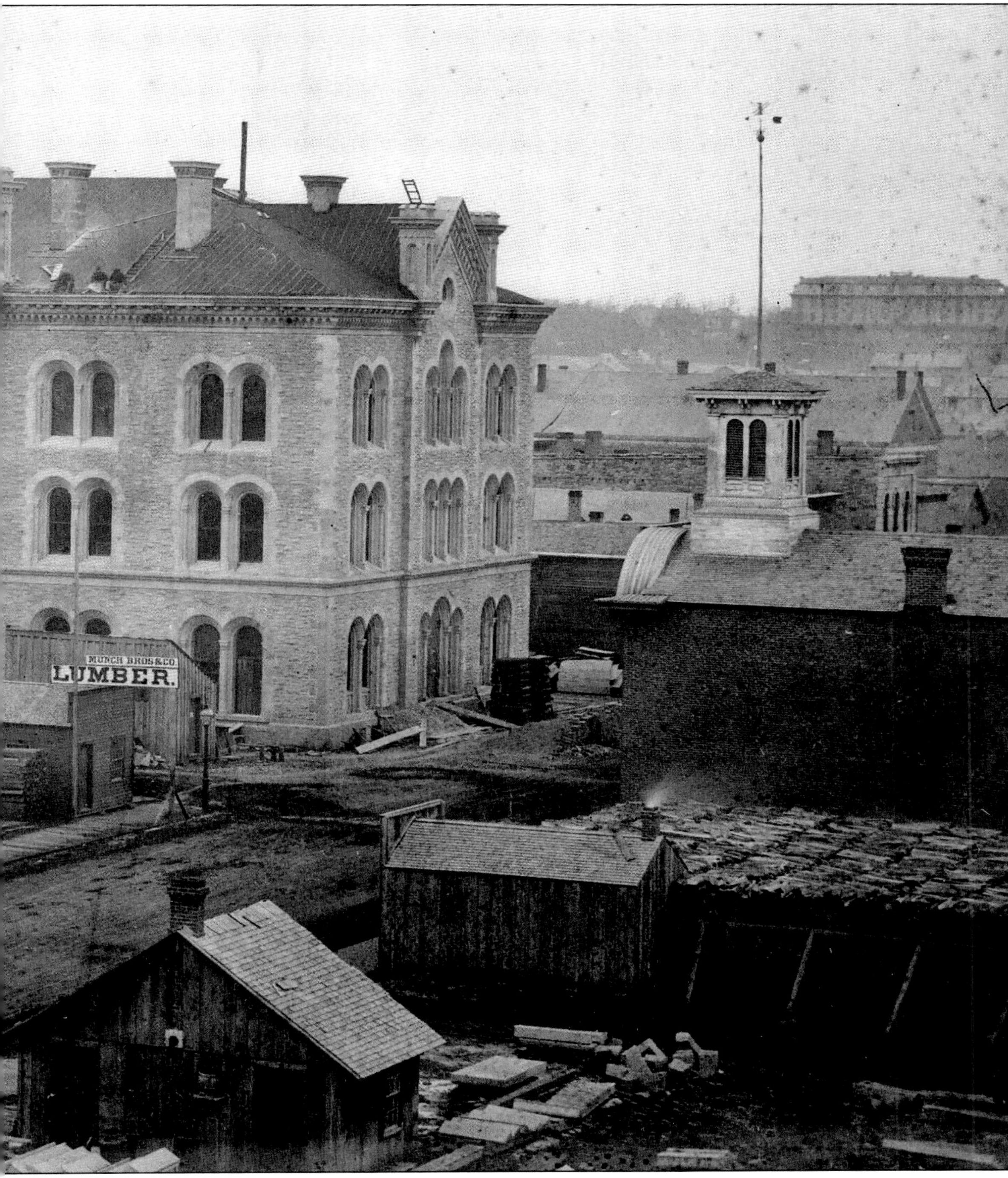

corner of Fifth Street and Wabasha. Judge Isaac N. Cardozo had his courtroom in this building. (From the photo archives of the Minnesota Historical Society)

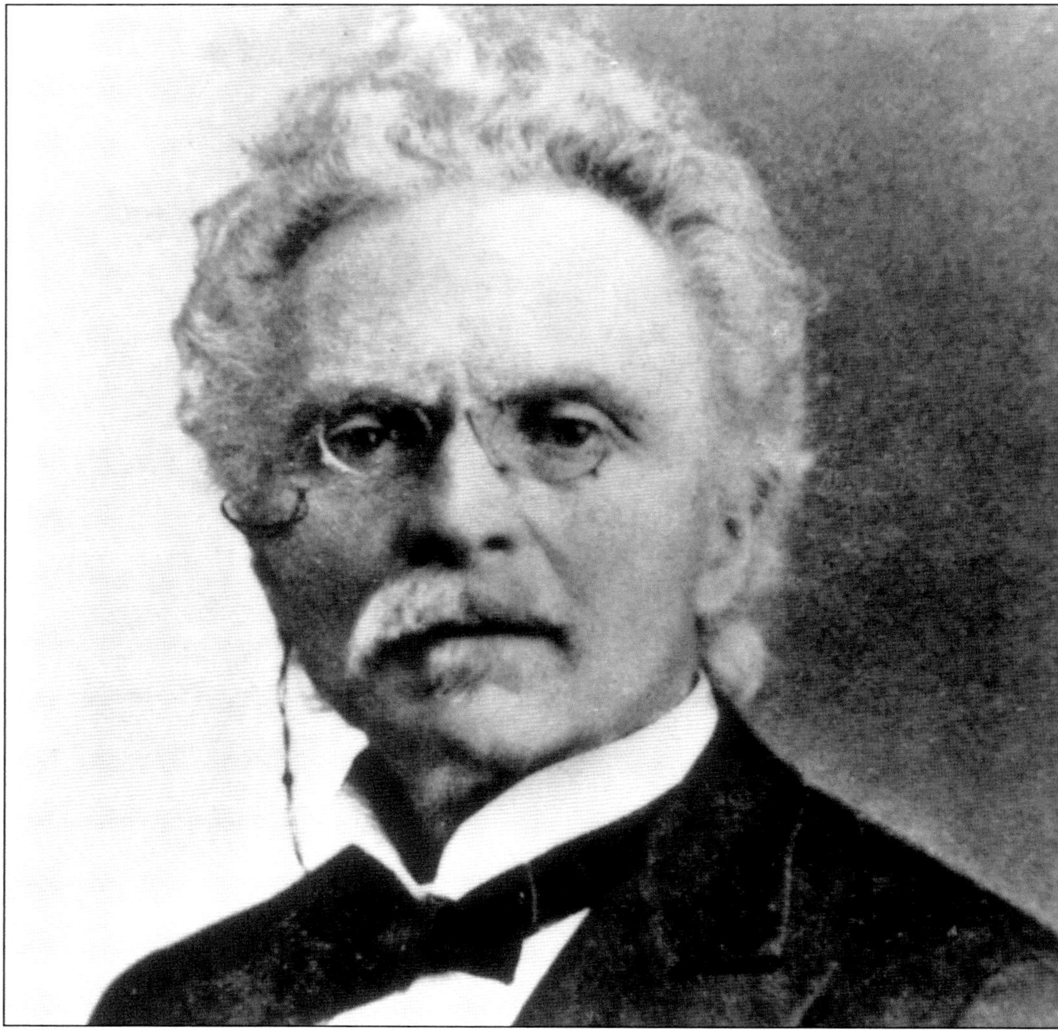

Rabbi Leopold Wintner, as the first Rabbi for the tiny Mt. Zion congregation, was also the very first rabbi in the state of Minnesota. He was hired in late 1871 and was paid $1200 per year. A. Applebaum was hired as shochet *(ritual butcher) for $600 per year. Rabbi Wintner served for two years until 1873. At the time, members were paying $2 per month for dues and an additional $6 per year for the privilege of buying* kosher *(ritually slaughtered) meat from the temple's official butcher. The official butcher paid the synagogue the sum of $50 for the privilege of being the official butcher. Rabbi Wintner brought to the tiny Jewish community a voice which, speaking in the name of Judaism, protested the effort by so-called Christian zealots to establish Christianity as the official American religion. When he left in 1873, he was acclaimed as a "man worthy of his profession, who openly and conscientiously proclaimed the free doctrine of Judaism." (From the photo archives of the Minnesota Historical Society)*

Hannah Leopold Austrian, large in spirit, influence, and size, was one of the "grande dames" of the pioneer Jewish women. Married before she was 19, she and her husband Julius were among the first white settlers in Fon Du Lac, Wisconsin. When they arrived in St. Paul in 1869, the Jewish community was in desperate straits. She founded the Hebrew Ladies Benevolent Society and served as its president for many years. She also helped to found the Neighborhood House on the old West Side Flats, and was the long-time sponsor of the Mt. Zion choir, and supervisor of its Sunday school after it was organized. She and her husband had at least three sons: Joseph, Edward, and Albert, and one daughter, Rachel. (from the Photo Archives of the Wisconsin Historical Society)

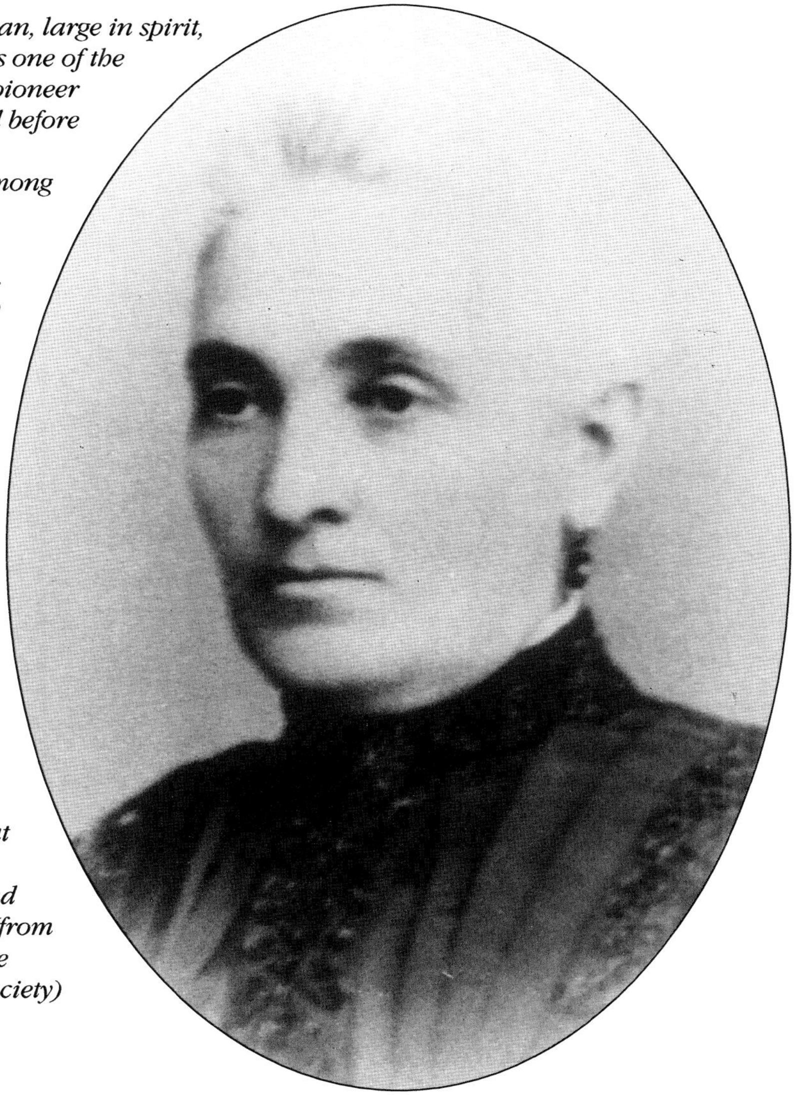

Chapter 3
AFTER THE CIVIL WAR

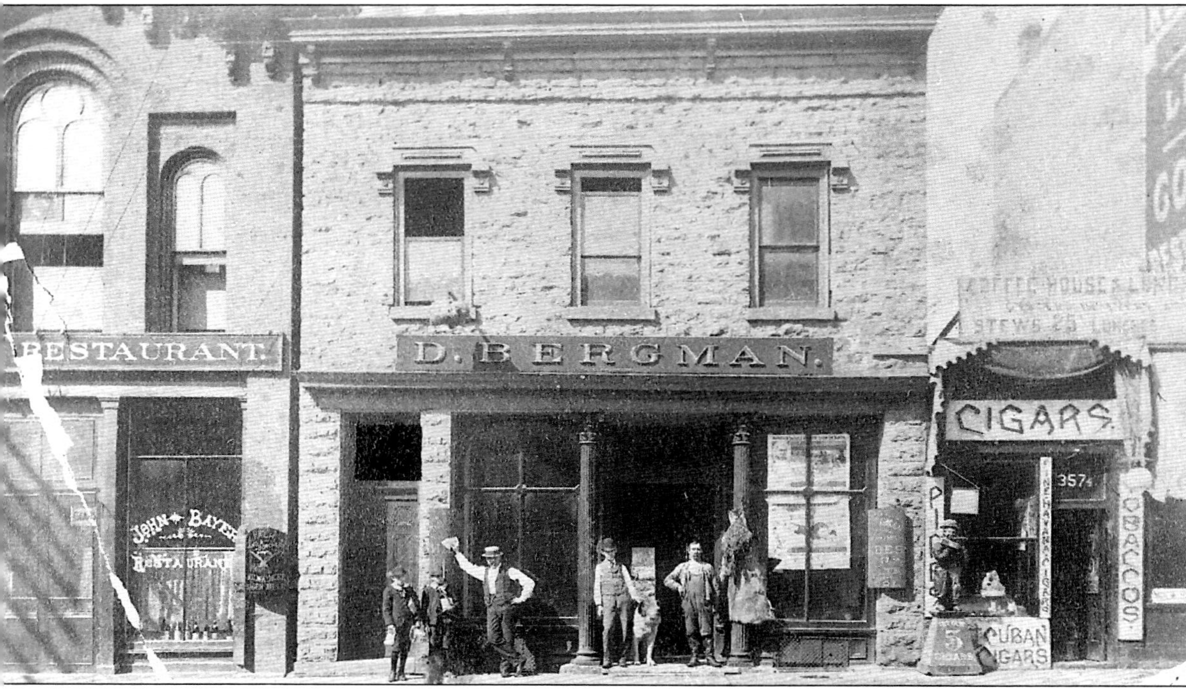

After Solomon Bergman died, his son David took over his fur business. His store was located on Jackson Street, right down the street from the Joseph Ullmann fur operation run by Isadore Rose. (From the photo archives of the Minnesota Historical Society)

The Civil War had a marked effect on the St. Paul community, for Jew and Gentile alike. It marked the end of the pioneering era and the beginning of expansion of the little river community from a frontier village to a major urban community. The end of the Civil War in 1865 also brought back to the community the prosperity that the Depression of 1857 had wiped out (72).

Prior to the Civil War, Jewish immigrants and settlers were faced with the necessity of adjusting themselves to a strange new civilization. Many of them had come from lands where the life of a Jew was hemmed in by medieval restrictions. They had all come to the United States to taste the nectar of freedom that was denied to them in their native lands. For many the taste of freedom was too much and many decided to abandon their Jewish affiliation, not by conversion, but by default. An early example had been set by many of the colonial Jewish pioneers who had chosen not to maintain their Jewish loyalties. Many of the early prominent American Jews who settled in the colonial period had intermarried and abandoned Jewish life.

Now that the Civil War was over, many of the early Jewish pioneers who settled in St. Paul were facing these same problems (73).

Jewish community life in St. Paul was in a state of chaos; many of its early leaders had left or died. The faint rumblings of

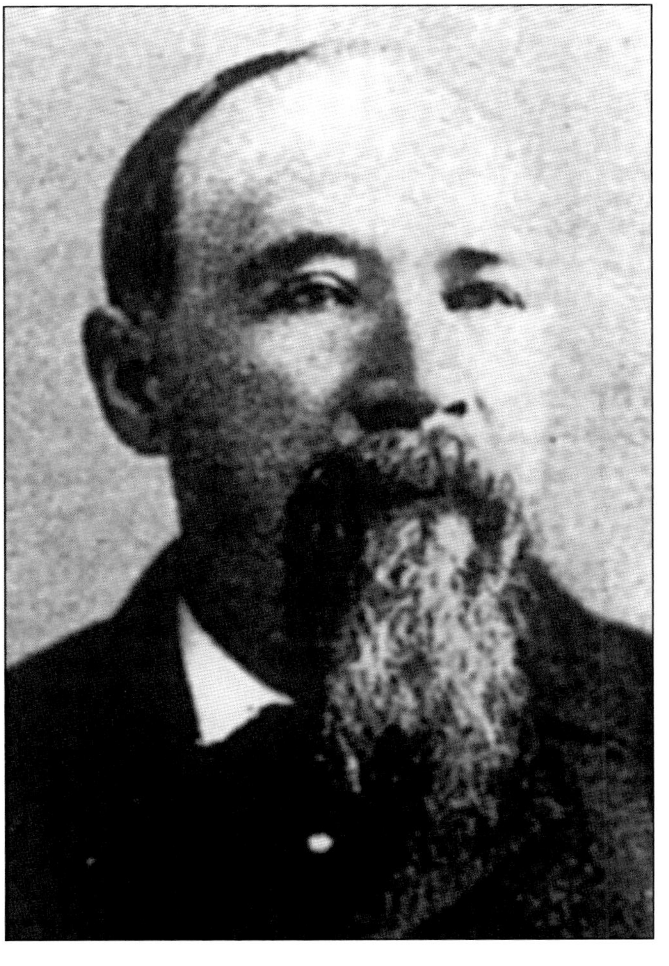

Some regard Solomon Bergman as a giant in the formation and development of Mt. Zion Synagogue. In 1870, he was president and served on the building committee that purchased the lot on which the first Mt. Zion Synagogue was built and supervised its construction. He returned as president of the synagogue in 1874, then from 1876–1880, from 1884–85, in 1889, and from 1894–1895. During his term in 1889, he led the movement to remove the old Mt. Zion cemetery to its present day location. Also during his term, he attempted to have a chapel constructed at the cemetery, which was not attained until after his death. Even as a synagogue leader, he still remained active in his business of wholesale furs and hides. He was never actively involved in public charity work. He died in 1895 while on business for the synagogue. (From the photo archives of the Mt. Zion synagogue)

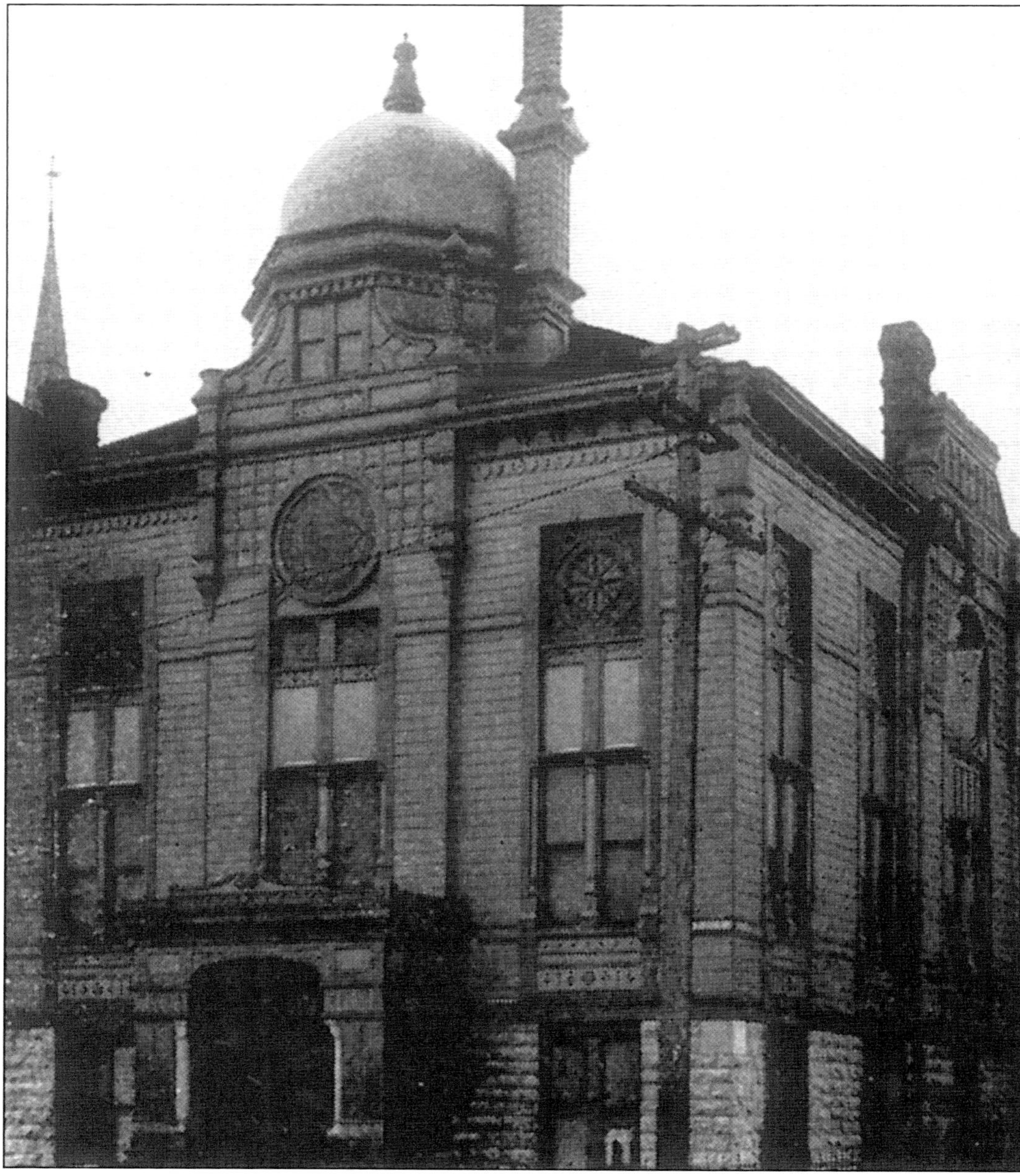

During the term of Rabbi Judah Wechsler, the old frame synagogue building, constructed in 1871, was removed and sold to an African American church group then located on Fuller Street. In 1882, a new and larger synagogue was constructed for $11,000. Mt. Zion remained in this building until about 1901. When a new synagogue was built, the building at Tenth Street and Minnesota Street, was sold to the Sons of Abraham, a newly organized orthodox group. (From the Archives of the "American Jewish World.")

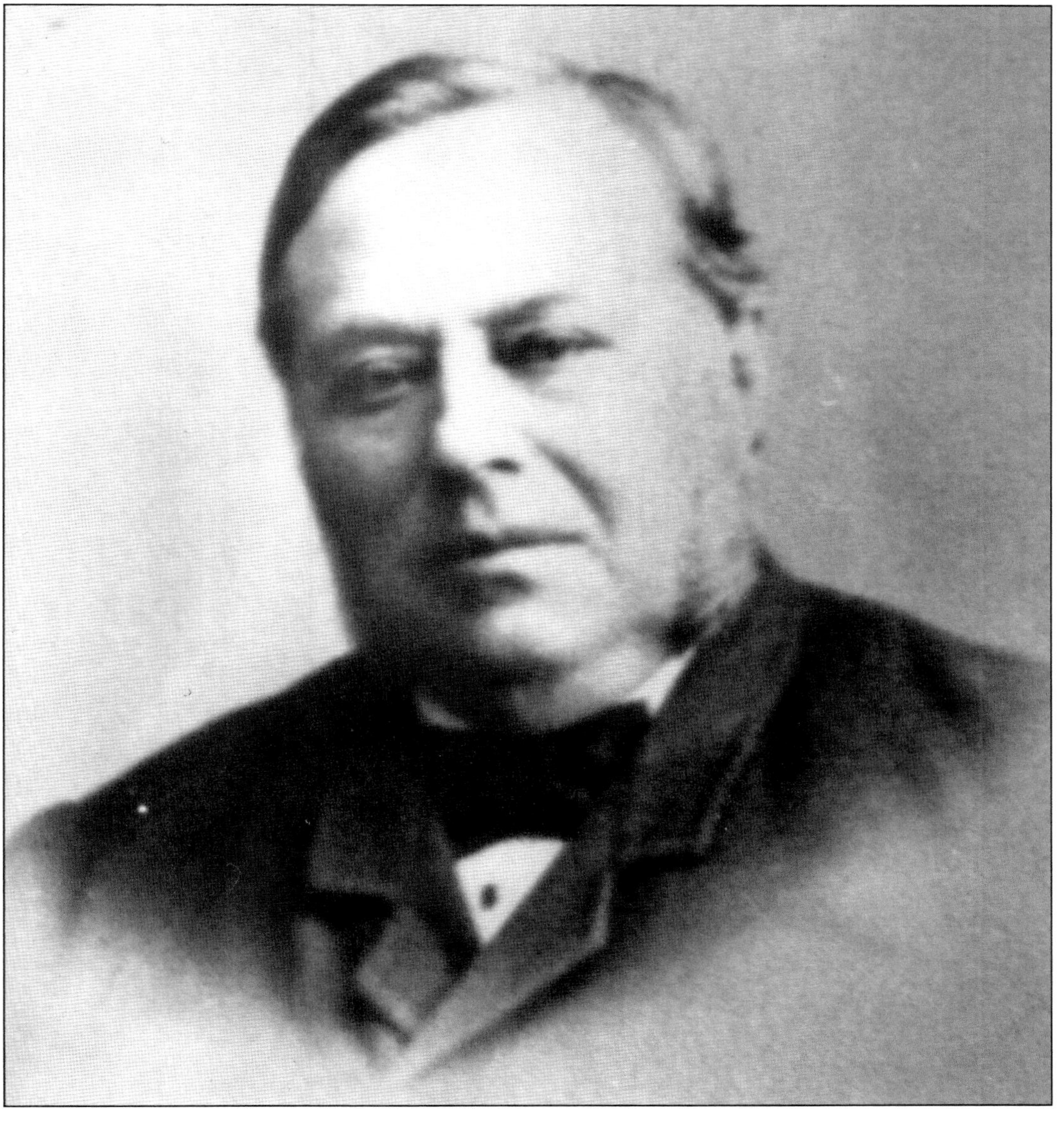

Julius Austrian was one of the more influential and colorful Jewish pioneers. In 1849, he and his wife Hannah Leopold Austrian were among the first white settlers in La Pointe and Fon Du Lac, Wisconsin, at a time when the Minnesota Territory was part of the Wisconsin Territory. In 1855, they had participated in the Jewish High Holiday services in La Pointe. He was already a successful businessman when he and his family came to St. Paul in 1869 from Wisconsin. He had a string of successful stores throughout the Upper Michigan Peninsula. He also had already acquired claims in mineral rights around Lake Superior, where the city of Duluth now stands. He was a man of great generosity, and when the fledgling Mt. Zion Synagogue was unable to hire its first rabbi, he guaranteed payment. He also was a moving force in the failed attempt to establish the Painted Woods colony in North Dakota. (From the photo archives of the Wisconsin Historical Society)

change were brought with the arrival of new German immigrants after the Civil War. The movement of Reform Judaism had its beginnings in Germany after the defeat of Napoleon and the return of oppression and tyranny in Germany. Many young Jewish men and women, tired of being discriminated against because they were Jews, and seeking the freedom and opportunities which were denied them because of their religion, left the faith of their fathers and became Christians. It was then that a number of Jewish leaders, hoping to keep their young people true to their own faith, began the movement known as Reform Judaism (74).

The influx of Eastern European immigrants encouraged the development of Reform Judaism and accelerated it psychologically (75). It was not ritual as much as social pressure that encouraged the separation. What had been strictly orthodox practice with variations of native religious customs (76) became a permanent division and the beginnings of the Reform Jewish movement in St. Paul. What had been a homogenous group was now bursting from within. New arrivals, some immigrants and some native born, would be men and women who would have to meet this challenge to the survival of the Jewish community.

One of the first to arrive during this period was an individual who was to have a momentous impact in stabilizing the religious life of these early Jewish settlers. He was Solomon Bergman. Mr. Bergman was born in 1830, in Olnhausen, Germany, and arrived in America at the age of 17. A year after his arrival found him in Cleveland, Ohio, as a partner in the clothing business under the firm name Wagerman Brothers and Bergman. He married Julia Schlesinger, traveled abroad during the Civil War, and on his return at the close of the Civil War in 1865, settled in St. Paul (77).

Mr. Bergman had come to St. Paul because he suffered from chronic laryngitis and the climate, as well as the fur trade, were beneficial to him. He spent his lifetime in the business of furs and hides. In 1868, he joined the ailing Mt. Zion congregation, which Julius Mendelsohn had struggled to hold together during the war. In 1870, Mr. Bergman succeeded Jacob Newman as president of Mt. Zion in a movement to invigorate and reorganize the old Mt. Zion group founded by the pioneers. He spent the rest of his active life outside of business devoting hours of time to Mt. Zion. He was a conservative influence against the impending struggle to abandon the traditional ways and move towards Reform Judaism. He had three sons who worked in his business—David, Oscar, and Clarence. The family lived at 381 Eighth Street in the "Lowertown" area (78). He died in 1895 while strolling down the street on synagogue business (79). Clarence Street on the East side of St. Paul was platted in 1886 and named after Clarence Bergman, his youngest son. (80) Others opposed Mr. Bergman's views on Reform Judaism.

Alexander Sternberg arrived in 1866 and opened a clothing store at 372 Third Street, eventually known as the "New York Clothing House." He was another in the group of young men who had asserted leadership in the ailing Mt. Zion after the Civil War. However, he was one of the early believers in establishing Reform Judaism in place of the existing orthodoxy that had been in place since the founding of Mt. Zion. He served in many capacities in Mt. Zion, including vice president (81). He was also a very prominent member of the business community, serving on the board of various banks in the city (82).

Alexander Sternberg and his two brothers, Herman (Ike) and Samuel, who later joined him in business, had come from Louisville, Kentucky. All were originally from Ellar, Germany, where their father, Lesman, and a sister, Bertha, remained (83). Herman, whose wedding in 1888 was one of the "social events of the season," later moved to Fargo, North Dakota (84). Alexander had four daughters—Hattie, Jennie, Flora, and Sadie. His wife had died in 1883 and is buried in Mt. Zion cemetery (85). Hattie, his daughter, served as a Sunday school teacher for Mt. Zion children, after a Sunday school was first organized (86).

Despite the impending struggle in Mt. Zion over the drift towards Reform Judaism, there were others in the Jewish community who were fairly ambivalent as to the outcome, and who were also above remaining in the orthodox fold with the Eastern European settlers. Among these was an old established Jewish Sephardic family.

When Benjamin Solomon Seixas—a descendant of the prominent old Colonial Eastern Jewish Seixas, Gomez and Levy families—died in 1866 in New York, his widow Zipporah, who was Mrs. Isaac N. Cardozo's sister, moved to St. Paul (87). She brought her 5-year-old daughter Rebecca, and 4 sons: Isaac Benjamin, age 17; Gershom C., age 12; Jacob C., age 10; and Harry, age 7 (88). They apparently had little more than the family's prestigious name when they arrived, and they were forced to live with Judge Isaac N. Cardozo and his family for a number of years (89).

Isaac Benjamin Seixas, the oldest of the Seixas sons, went to work for Moritz Auerbach, a Jew by birth but not practice, who was a prominent dry goods merchant and banker, and who had married Senator Henry Rice's daughter, Mathilda. Isaac later worked as an entry clerk, bookkeeper, and finally as cashier for Joseph Oppenhim, prominent milliner (90). Isaac married Rachel Hart of New York, and with his three brothers moved into a house on Sherman Street in Irvine Park. Eventually they moved to 344 Iglehart and then to 255 Louis on St. Anthony Hill, and they all resided together until about 1887, (91) when Judge Isaac N. Cardozo died. Isaac B. Seixas was active in B'nai B'rith and served as vice president in 1876 (92). The next year when his uncle Isaac N. Cardozo died, he served as the executor of his uncle's estate (93). In 1889, he appears on the Mt. Zion membership list, (94) although none of his brothers do.

In 1895, Isaac B. Seixas left the Oppenheimer millinery firm (which had succeeded the Joseph Oppenheim firm) when Mr. Oppenheim returned to New York (95) and went to work as a salesman for S. Weiss, a clothing merchant. He died in 1903 at the age of 53, leaving his wife Rachel, and at least 2 daughters, Rachel and Jeanette. They apparently returned to New York after his death (96).

Jacob B. Seixas, or Jay as he was commonly called, went to work for the Minnesota Steam Laundry, and then the Troy Laundry, first as a manager and eventually acquiring a partnership (97). In June of 1877, it was reported in the *St. Paul Daily Dispatch* that Jacob had been elected as new president of B'nai B'rith (98). This is supported by the city directory of that year (99). However, B'nai B'rith records do not show that he assumed or held the office for its full term, for whatever reason (100). For many years Jacob was active in and served as recorder of the Banner Lodge of the Ancient Order of United Workmen, a secret fraternal group (101). In 1899, Jacob Seixas was employed in the cigar business and lived at 372 N. Smith (102). He probably never married and disappeared from the scene.

Harry Seixas, or Henry as he sometimes called himself when listed in the city directory, lived with his mother at the Cardozo's until Mrs. Seixas' death, and then alternately living with his brothers Jacob, Gershom, and Isaac. He worked with his brother, Isaac, at Auerbach and Finch's. Even after Isaac left the Auerbach firm, Henry stayed on as a salesman and continued on after it became Finch and Van Slyke, until he died. He never married. (103)

Gershom Seixas, namesake of the Revolutionary War "Patriot Rabbi," lived the longest. He worked at many trades; his first job was with Kelly Mercantile, for a while he worked as foreman for Minnesota Steam Laundry, and then he was a manufacturer's agent for Foley Mercantile. He finally became a merchandise broker (104). He married and he and his wife, Sibba, had at least three daughters—Joette, Isabelle, and Harriet—

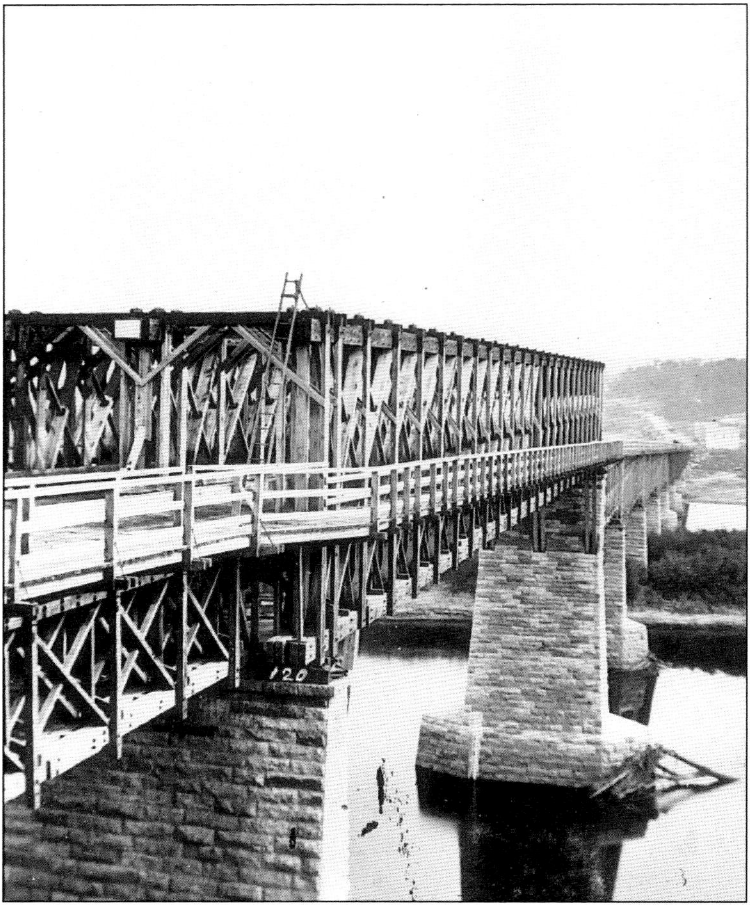

The first Wabasha Street bridge across the Mississippi River is shown here c. 1859, over to the West side of St. Paul. It was replaced shortly after this picture was taken. The so-called "West Side" remained a part of Dakota County until 1874, when it was annexed to St. Paul, and shortly thereafter the "West Side Flats" became home to many Jewish immigrants, and a lively Jewish community with many of its own synagogues. It frequently flooded, and urban renewal programs in the 20th century eventually wiped this community out. Photo by William H. Illingworth. (From the photo archives of the Minnesota Historical Society)

and a son, H. Dwight Seixas. He lived in White Bear for a number of years, but after the Great Depression of 1929, he went to live with his son (105).

Whether Abbie I. Seixas, who died on July 20, 1884 (106), was possibly a maiden aunt or a cousin of the Seixas' we do not know, but she appeared in 1879 living with the Seixas brothers on Sherman Street (107). Hers was one of the early burials in the old Mt. Zion Cemetery, then located adjacent to Oakland Cemetery on Front and Jackson (108).

Rebecca Sexias, the baby, lived with her brother, Gershom, for a number of years, and was living with her brother Isaac when he died. Whether she returned to New York with Isaac's widow and daughters to rejoin the large Seixas clan, or whether she married, we do not know, but she disappears from the scene after 1903, the year of Isaac's death (109).

Not all the settlers of the Jewish faith were from Germany. Some came from Austria-Hungary (Bohemia), France, and England, and many—like the Elfelts and Judge Isaac N. Cardozo who were native born Americans and had been born elsewhere in the United States— settled in St. Paul.

Zsigo, or Z. Weiss as he was most often called, was born in Hungary and arrived in St. Paul in 1868. He was a manufacturer and dealer in hoop skirts and women's corsets when he first arrived, and later was a prominent milliner (110).

Mr. Weiss was another of the leaders in the Mt. Zion synagogue that had joined and almost immediately became influential in the destination of what was then St. Paul's only organized Jewish congregation. Mr. Weiss served as secretary of Mt. Zion in 1871 (111). He had at least four sons: Phillip, Sigmund, Adolph, and Herman (112). He also had a brother, Phillip H. Weiss, who was his business partner in Weiss and Weiss, located at 97 E. Seventh for a number of years (113). Z. Weiss lived at 243 Twelfth Street (old Norris), and his brother, Phillip, lived at 626 Temperance and the 345 Pleasant Avenue (114).

Sylvester Sulzbach was born in France (115) and arrived in St. Paul in 1867. In the 1869–70 St. Paul Business Directory, he is listed as a "cigarian artist" (116). He later went to work for John Hart as a cigar maker (117). He had two sons, Moses and David, (118). In 1879 he was elected president of the Minnesota Lodge of the B'nai B'rith and was re-elected again in 1891 (119). At the turn of the century he was living at 525 L'Orient. Gustave Sulzbach, another cigar maker, may have been his brother (120).

For those Jews who were determined to remain faithful, a vague and amorphous pattern of communal life centered in the synagogue. The synagogue was not merely a house of worship, but also the communal center; educational, philanthropic, and social activities were carried on within its precincts. In the average community, parochial schools, charitable and philanthropic societies, and fraternal organizations were all part of the synagogue complex (121).

Two significant events took place in 1869 that had a permanent impact on the pattern of communal life within the St. Paul Jewish community. The first event involved the more orthodox of the settlers. Dissatisfied with Mt. Zion, they began to gather together for private prayers in a frame house on Payne Avenue near Seventh Street in the Dayton's Bluff near East Side area (122). They were the roots for the first strictly orthodox synagogue in Minnesota and established what later became the Sons of Jacob Synagogue (123). At this point, Mt. Zion began its slow evolution toward Reform Judaism. The second event involved a husband and wife team who were to have far reaching influence. Julius Austrian and his wife Hannah arrived in St. Paul in 1869 when the Jewish communal institutions were in very poor circumstances (124).

Julius Austrian was one of five brothers. In the old country their name was Oestrreicher. In the late 1840s, his older brothers, Marx Austrian and Lewis Leopold, had gone to La Pointe, Wisconsin, on Lake Superior, where they were among the first white settlers. As early as 1855 they held High Holy Day (Yom Kippur) services in La Pointe, Wisconsin. In 1849, Julius married Lewis Leopold's sister Hannah, who was not quite 19. In 1851, he made a trip south to St. Paul in the dead of winter and arrived with two dog trains and several hundred pounds of freight (125). Their business prospered and stores were established on the northernmost part of Michigan's Upper Peninsula (126). The Austrians had an immediate impact on the community. They engaged in building the Mt. Zion synagogue's membership. They helped find money necessary to erect the first synagogue building in Minnesota in 1871, in St. Paul. Hannah founded the Mt. Zion's first women's group, the Hebrew Ladies Benevolent Society, and helped found the St. Paul Neighborhood house (127). She was a stocky woman, large like her husband and the authority of her leadership was coupled with a wonderful sense of humor (128). Unlike his wife, Julius preferred a quiet, behind-the-scenes type of leadership. He was active in the Standard Club (129), the Hebrew Relief Society (130), and the Mt. Zion Cemetery Association (131). He first worked in coal and iron, then clothing, and finally was a produce commission merchant. He died in 1891. The Austrians lived at 478 E. Ninth Street in the "Lowertown" area for many years (132).

Hannah Austrian was a true community leader. The highlight of the 1897 social season was a huge celebration in her honor, on the occasion of her 25th anniversary as president of the Hebrew Ladies Benevolent

Society and long time sponsor of the Mt. Zion Choir and supervisor of its Sunday school. By 1900, with Hannah Austrian as their leader, Jewish women had collected thousands of dollars for philanthropic causes (133). No one else but Hannah Austrian could have gone to the mayor's office and chamber of commerce and raised money and housing for the several hundred Jewish refugees who suddenly appeared on St. Paul's doorstep in 1882 (134). After 1901, she went to live in Chicago with her daughter, Mrs. Emil (Rachel) Hart, until her death. The Austrians also had three sons: Joseph, Edward, and Albert. Albert served five terms as president of Minnesota Lodge No. 157 of B'nai B'rith (135), and was also president of the St. Paul Railway Company (136). Joseph remained in Wisconsin (137).

Marx Austrian was blind from his youth. However, he married Caroline Wilner and was successful in the clothing business and later in the jewelry business with Marx Wittleshofer (138). He had pioneered with the rest of his family and the Native Americans at Lake Superior loved the handicapped white man (139). For many years Marx Austrian was the *shofar* blower for the Mt. Zion congregation. The Jewish New Year has traditionally used the blowing of a ram's horn (*shofar*) to call the faithful to worship. It was considered the highest honor a congregation could bestow on one of its lay members. The *shofar* blower was a respected member with a substantial lung capacity, as the ram's horn was indeed an animal horn, sans valves or conventional mouthpiece of modern instruments. Marx was replaced as *shofar* blower in the 1880s by a cornet (140). The break with tradition was symbolically significant of how far the Reform Judaism movement had gone in a short period of time. Marx outlived his brother by 12 years, and his wife Caroline died in 1910 at the age of 90 (141).

There were others who arrived after the Civil War who struggled to make ends meet, to educate their children in the ways of their fathers through a knowledge of Hebrew and the reading of scripture, and to simply survive. Some did not make it and left. Others did not like the climate and moved on. Early death also played a major role in adding to the harshness of life in the new world, especially in this remote outpost and wilderness. Of the first 100 burials in the old Mt. Zion cemetery of Front and Jackson, more than 30 were babies, who died stillborn or of cholera, heart failure, brain tumors, or diphtheria (142).

Some of these settlers stayed a while and then are lost. Samuel Levy was a cigar maker for William L. Hart and lived on 9th between Wabasha and St. Peter Streets for a while. Joseph Kahn and his widowed mother, Mrs. Solomon Kahn, lived briefly at 98 E. Seventh Street. He was a horse dealer. Abraham Leopold, a Pennsylvanian by birth, came to St. Paul and lived at 25 West Tenth St. He buried a son who had moved to the Montana Territory (143). Leopold Schlesinger, related to Solomon Bergman's wife, came to work for Mr. Bergman and lived in his house for a short while. Samuel Levi was a glazier who died in 1879 leaving a wife and a 12-year-old son (144).

Charles Burnstein, Jacob Levi, Julius Cohn, Ruben Goldstein, Abraham Goldstein, and Abraham Marchofsky were all peddlers. Eva Frank and Jennie Koenigsberg both ran clothing stores. Others like Moses Coddon, David Goodman, Mayer Rosenholtz, Abraham Kaufman, and David Goldman were to be among the early settlers who organized a more orthodox synagogue, Chevrah B'nai Ya 'akov (Sons of Jacob) (145). However, only a handful stayed and all trace is lost of the others. Many who came did not affiliate with any synagogue and their names do not appear on any synagogue organization list. There were Jews in name only and defaulted in maintenance of their faith.

Some who did stay assumed leadership roles in the Jewish community, but stayed only briefly and moved on. Isacc Bondy and his sister Sarah came to St. Paul from New York (146). Isaac went to work for Benjamin Plechner, became president of the B'nai B'rith (147), and then moved to Duluth

(148). Leopold Isaacs was another. He was of German birth and in the wholesale wine and liquor business. He and his large family lived on Canada Street for a while (149). He served as president of Mt. Zion Synagogue in 1872 (150) and B'nai B'rith in 1876 (151). He also took a commanding interest in the newly established Hebrew Union College in Cincinnati, Ohio and collected funds for it in St. Paul (152). His daughter, Carrie, was in the first recorded confirmation class at Mt. Zion in 1870 (153). He and his family later moved to Montreal, Canada (154).

Joseph Abeles (or Ables) was the last of the "October, 1869" group of young men who had a significant impact on the St. Paul Jewish community. But his life and time was short. Mr. Abeles had moved to St. Paul from upstate New York because of his health. He was not quite 40 years old when he arrived with his wife Eva and their four sons: Julius, Herman, Simon, and Sigmund (155). He entered the clothing business and showed a remarkable talent for community work. He was elected secretary of Mt. Zion in 1870, and in 1871 he was elected president when the congregation moved into its first home at Tenth and Minnesota Streets. However, he died suddenly during his presidency in March of 1872 (156). His burial in the old Mt. Zion Cemetery, then located at Front and what is now Jackson, next to Oakland Cemetery, was the 19th burial in that location. His widow was given a pew of her own, and in her own name, as the women now sat with the men in the synagogue, contrary to orthodox tradition (157). In 1888, his son Julius was elected president of B'nai B'rith (158).

In 1889, Mr. Abeles' body, along with approximately 100 other bodies then buried in the old cemetery, which was only about an acre of ground (159), were disinterred and moved to the present location on Payne and Larpenteur (160). After 1890, the family seems to have disappeared from the scene. For most of their stay in St. Paul, the Abeles family lived in the "Lowertown" region at 333 E. Ninth St. (161).

Another who was here only too briefly was Simon Rosenfels. He came from Chicago and went into the liquor business with Max Frankel (162). He was born in Virginia and had arrived in St. Paul with six members in his family. His wife, Bertha, died suddenly in the early 1880s and was the 23rd person to be buried in the old Mt. Zion Cemetery (163).

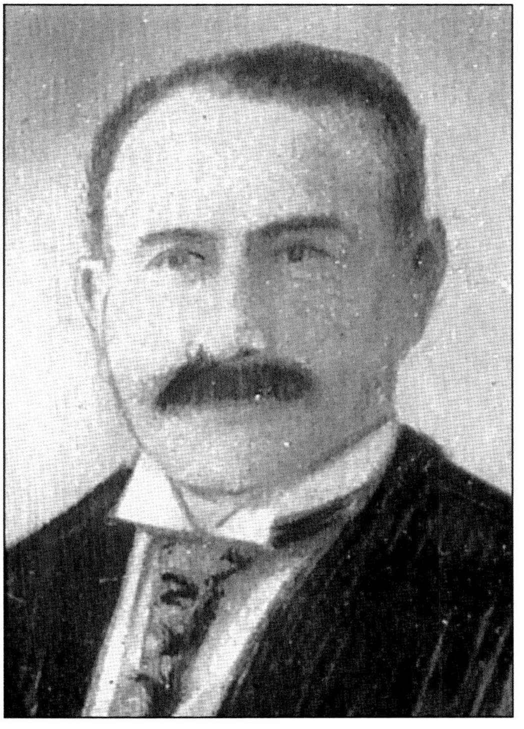

Originally from upstate New York, Joseph Abeles arrived in St. Paul in 1869, and immediately became heavily involved in Jewish community life. In 1871, he lead the initiation of the founding members of Minnesota Lodge No. 157 of the B'nai B'rith and became president of Mt. Zion Synagogue after having served as secretary in 1870. He died suddenly in March of 1872, and his widow was given a pew of her own. In 1888, his son, Julius, was elected as a president of Minnesota Lodge of the B'nai B'rith. (From the photo archives of the Mt. Zion Synagogue.)

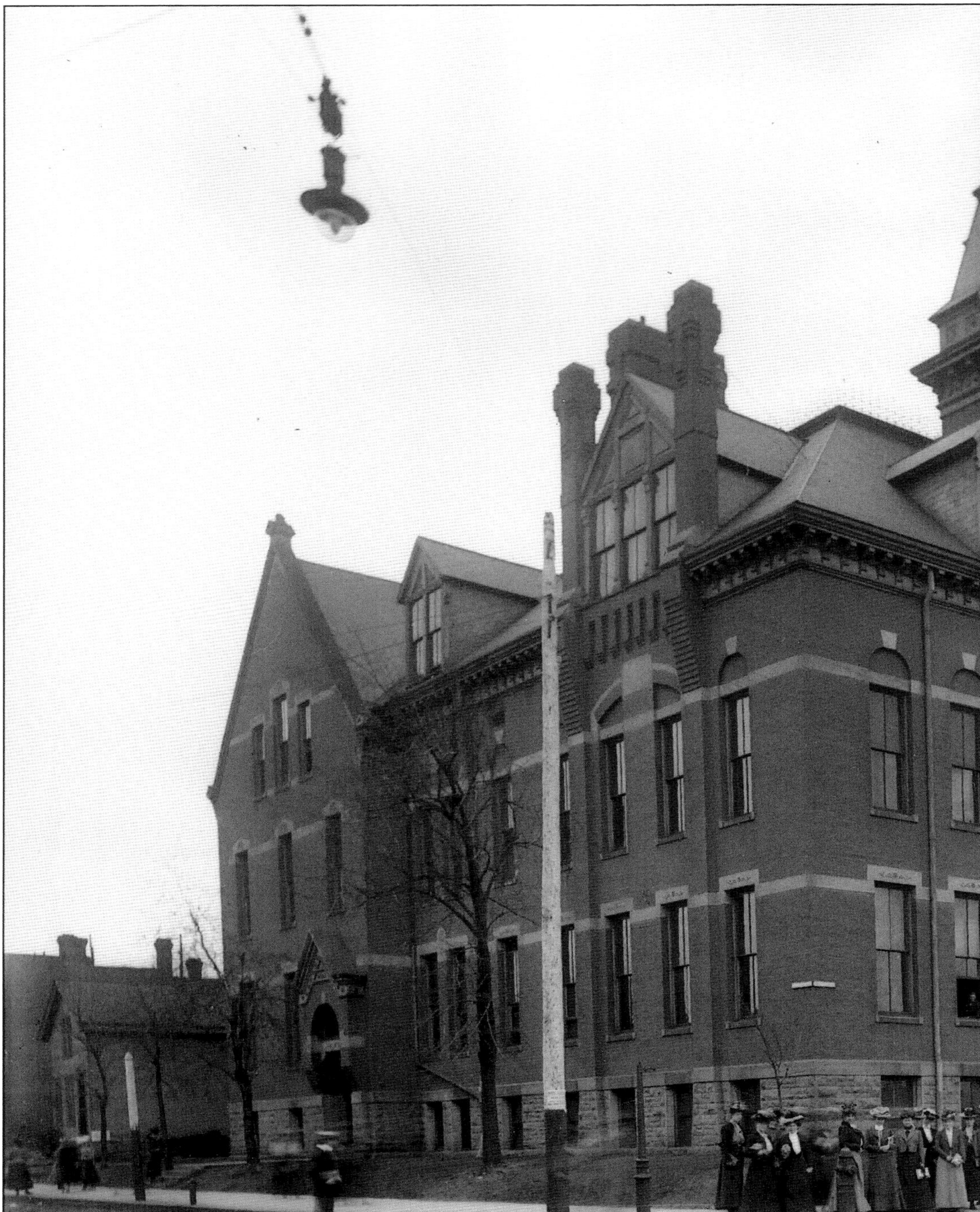

St. Paul's Central High School, which was St. Paul's first high school, was constructed in 1883 on a block bounded by Tenth, Eleventh, Minnesota, and Robert Streets. The school was built on the site of the old Adams school and near the neighborhood of most of the early

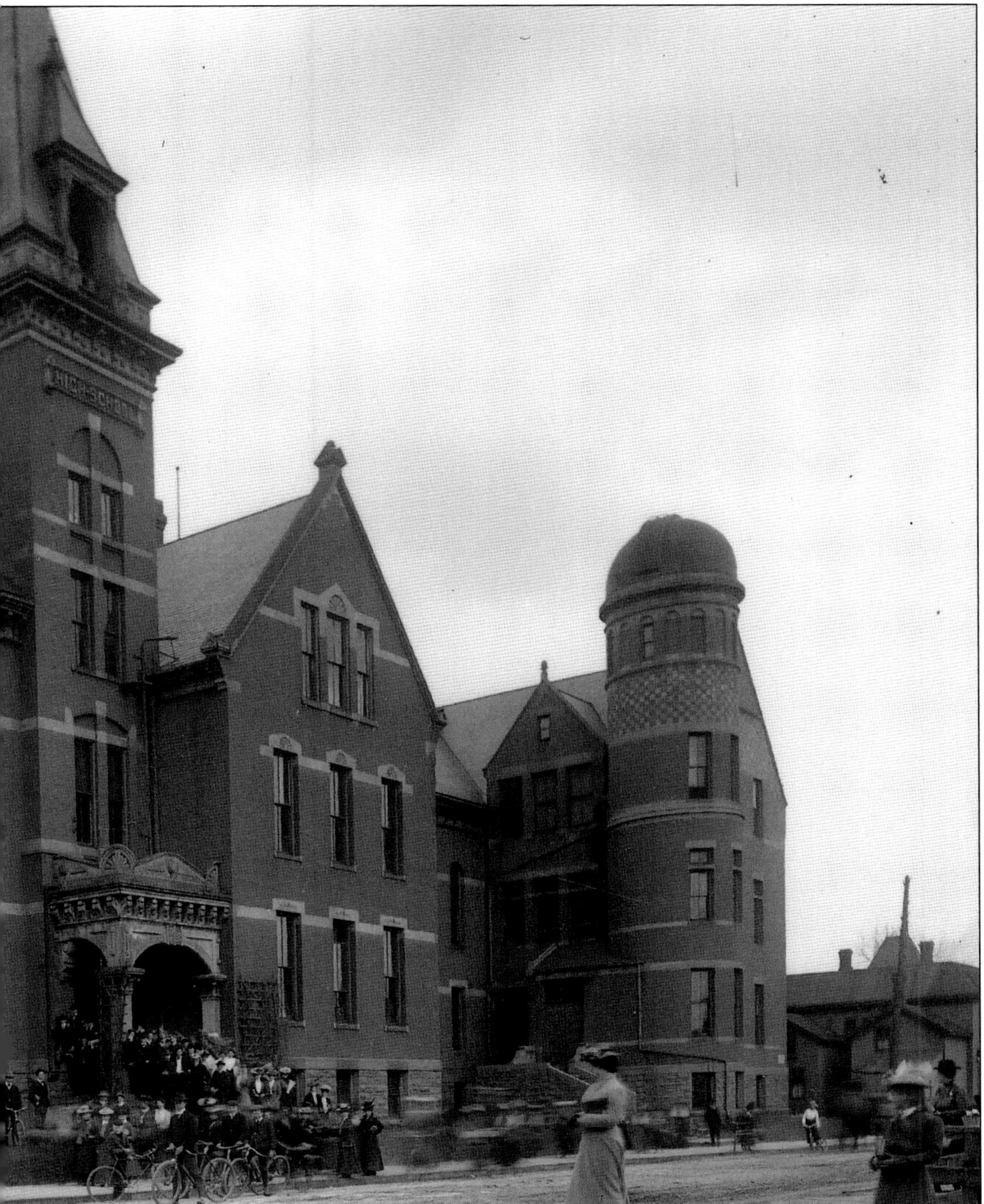

Jewish pioneers. Both the original and second Mt. Zion Synagogues were directly across the street from the school. Photo by C.P. Gibson. (From the photo archives of the Minnesota State historical Society)

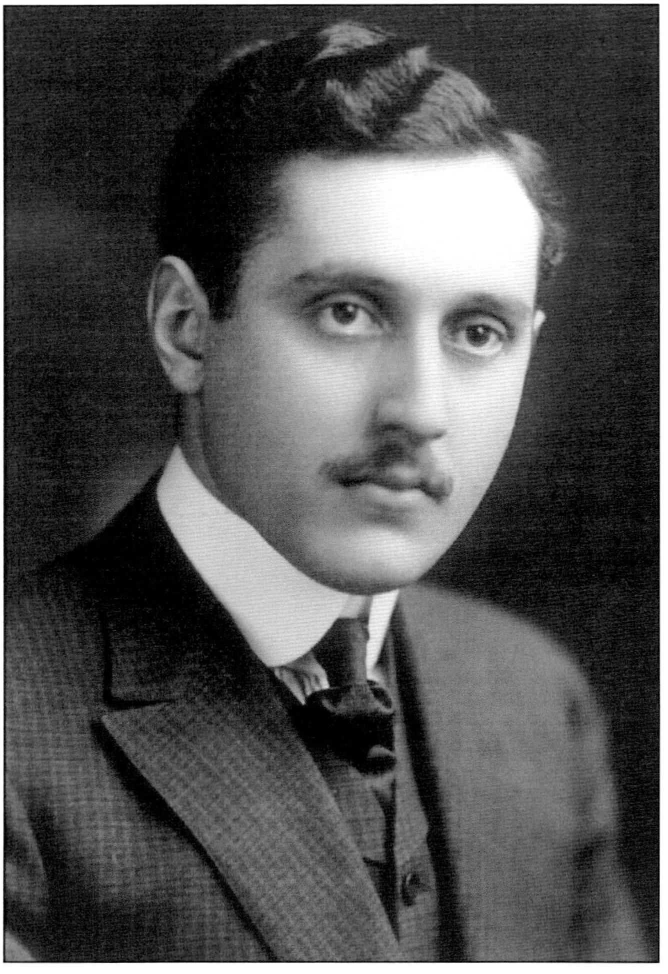

Pictured here is Ralph N. Cardozo. This photo was taken by Rembrant. (From the photo archives of the Minnesota Historical Society)

Simon served as president of the B'nai B'rith in 1872 and again in 1875 (164), and went on to serve as president of the District Grand Lodge in Chicago and play an important role in the B'nai B'rith. He died suddenly on May 22, 1885 (165).

Max Wittleshofer (or Wittlehofer) arrived in 1870 and bought out a pioneer jeweler and watchmaker. He was single, had been born in Germany, and was in business for a while with the blind Marx Austrian (166). In 1879 he served on the board of Mt. Zion (167) and as president of B'nai B'rith (168). He disappeared from the scene as suddenly as he appeared.

Permanency was becoming the rule rather than the exception as the Jewish community's roots strengthened. Jews not only came to stay, but also established some firsts.

In the early 1870s, another Cardozo family arrived on the St. Paul scene. They were part of the English branch of the Cardozo family that had fled Spain but did not immigrate to America approximately 200 years earlier. George N. Cardozo was a native of London, England, and he came to America with his wife Rachel, five sons, and a daughter. They first settled in La Crosse, Wisconsin, but moved to St. Paul in 1870 (169).

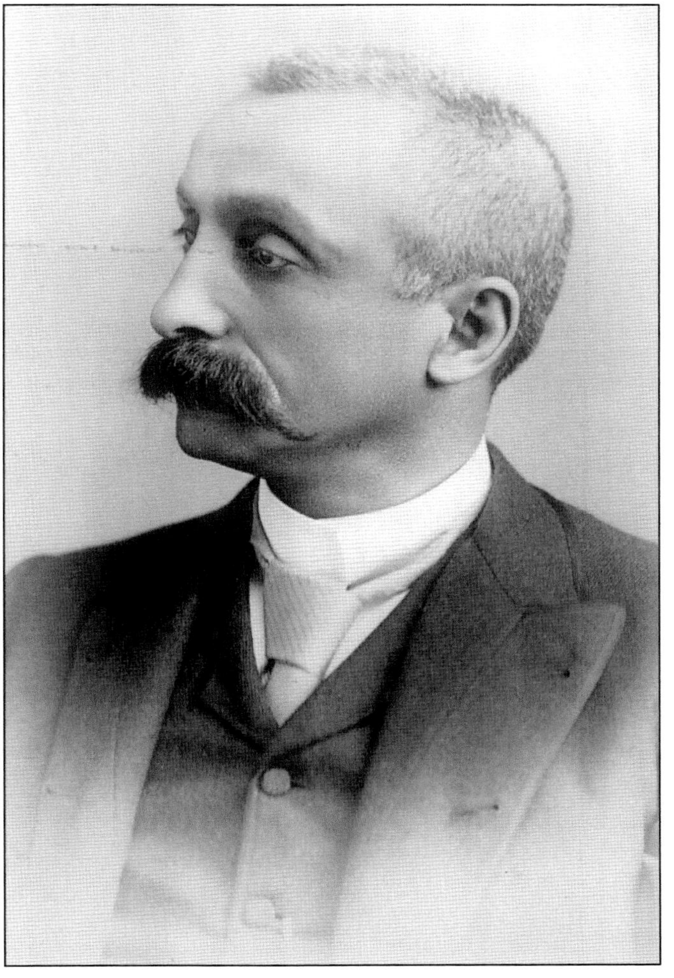

Rudolph B. Frankel was the brother of Max Frankel. This photo was taken by Palmquist and Jurgens. In January of 1871, when Rabbi Epstein from Milwaukee came to St. Paul to dedicate the little frame building as Mt. Zion's first home, he also brought with him a petition to collect signatures to establish a B'nai B'rith Lodge. Rudolph B. Frankel, together with 26 other prominent Jewish men from Minneapolis and St. Paul, were the first charter members of Minnesota Lodge No. 157. On February 20, 1871, Rabbi Epstein returned with Simon Rosenfels of Chicago, and together with Joseph Abeles conducted the first initiation ceremonies. Judge Isaac Nunez Cardozo was elected as the lodge's first president, Abram S. Elfelt as vice president, Benjamin Rose as recording secretary, Daniel Goodman as financial secretary, and Julius Austrian as treasurer. (From the photo archives of the Minnesota Historical Society)

George N. Cardozo was a cigar maker and established a small factory and store at Jackson and Fourth Streets. From time to time he would invest in pieces of furniture at second-hand stores. Gradually the furniture business grew so that there was little room in his small shop for both furniture and tobacco. Mr. Cardozo began storing the tobacco in the attic over the store. His family grew up in an atmosphere of furniture and household necessities, mixed with the odor of tobacco leaves and finished cigars. There were lulls between the times when he disposed of his stock of second-hand furniture and another auction sale would enable him to replenish his supply. During these times he brought his tobacco stock down from storage and made fresh supplies of cigars (170).

He set up his two oldest sons, Phineas N. and Benjamin N., to finally establish a separate furniture business, as P.N. Cardozo Company. The store was at Sixth and Wacouta (171). For many years the business was conducted under various names in a two-story frame building on Jackson between Sixth and Seventh Streets under the names B.N. Cardozo and Cardozo Brothers (172). In 1889, George sold out all of his interest in the business to his sons and retired. The family was then living at 267 Ramsey (173). That year Levi Cardozo, the younger brother, moved to California.

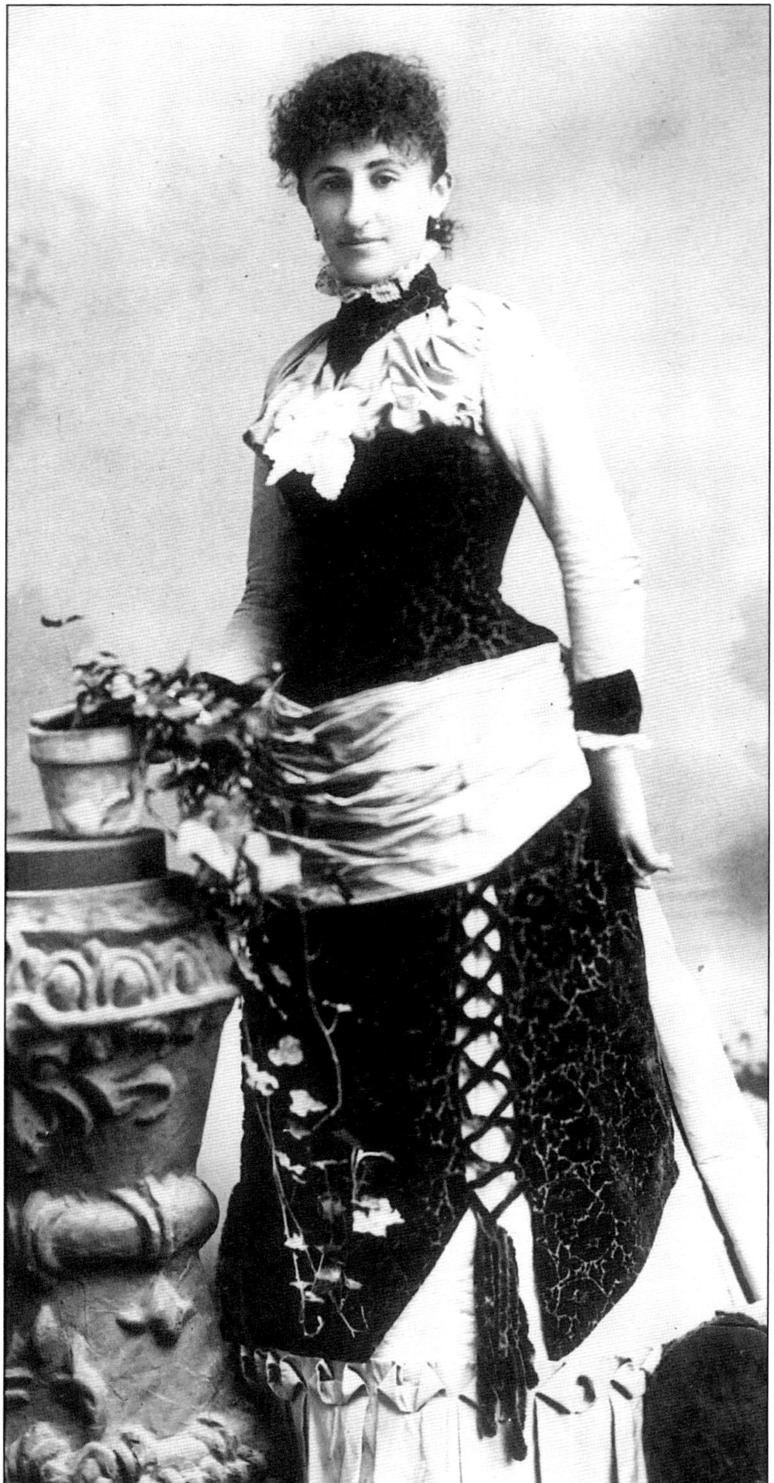

Josephine Newman Frankel is pictured here (Mrs. Max Frankel). Her father was Jacob Newman, one of the first pioneer Jews in St. Paul. She was born in the state of Virginia. Early on they lived on Robert Street, in what is now downtown St. Paul, between Sixth Street and Seventh Street, where many of the early pioneer Jewish families lived. They lived with the Appels, the Meyers, and the Frankels, one of whom Josephine married. Her father remained faithful to the original but smaller Mt. Zion faction. He eventually removed to Philadelphia where he died. Josephine and Max Frankel had three sons: Michael, Louis, and Hiram. In 1901, after the Mt. Zion congregation voted to build a new synagogue building, Josephine Frankel organized the Ladies Guild, which through a series of social events raised $8,500 for the purchase of an organ for the now Reform Synagogue. (From the photo archives of the American Jewish World, September and October, 1979)

William Cardozo and Simon Cardozo, other brothers, were soon into the business (174). George's eldest child, Sophia, married Siegmund Adler and she opened her own business of wholesale furniture (175). Sophia was also very active in the Daughters of Rebekka organization (176).

In August, 1895, George N Cardozo died. His son Benjamin had other interests and soon became secretary of St. Paul Cartage Company and eventually moved to New York in 1898. Shortly thereafter, Ralph N. Cardozo assumed control of the business (177). At the time of their father's death in 1895, William, Phineas, and Levi had left Minnesota as had their sisters, Deborah (Silber) and Julia (Raphael). In total, George left 11 living children and his widow, Rachel, surviving him at his death. Rachel Cardozo apparently had some business dealings with Charles Elfelt, as a note in the sum of $2,000 was found among Mr. Elfelt's papers at his death (178).

Ralph Cardozo's father-in-law, Nathan Solomon, a prominent wholesale liquor dealer, bought the Cardozo family home after George's death (179). Mr. Solomon also served as a president of B'nai B'rith (180) and was very active in the Mt. Zion Synagogue (181). Many of George Cardozo's descendants have continued to contribute much to the St. Paul civic community.

Another who arrived early in 1870 was David Greenblat (also spelled Ginblot and Grinblot). His father died in their native Poland at an early age in a cholera epidemic. David came to the United States in 1866, leaving behind his widowed mother, his brothers, and his sisters. Four years later he came to St. Paul as a peddler (182). For a short time he lived on Ninth Street and then on Eagle Street near the steamboat landing (183). In 1886 he sent for his elderly mother, who was then 82. She lived to be 107 and died as a resident of the Jewish Home for the Aged, which was then on Wilken Street. The St. Paul Dispatch made much of her age, comparing it to the fact that her father lived to be 115 (184). Mr. Greenblat later had a fancy goods store on St. Peter and lived at 424 Nina (185).

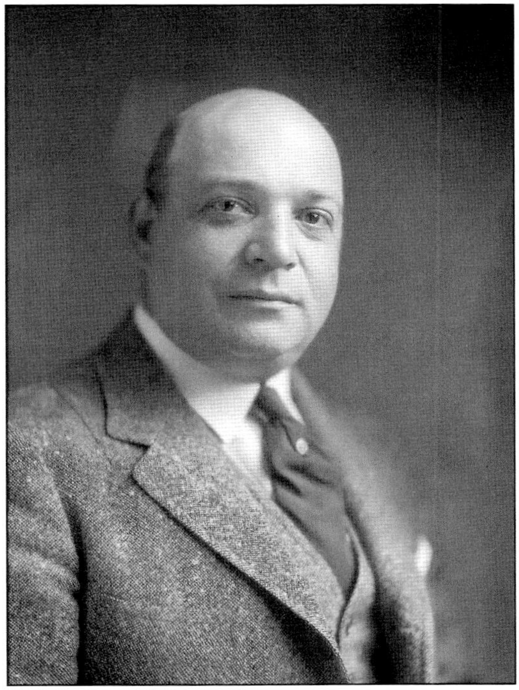

Hiram D. Frankel was a journalist, attorney, and author of first comprehensive history of the St. Paul Jewish community in 1907. His article in the Reform Advocate, *a publication by Rabbi Emil G. Hirsch, a national publication that ceased in the 1930s, turned out to be full of omissions and errors. (From the photo archives of the American Jewish World)*

Max Frankel and his brother Rudolph arrived in the early 1870s. They were born in Germany and were among the first initiated into B'nai B'rith after it was established in 1871 (186). Max Frankel also went on to have profound influence in making the secret fraternal Jewish organization of B'nai B'rith more than just a social or fraternal club, and helped transform it into a world-wide service organization. He married Jacob Newman's daughter, Josephine, and lived with the Newmans for a number of years on Robert Street. He became a very active member of Mt. Zion and the entire community (187). More importantly, he was the first of the second generation who was taking over the community. His influence and the influence of his sons—Michael, Louis, and Hiram—over the direction of the Jewish community, the Mt. Zion congregation, and the cultural life of the Jewish community were immense.

B'nai B'rith was the order of tradition and prestige amongst the established Jewish community. Max Frankel was first elected president of B'nai B'rith in 1877 (188). He apparently was elected in place of Jacob B. Seixas, whom the newspapers reported as being elected to that office (189). Max Frankel was not to have influence again in B'nai B'rith for another 15 years. He apparently devoted the intervening years to building up his wholesale liquor business into one of the largest in the Northwest.

A Civil War veteran, Benjamin Plechner and his brother William first settled in Minneapolis. Benjamin moved to St. Paul in 1871 and opened a clothing and furnishings business. More than any other person, he was most responsible for Mt. Zion becoming a Reform synagogue. (From the photo archives of the Mount Zion Synagogue)

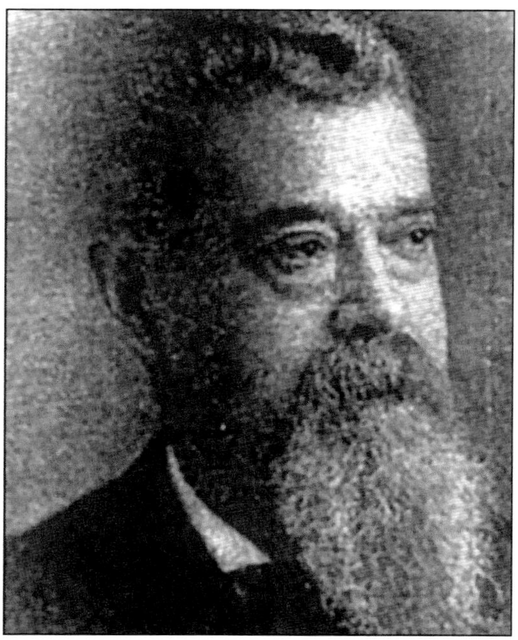

In 1892, Max Frankel was again elected president of Minnesota Lodge No. 157 of B'nai B'rith (190). However, things were in turmoil. The young men of the community were repeatedly being excluded from Minnesota lodge by the older members. Things came to a head when a competing B'nai B'rith lodge was formed among the young leadership of the community (191). Max became busy with the affairs of Mt. Zion in 1895 when old Solomon Bergman had died and Charles Fantle, Ben Plechner's son-in-law, refused to succeed to the presidency of Mt. Zion. Max Frankel thus became the first of the second generation to assume leadership in Mt. Zion. Other synagogues had been forming in St. Paul, and Mt Zion was now the "Reform" synagogue. New challenges like the retirement of the synagogue's Rabbi, the pressing building needs, and the change in the life-styles of the Jewish community, all pressed in on the new president of the synagogue (192).

Max Frankle's son, Michael, assumed the presidency of Minnesota Lodge of B'nai B'rith in 1900 (193), and a new generation of leadership moved swiftly, causing the older group of leaders to languish into inactivity (194). The competing lodge of B'nai B'rith quickly folded (195). In 1903, Max Frankel reassumed the presidency of the B'nai B'rith and his son Louis succeeded him in 1904 (196).

Louis R. Frankel was a dedicated citizen with varied interests. He had served as assistant city attorney of St. Paul three years after being admitted to the bar and later became the first Jew to serve as St. Paul city attorney (197). He was a prominent Democrat (198) and taught English at night at the new Neighborhood House on the West Side. He served as recording secretary of Mt. Zion, and was for many years a trustee of that synagogue (199). He also became chairman of the Mt. Zion Cemetery Association. He lived at 936 Ashland for many years (200).

Hiram D. Frankel was also very talented. He was an attorney and journalist, having been city editor of the old *St. Paul Daily*

News before being admitted to the bar (201). His collection of papers donated to the Minnesota Historical Society is contained in 34 boxes, and sheds much light on Jewish life in St. Paul. In 1899, he taught Sunday school at Mt. Zion (202). In 1907, he wrote the first comprehensive history of the St. Paul Jewish community for publication in the special Minnesota edition of the *Reform Advocate*, a national Jewish publication (203). In 1922, he was elected president of Mt. Zion (204). He later became Executive Secretary of the District Grand Lodge of B'nai B'rith and moved to Chicago (205).

Shortly after the Civil War ended, Benjamin H. Plechner and his brother, William, settled in Minneapolis. Benjamin, an Austrian (Bohemian) by birth, had been a Civil War veteran (206). In 1871, he moved to St. Paul. In addition to his clothing and furnishings business, he had displayed a profound interest in Jewish affairs, and his qualities as a leader were quickly apparent. He was a multi-talented man; besides his business interests, he was also a cabinet-maker and a poet on the side, with a book of poems to his credit (207). When Benjamin Plechner moved to St. Paul, his brother William remained in Minneapolis.

After Benjamin Plechner moved to St. Paul, his rise in the leadership circles of the community was swift. In 1874, he was elected as a trustee of Mt. Zion congregation and president of Minnesota Lodge on B'nai B'rith (208). In 1875, he was elected president of Mt. Zion. In 1878, Plechner attended the Union of American Hebrew Congregations convention in Milwaukee, Wisconsin. This was the national Reform Judaism movement's national meeting. While there, he addressed an urgent letter to his congregation back home. "No one can conceive the magnitude of that assembly, unless he was present . . . When I have seen what interest a great many young co-religionists take in Judaism, I only then could see how sadly our religion is neglected in St. Paul."

He recommended an immediate membership in the Reform Movement, and from that moment on, Mt. Zion was officially a Reform congregation (209). German was no longer to be used as the exclusive language of prayer at Mt. Zion, and the women could sit with the men in prayer. *Kashrut*, the

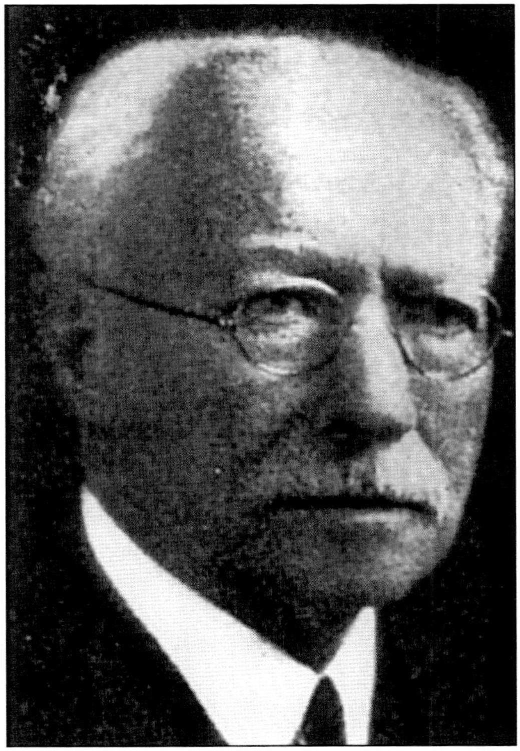

Max Frankel and his brother Rudolph Frankel arrived in St. Paul in the early 1870s. They lived with the Aaron Meyer's, the Jacob Newman's, and the Morris Appel's on Robert Street between Sixth and Seventh Streets, where Morris Appel had a clothing store. He became a giant in both the B'nai B'rith and the Mt. Zion Synagogue. He and his brother Rudolph were one of the first initiates in February of 1871, of the Minnesota Lodge of B'nai B'rith. He also found time to build up a very large liquor business. In 1901 he headed a committee of 15 to raise funds for a new Mt. Zion temple, and $66,000 was raised for the new building on Holly Avenue and Avon, in the Crocus Hill district. (From the photo archives of the Mount Zion Synagogue)

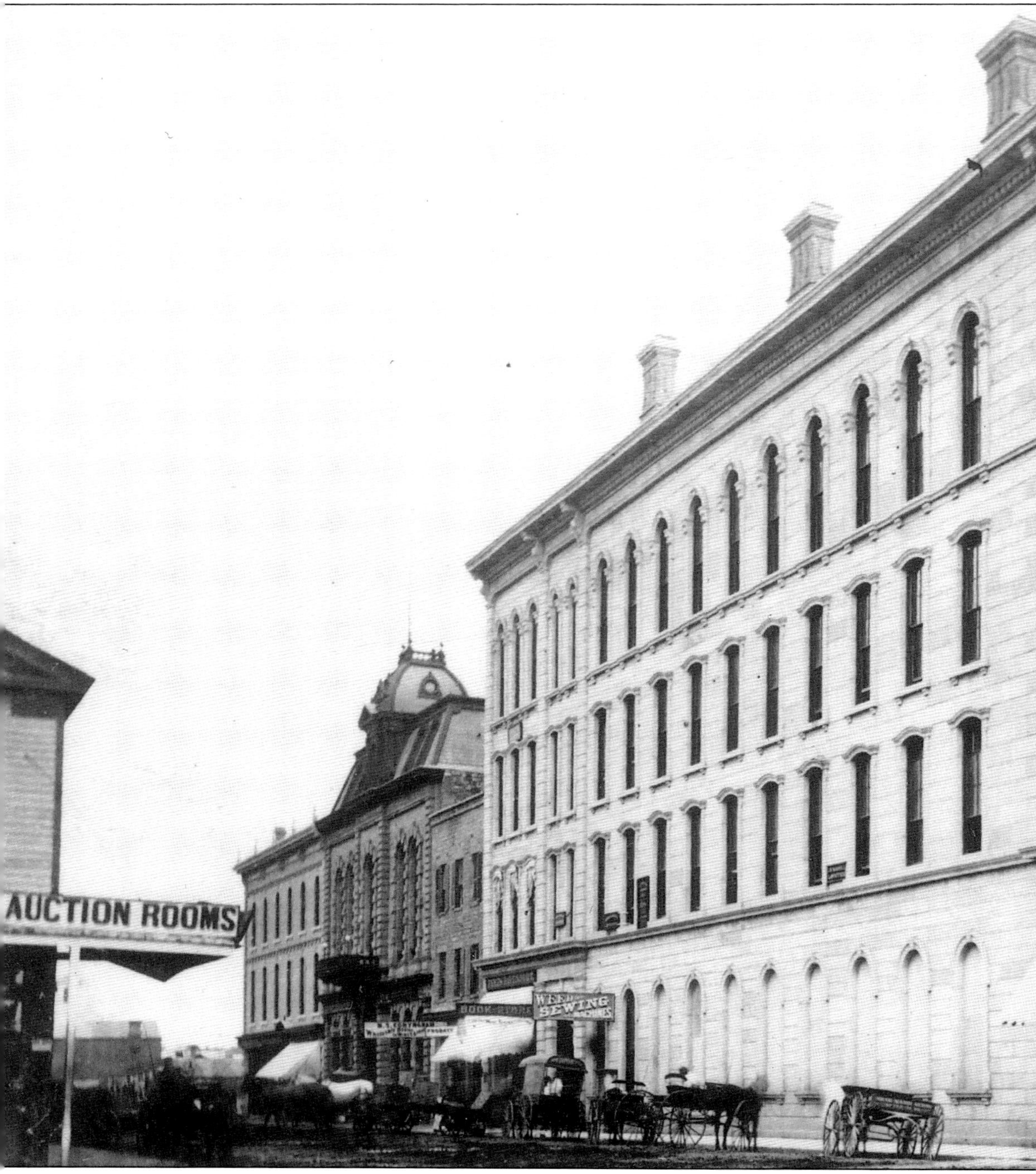

The first Mannheimer and Goodkind "Dry Goods" store opened in 1871 at 7 East Third Street (now Kellogg Boulevard) at Wabasha Street, in the McQuillan Block. Henry J. Strouse, pioneer Jew, who came to St. Paul in the early 1870s representing A.R. Strouse, prominent New York

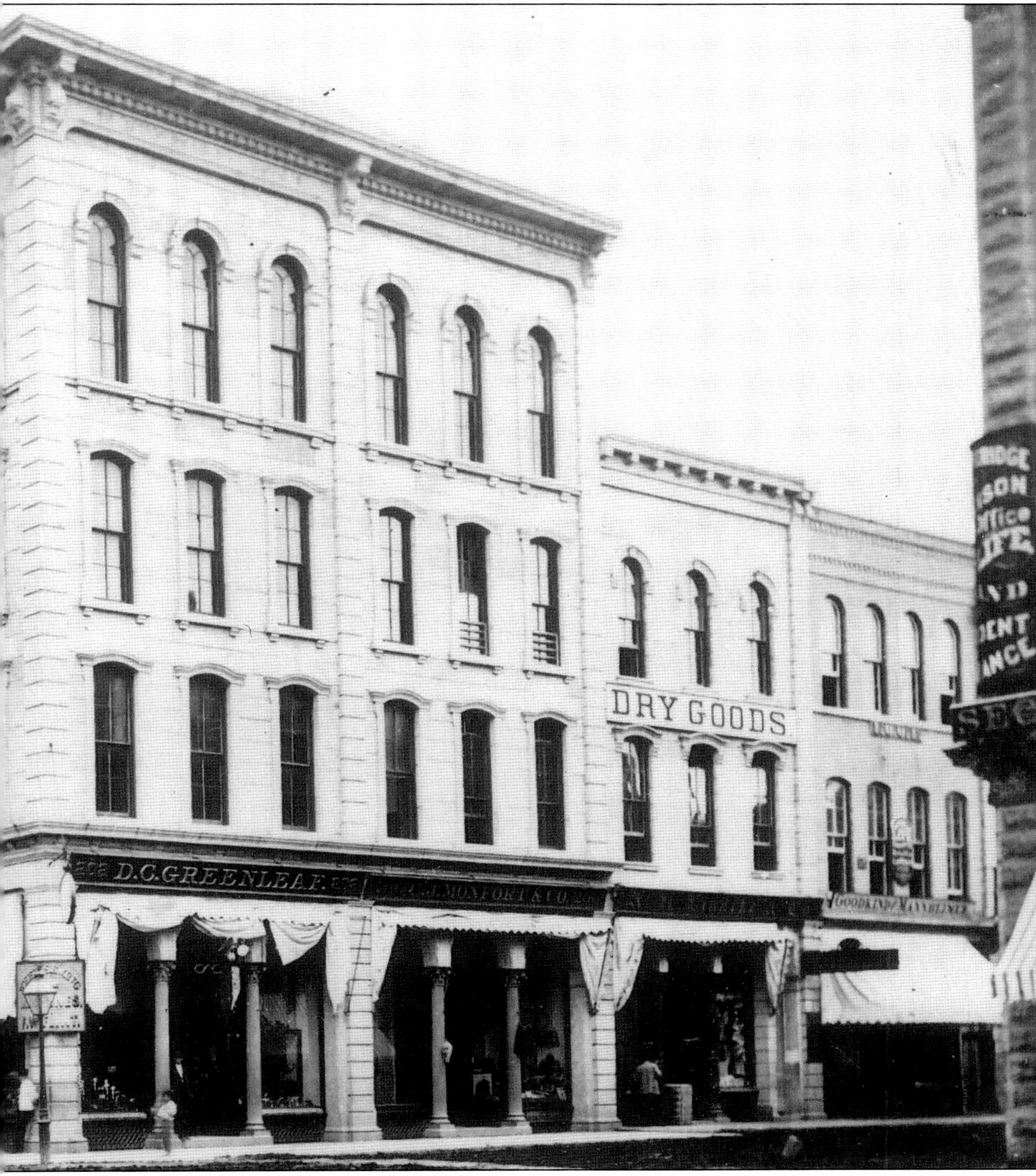

Dry Goods firm, also lived in the McQuillan Block for many years. He served as a president of Minnesota Lodge of the B'nai B'rith, and in 1894 was elected to the St. Paul city council. Photo by William H. Illingworth. (From the photo archives of the Minnesota Historical Society)

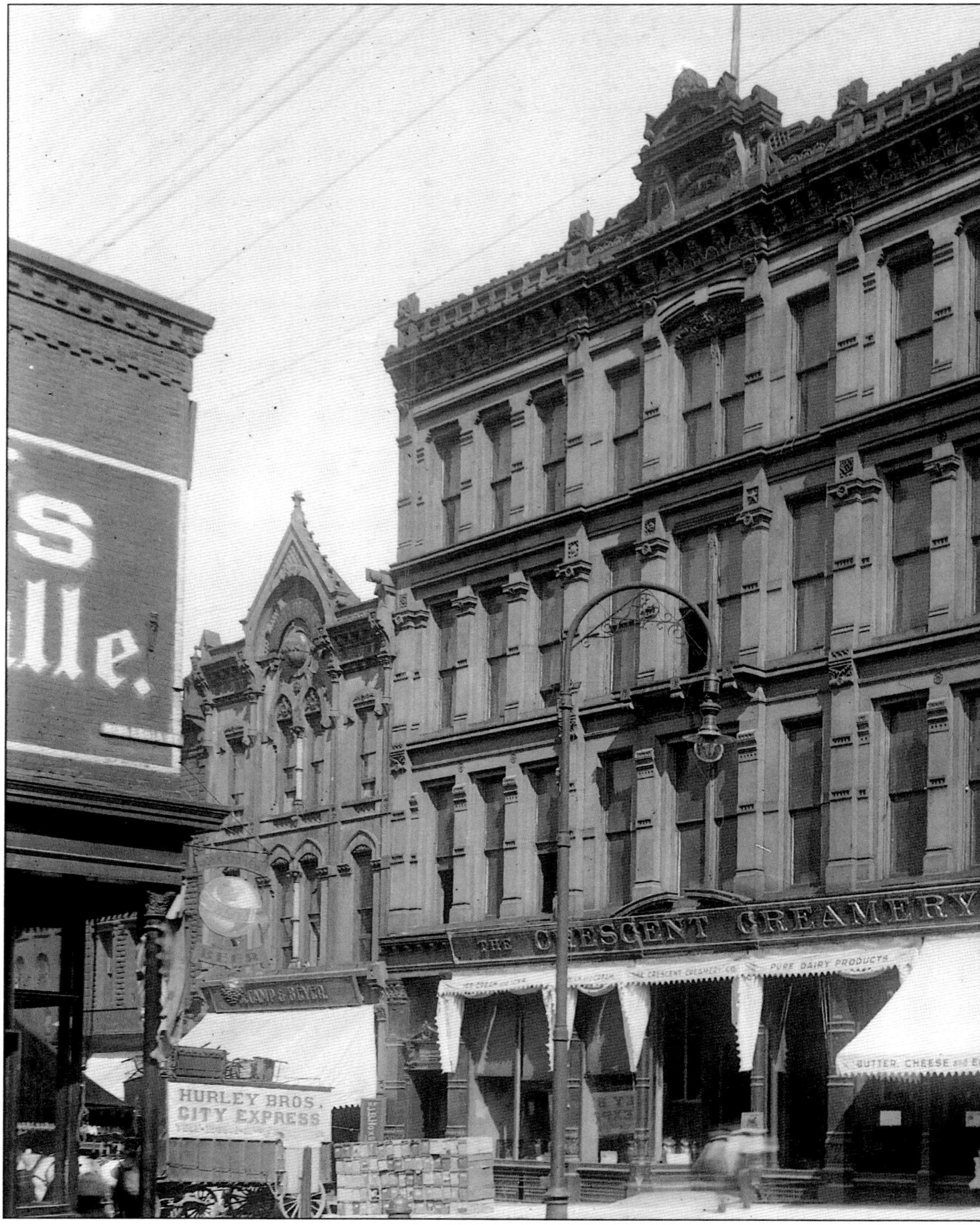

The second Mannheimer and Goodkind "Dry Goods" store, opened in 1882 in the so-called Mannheimer Block located at Third Street (now Kellogg Boulevard) and Minnesota Street, where it remained until 1893, when Crescent Creamery took over the block. The third store

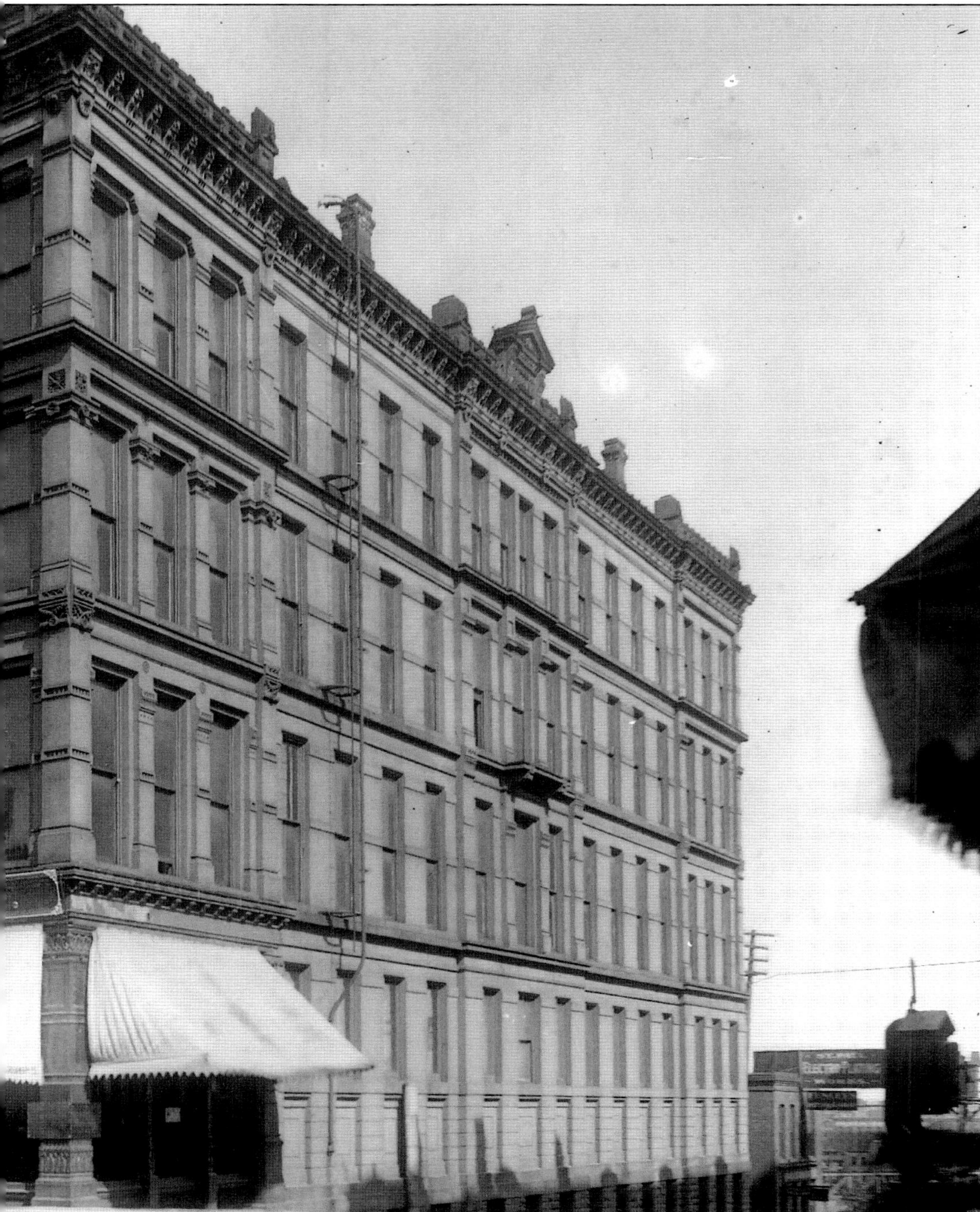

was located at Sixth Street and Robert Street and was the largest store of its kind between Chicago and the West coast. Photo was taken by pioneer photographer, C.P. Gibson. (From the photo archives of the Minnesota Historical Society)

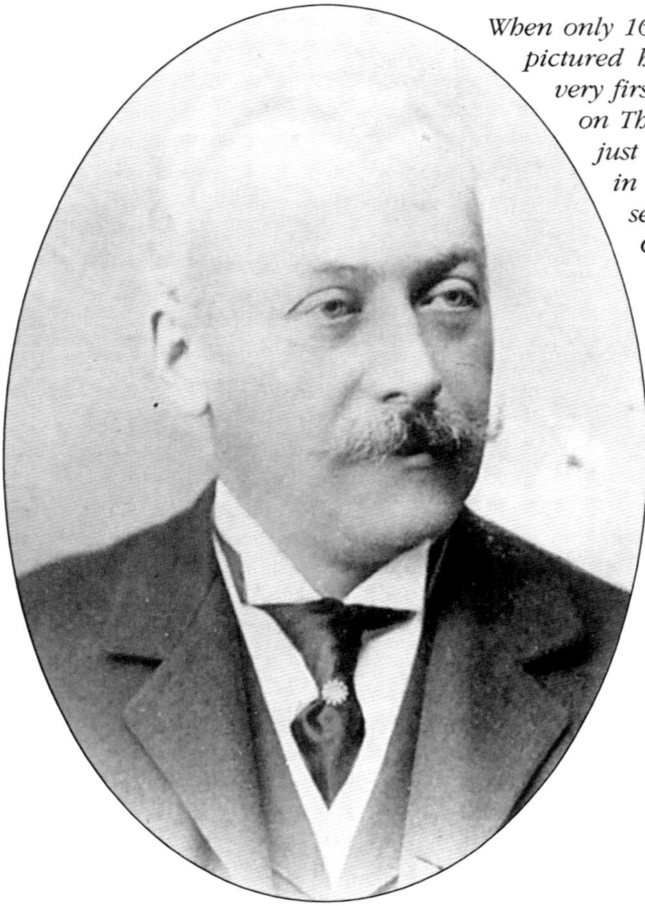

When only 16 years old, Benjamin L. Goodkind, pictured here, witnessed the opening of the very first Goodkind and Mannheimer store on Third Street (now Kellogg Boulevard) just below Wabasha Street. On that day, in April of 1871, the Indians and the settlers mixed and his father, Louis Goodkind, knew all of his customers by their first names. (From the photo archives of the Ramsey County Historical Society)

maintenance of dietary laws through the use of ritually clean meat, would be no longer stringently enforced. Many Jewish laws observed by their forefathers were no longer necessary. The reforms came slowly, but they came, and thus divided the community.

Benjamin Plechner died in 1893 leaving his wife Babette, and 7 children, the youngest being 15 years old. He died without a will and left life insurance totalling $4,918.40 (210), and a host of descendants who have remained active in the community. The family lived at 555 Westminister on the East side for a number of years (211). His son Samuel worked for James J. Hill and the Great Northern Railway as a purchasing agent, and was killed in a tragic accident near the Hill farm at North Oaks when his car overturned (212).

Charles Hostetter was also a Civil War veteran and served under the Confederacy (213). He had been born in Germany in 1839. His brother Abraham was born in Pennsylvania, when the Hostetter family had moved to America to Lancaster, Pennsylvania (214). In 1871, the two brothers moved to St. Paul. Charles married Annie Lowenstein in Mississippi in 1865. For nine years after his arrival, Charles worked for the Powers Dry Goods Company (215).

In 1874, Charles Hostetter was elected a trustee of Mt. Zion (216). In 1880 he went into the liquor business. He had four children: Florence, Benjamin, Sidney, and William (217). His brother Abraham worked for the

Lake Superior and Mississippi Railroad for four years then joined the Chicago, Milwaukee, and St. Paul Railroad (218). Abraham lived in Irvine Park for a number of years, and at the turn of the century was one of the first Jewish settlers in the Merriam Park area, living at 442 North Fairview (219).

Louis Goodkind and Jacob Mannheimer then arrived in St. Paul in 1871. These two men were to have a very significant influence on the commercial life of early downtown St. Paul and its development into a commercial center. Louis Goodkind was the older of the two men. He had been born in Bavaria on November 13, 1825 (220). He married Jacob Mannheimer's sister, Mina, and lived in Adrian, Michigan for a time where his son, Benjamin, was born in 1855 (221). They later moved to Chicago, where he engaged in the dry-goods business (222).

In April, 1871, the first Goodkind and Mannheimer store was opened at old 193 Third Street (now Kellogg Boulevard), which later was renumbered 7 East Third Street, just below Wabasha. At the opening, St. Paul's total population was 21,000 people. This opening was long remembered in St. Paul and the surrounding territory and was the occasion for a huge celebration. Native Americans mingled with townsfolk and the business got off to a prosperous start. Louis Goodkind knew all of his customers by their first names and the business prospered (223). Benjamin, only 16 years old, was with his father that opening day, as was the partner, Jacob Mannheimer (224).

Jacob Mannheimer was the son of Moritiz Mannheimer, a doctor in the little town of Dinkelsbuhl, 8 miles west of Wittleshofen, the home of the Austrian family in Germany. Dr. Mannheimer could not move without receiving a special permit and could not practice where he wished. He counseled his children to move to America. Many of Germany's Jews emigrated not merely because of acute economic need after the revolution of 1848, but also because the Jews had no future in Germany. The unsuccessful revolution had produced reactionary repressions, including military conscription. Many older German Jews stayed, but their children set out for America, having no intent of returning (225).

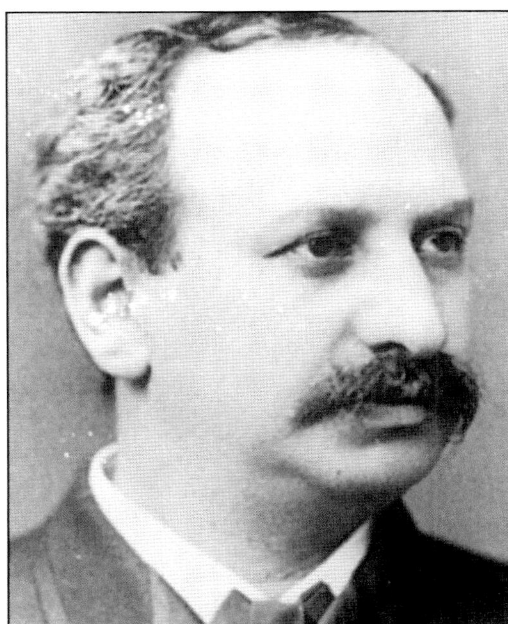

In 1880, Ansel Oppenheim, pictured here, constructed one of the larger homes on Summit Avenue, at 275 Summit Avenue for approximately $ 9,000. In 1895, when he was vice president of the Chicago Midwest Railroad, one of the most destructive fires to occur on Summit Avenue, St. Paul's premier street for the affluent, destroyed the Ansel Oppenheim home and all of its contents. The family never rebuilt the house, and lived in the then newly completed Aberdeen Hotel for many years prior to his death. (From the photo archives of American Jewish World, September and October, 1979)

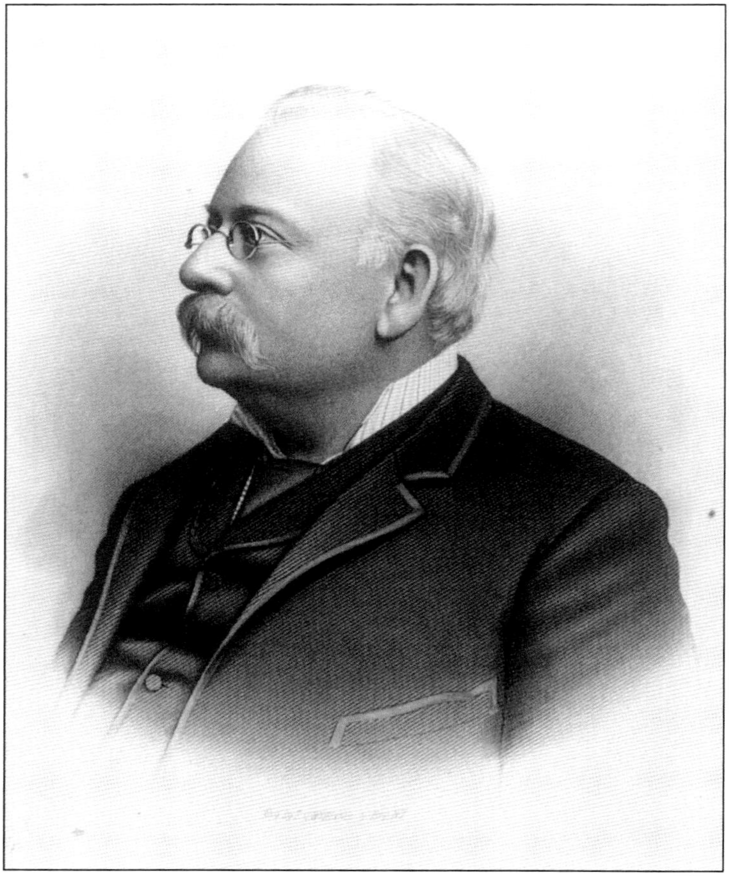

Pictured here is Robert Mannheimer, from "Andrews History of St. Paul." (From the photo archives of the Minnesota Historical Society)

Jacob Mannheimer was born before the 1848 revolution on January 17, 1847, and received his formal education in Germany. As an 11-year-old boy, he came alone to America and joined his mother and brothers and sisters who had preceded him here and were then living in Chicago. When he moved to St. Paul in 1871, he lived at Gruber's Hotel and later married Louisa Gruber, a daughter of the owner and had five sons and a daughter (226).

With substantial growth, the firm of Goodkind and Mannheimer soon needed assistance. The partners decided to send to Chicago for Jacob Mannheimer's two brothers: Robert and Emil. This change in 1873 resulted in the store being renamed Mannheimer Brothers (227). It remained such until 1903, when it was incorporated. In 1926, Mannheimers merged with Schuneman and Evans and in 1928 it became Schuneman's Department Store. It then merged with Dayton's of Minneapolis and became Schunemann-Daytons and then just Daytons, as it is today. In 1882, the business moved to the newly constructed "Mannheimer Block" at Third St. and Minnesota, then again in 1893 it moved to Sixth and Robert, where it remained for many years (228). It was the largest store of its kind in the northwest and dealt with goods from all over the world (229).

In 1880, Louis Goodkind became president of Minnesota Lodge of B'nai B'rith (230). In the 1870s he had served on the board of Mt. Zion and also helped organize the Standard

Pictured here is Mrs. Ansel (Greve) Oppenheim. (From the photo archives of Minnesota Historical Society)

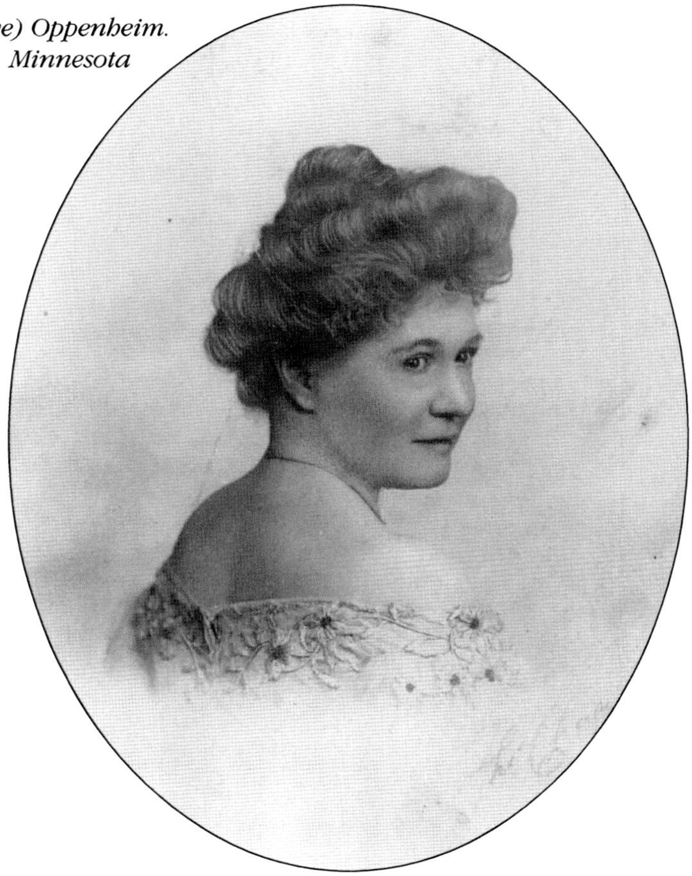

Club, the first private Jewish social club. For a full generation, the Standard Club was used for balls, dinners, weddings, and various other parties. It occupied two floors of rooms on 226 East Sixth Street. Some of the most prominent weddings included: Fannie Goodkind to Ambrose Guiterman in 1887 (231), and Edith Goodkind to Lessing Rosenwald (of the Sears-Roebuck Rosenwalds) in 1913 (232). Its members were a list of "who's who" in St. Paul Jewry, and in 1887 the *Dual City Blue Book*, St. Paul's unofficial social register, printed a list of the members of the Standard Club in a rare glimpse of those who occupied the top social strata of the Jewish community (233). Its members were primarily the so called "upper-group," which consisted of Jews from Germany, Austria-Hungary, Bohemia and Alsace-Lorraine; they were western Jews, who had in common that they spoke German as their native tongue, or knew it as their old family language (234). In August of 1902, the St. Paul newspapers described the Standard Club as the "most sumptuous and elaborate of all the denominational clubs in the city" (235). When the St. Paul Athletic Club was organized and constructed, the Standard Club disbanded, as most of its members had joined the new facility (236).

Between 1899 and 1904, the three Mannheimer brothers and Louis Goodkind all died, leaving the business to their sons (237). The sons and daughters of both families became very prominent and were considered "old settlers," even though they arrived a full generation later than the first Jews of St. Paul (238). There are still Mannheimers in the

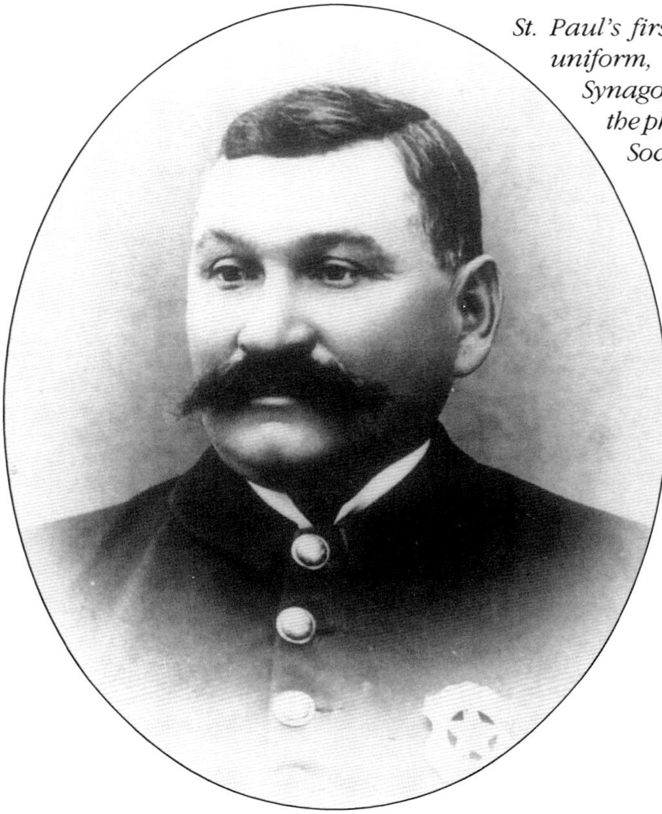

St. Paul's first Jewish policeman, shown in his uniform, was Moritz Kafka, also Mt. Zion Synagogue's first Shamos *or sextant. (From the photo archives of the Jewish Historical Society of the Upper Midwest)*

community, and the Goodkind-Mannheimer family home at 270–272 West Seventh (in Irvine Park) was recently torn down after efforts to save it failed (239). Mrs. William Goodkind, a cousin of James Oppenheim, the prominent author (240), helped to organize the St. Paul Jewish Day Nursery on the "West Side" of St. Paul. The nursery was later taken over by the Neighborhood House, where it continued on a nondenominational basis to service the residents of the West side area (241). Louis Goodkind, along with the Frankel family, is given credit for changing the direction of the B'nai B'rith to make it a unifying force in the Jewish community and giving status to the newly arrived East European group of Jews (242).

Joesph Oppenheim was born in New York and came to St. Paul in 1872 as a traveling agent for I. Oppenheim Co., a wholesale millinery business out of New York City. Joseph's father, Isaac, partnered with August Oppenheimer forming I. Oppenheim Co. The elder Oppenheimer had emigrated to America in 1842 from Germany (243). Joseph's two brothers, James and Ansel, came to St. Paul at the same time to represent the family business (244).

Joseph Oppenheim was 26 years old when he was elected as the first Jew to serve in the Minnesota State legislature of St. Paul in 1879, the same year his father died (245). Four years earlier, he had served as one of the founders and first president of the Standard Club (246). One year later in 1876, he served as president of B'nai B'rith (247). He later served several terms as the first Jew on the St. Paul Board of Education, from the second ward (248). Joseph Oppenheim returned to New York City during his last term on the school board in 1884–1885 (249), probably to help handle the family's business interests. He had a son, James, who was born in St. Paul in 1882 (250), and who later went on to become an author of national prominence (251). When Joseph Oppenheim left for New York, August Oppenheimer came to take over the business in his own name (252).

Ansel Oppenheim became a prominent St. Paul attorney and civic leader. He served on the St. Paul city council for one term in 1890, and was the first elected Jew. He was active in real estate and banking interests with his father-in-law, Herman Greve (253). He also served as State Democratic Chairman and as Secretary to the National Democratic Convention that nominated Grover Cleveland for President of the United States (254). Although never actively identified as a practicing Jew, nevertheless Ansel served on a committee that was hastily organized to handle the relief of over 200 Jewish refugees who suddenly appeared in St. Paul in the summer of 1882 (255). He died in the winter of 1916 (256). His son Herman Oppenheim briefly served as assistant city attorney (257).

Henry T. Sattler, David C. Sattler, and Jacob B. Sattler were born in Germany and they arrived in St. Paul in the early 1870s. They soon organized the David C. Sattler and Brothers clothing firm at 76 East Third Street. There is no indication whether they were related to the Louis Sattler who served in Company A of the First Minnesota Regiment during the Civil War and the Indian Wars (258). They were active in Mt. Zion congregation with David serving as trustee and financial secretary in the late 1870s (259).

Jacob Sattler later moved to Duluth to become a pioneer leader (260). Two of Jacob's children were stillborn and among the early burials in the Mt. Zion cemetery. Henry Sattler also buried an infant girl in the same cemetery located at the intersection of Front and Jackson (261). Joseph Sattler was one of the members of the first confirmation class at Mt. Zion in 1880 (262), and was probably David's son. Joseph also became

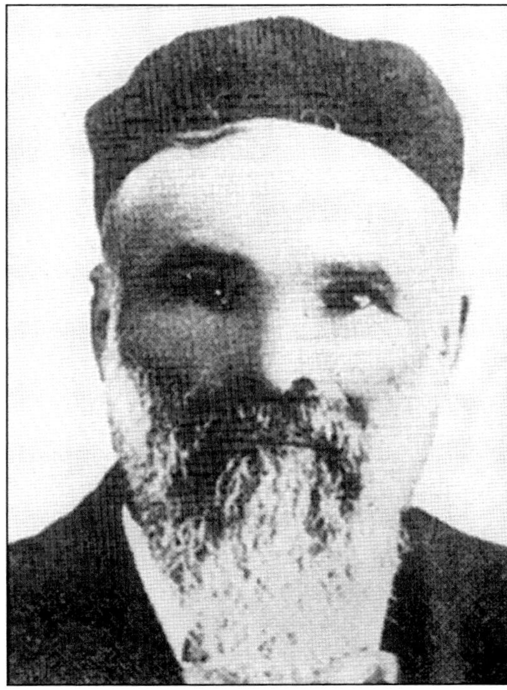

Aaron Mark is regarded as the founder and leader of both the orthodox and conservative Jewish communities of St. Paul. From his home on the East side of St. Paul began the roots of what became the Chevra B'nai Yaakov, Sons of Jacob, in 1873. Later, his widow Bessie Mark presided over the laying of the cornerstone of the Temple of Aaron, a conservative synagogue, in 1910 which was named after Mr. Mark. (From the photo archives of the American Jewish World, September and October, 1979)

the first president of the so-called "Social Club," which was founded by the younger men of the community who were unhappy with the Standard Club. The members of the Social Club were involved in discussions and debates as well as the usual social entertainments. Debates included: "Is fire or water more destructive?" and "Should Grant run for a third term?" Jewish subjects were avoided (263).

Moritz Kafka also arrived in the early 1870s. He was a peddler, born in Germany.

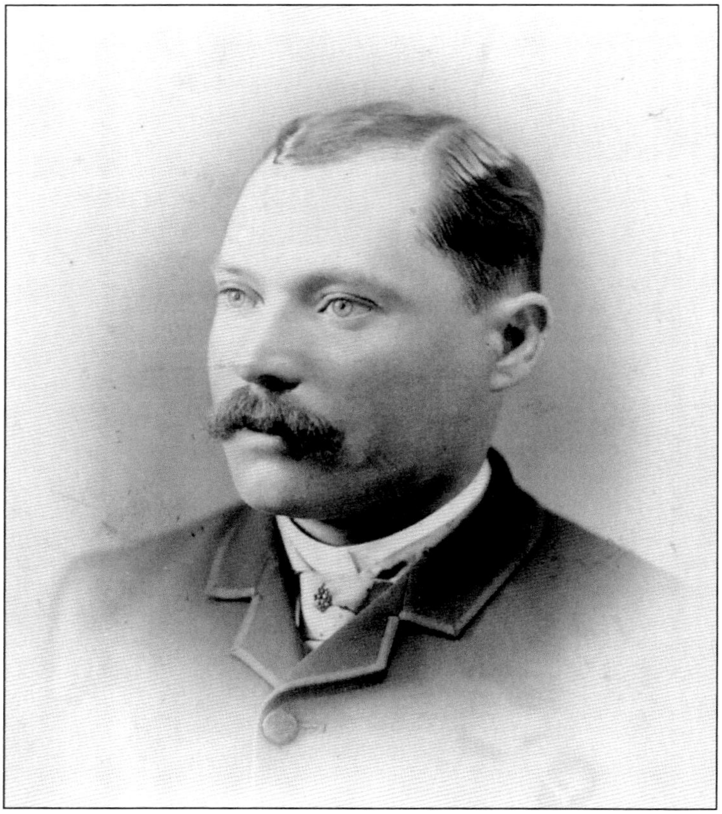

Dr. Joseph Mark was the first registered Jewish physician in Minnesota. Born in Lithuania, he was the father and grandfather of other doctors. Photo by Greenleaf. (From the photo archives of Minnesota Historical Society)

Five members of his family came with him when he arrived. In 1874 he became the first *Shamos* (custodian) of the first Mt. Zion congregation building. His duties included: "....take care of the Temple and keep it in good order, prepare lights and extinguish them; keep fire burning during divine services and school and attend to all collections for the congregation and obey orders from the president during divine services..." (264).

Mr. Kafka later became St. Paul's first Jewish policeman (265). The family lived at 590 Rice and later moved to 268 E. Congress on the West Side—the house is still standing (266). When he died in 1917, his children had pioneered through the area and were living in the communities of Milnor and Edgely, North Dakota, and Staples, Minnesota. (267)

Henry J. Strouse arrived in St. Paul representing the New York firm of A. H. Strouse, a prominent dry goods establishment in the early 1870s. He stayed on to become very active in the community, serving as president of B'nai B'rith in 1884 (268), and in 1894 he was elected to the St. Paul City Council. He was also very active in the Odd Fellows organization (269). He lived in the McQuillan Block at Third Street (Kellogg Boulevard) and Wabasha for many years. He does not appeared to have married (270).

The early 1870s had brought far-reaching changes that affected the unity of the Jewish community in the practices of their religion. These disruptions were of a socioeconomic origin and occurred first in the oldest community. New settlers had arrived who were generally referred to as Polish and whose native tongue was Yiddish, a mixture of High German, Polish, Hebrew, Russian, and English. This later group of settlers were

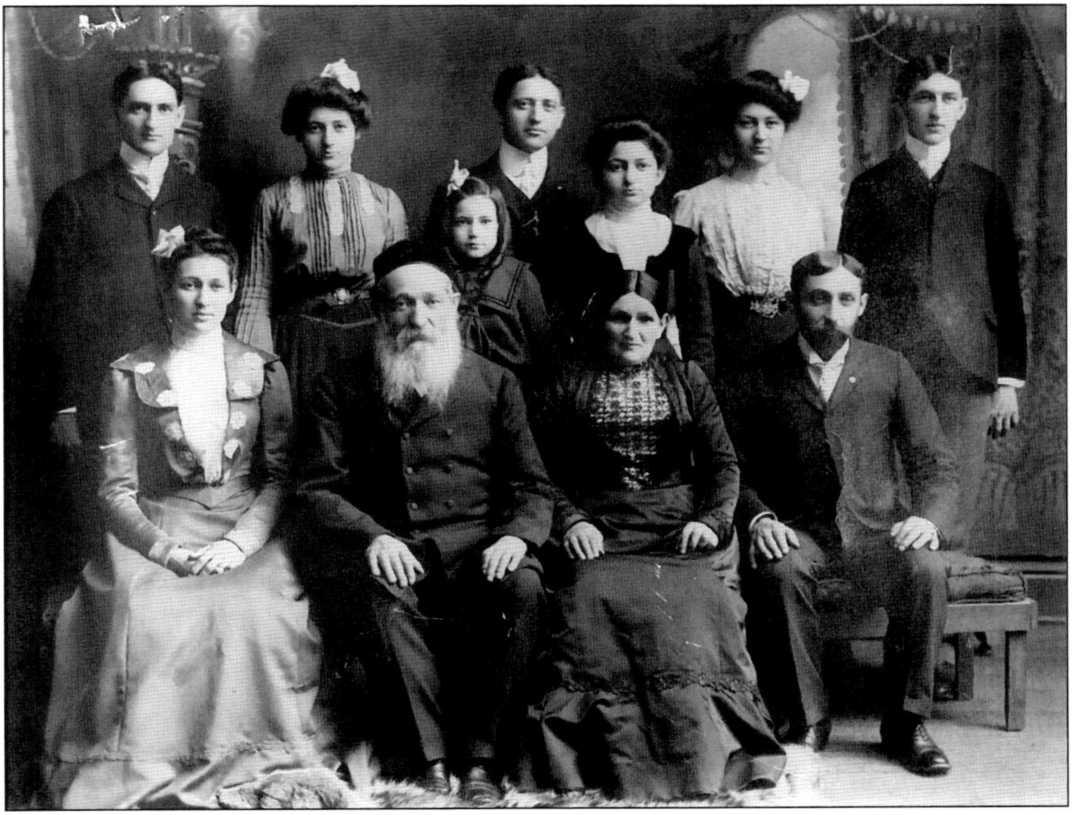

Moses Calmenson and his family are pictured here, from left to right: (top row) Sam Calmenson, who settled in Aberdeen, South Dakota; Marcia (Calmenson) Goldberg, who moved to Calgary, Alberta, Canada; Rose (Calmenson) Rosenthal, who resided in St. Paul; Phil Calmenson who moved to Montevideo, Minnesota; Florence, (Calmenson) Sloan who moved to California; Mamie (Calmenson) Yukman, who moved to Chicago, Illinois; and Ben Calmenson, who was an attorney in St. Paul; (bottom row) Jenny (Calmenson) Levine, who lived in Duluth, and then removed to St. Paul; Moses Calmenson; "Bas Sheva" Calmenson, Moses's second wife and mother to all children born in the United States; and Cain Calmenson. Louis Calmenson, the other son of Moses, is not in the picture. Moses Calmenson and Aaron Mark are considered the two most influential Orthodox Jews who helped to create the Sons of Jacob (now Beth Jacob) Synagogue. Both men left the little town of "Pren," Lithuania, in 1865, hidden in the bottom of a farmer's truck, covered by farm produce. They both went into the "junk" business. Photo taken by Geoffrey Marshall. (Photo courtesy of Mrs. Harold (Connie) Field, Moses Calmenson's granddaughter)

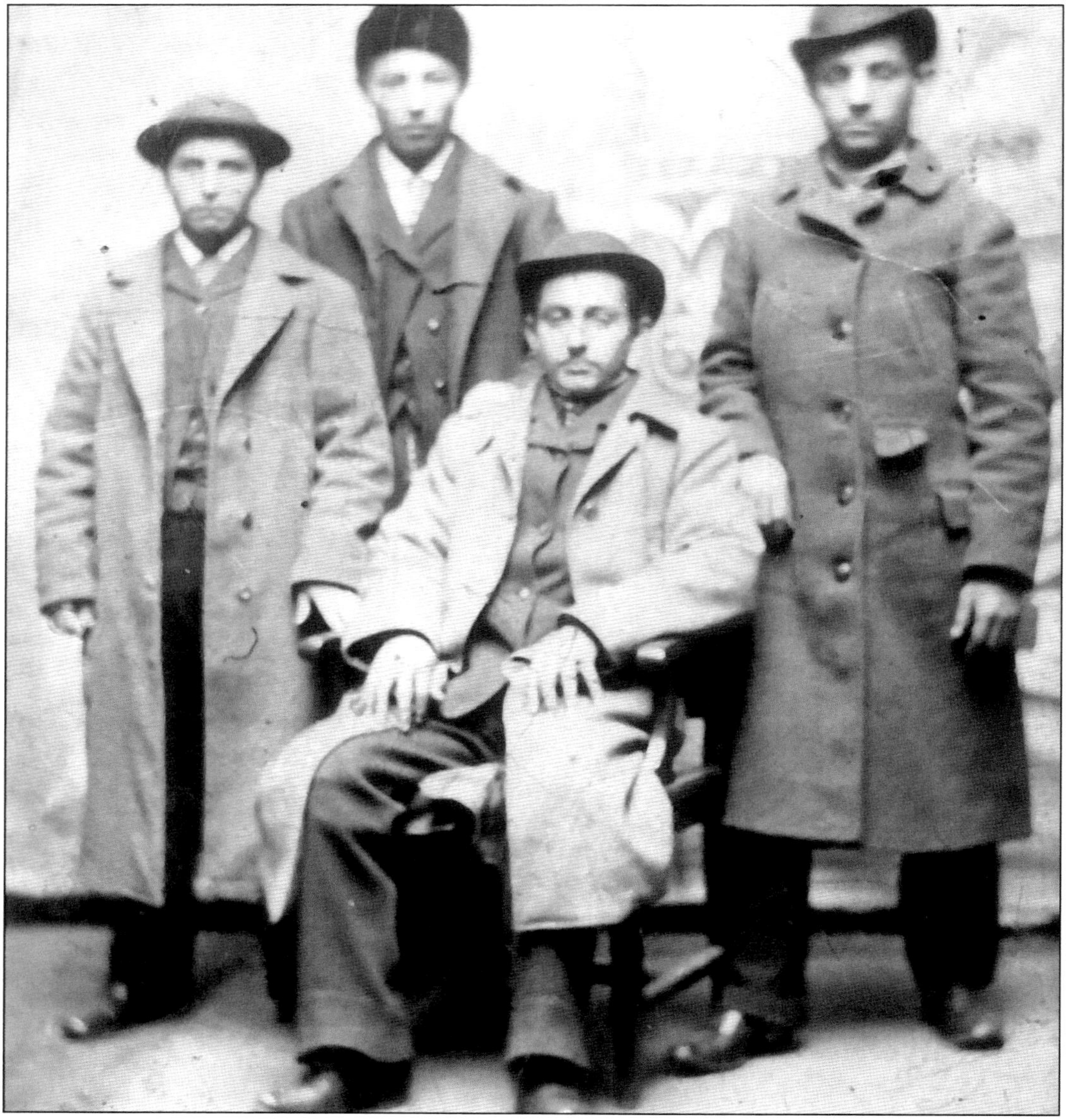

Cain Calmenson and Louis Calmenson are shown in this photo with their cousin, Joe Cohen (standing left), and an unidentified friend or relative. Standing on the right is Cain, whose original name in the old country was Calmen. Sitting is Louis Calmenson. Moses Calmenson, their father, was 18 years old when Cain was born. Moses and Aaron Mark fled Lithuania to America, but after Moses had lived in the United States for several years as a peddler, he returned to St. Paul, bringing both boys ages nine and seven, and a new bride, Bas Sheva, who was the daughter of Reb Lippe Ha Cohen. A year after Cain came to St. Paul he was peddling matches on the streets of St. Paul. Cain later married Annie Cohen, sister of Reb Lippe Ha Cohen. Both he and his father, Moses, were among those Orthodox Jews who organized the Sons of Jacob Synagogue in 1873. (Photo courtesy of Mrs. Harold (Connie) Field, Moses Calmenson's granddaughter)

presumed not to know what it was like in the "old days." This presumption did not carry over, however, to the newly arrived German Jews, who were considered family (271).

The first Eastern European Jewish were not desperate refugees like those who would arrive in the 1880s and thereafter. Like many of the German Jews, they first settled along and around Jackson and Robert Streets, on Eight, Ninth, and Tenth into the near East Side area along and around Payne Avenue (272). These Jews from Eastern Europe were generally more meticulous in their observances of their religious rituals (273). As the German Jews moved toward Reform Judaism, the Eastern European Jews moved closer to orthodoxy.

One of the first of the more orthodox Jews to arrive was Aaron Mark. Aaron Mark had been born Aaron Joseph, in Vilna, Poland, in 1831. He had first married in Kovno, Lithuania, where his first son Abraham had been born in 1857 (274). He married a second time to Bessie Mark in 1861, and took the name of her deceased cousin in order to avoid conscription in the Army (275). They came to America in 1868 and lived in New York for a time, moving to St. Paul in 1873 (276). At first he peddled and then opened a junk yard called Aaron Mark Iron Works on Robert Street between Seventh and Eighth, where the Golden Rule department store stood, now the site of the Metro-Square Building (277). Aaron Mark was one of the founders and supporters of the more orthodox Sons of Jacob or Chevrah B'nai Ya'akov. There had been some informal organization prior to Aaron Mark's arrival, as it only required the traditional 10 adult men to organize a *minyan* prayer group, without a rabbi or formal synagogue building. Women were not counted in composing a *minyan* group, nor were young men under age 13 (278).

In 1873, shortly after Aaron Mark's arrival, a meeting was held in his home where it was decided to formally organize the Orthodox Jewish community. Thereafter, Aaron Mark's home became the meeting place of the orthodox community and served as place of

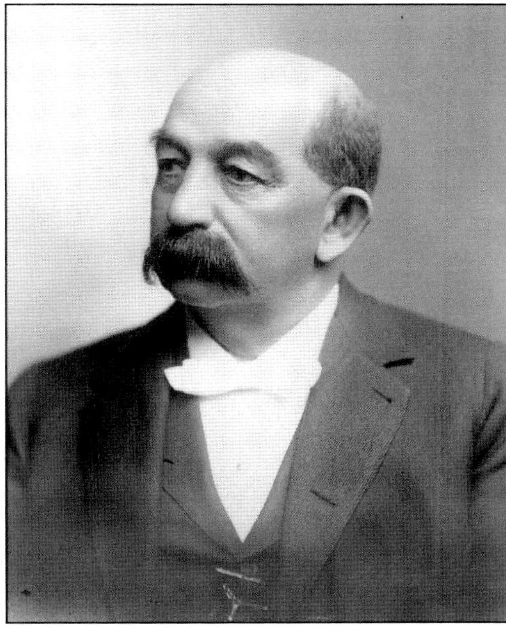

This photo of Henry J. Strouse was taken by C.N. Zimmerman. (From the photo archives of Minnesota Historical Society)

worship until a more permanent place was purchased (279). On March 25, 1875, the Sons of Jacob was formerly incorporated with 12 families, with Aaron Mark as one of the incorporators. More importantly, Aaron Mark was also influential in laying the groundwork for the first conservative synagogue in Minnesota, the Temple of Aaron in St. Paul, which was named after him after his death (280).

Orthodox Jews believed that the Torah (sacred scriptures) was given to the Jews by God on Mount Sinai. Therefore, they said that every word was holy. When the realities of life came into conflict it was the realities of life that had to yield, for the Torah, being God's will, was unchanging. Any of the rules or the traditions long in use were unchangeable. No law, said the leaders of Orthodox Judaism, must ever be revoked. Conservative Jews opposed orthodoxy because they felt it was unyielding. They also opposed the Reform movement because they felt it was breaking with many ideas basic to

Judaism. Conservative Judaism did not come to St. Paul until after the 20th century had begun (281).

Aaron and Bessie Mark had six children from their marriage: Emmett, who moved to Willow River, Minnesota; Lena (Moses); Mary (Mark); Sarah (Mark); Fannie (Litman), and Sadie (Rubenstein) (282). Abraham, Aaron's son by his first wife, married Moritz Kafka's daughter, Lena, in one of the first Reform Orthodox marriages in the community. They moved to northern Minnesota, where Abraham Mark became a prominent merchant until his death (283).

Mrs. Bessie Mark, Aaron's widow, was one of the most active and philanthropic women in the community. Mrs. Mark was a founder of the Jewish Home for the Aged, which bought the old Banning house on Wilkin Street, and the Jewish Educational Center, formerly at Holly and Grotto (284). She had the unique experience of laying the cornerstone for both the original Sons of Jacob building on Tenth and College in 1881, and the original temple of Aaron building at Ashland and Grotto in 1913 (285). The latter still stands but is used as a community theater building. For many years, after the Sons of Jacob building was dedicated, the Mark family home was at 835 Reaney (286) on the near East side. Mrs. Mark's nephew, Joseph, was the first registered Jewish physician in Minnesota in 1883. He came from Lithuania and had received his medical degrees in the old country, and was the son and grandson of doctors (287).

Another newcomer in 1873 was Moses Calmenson, who, like Aaron Mark, was to have a significant and profound impact on the religious and cultural growth of the St. Paul Jewish community. He arrived in St. Paul with his sons Cain and Louis, ages nine and seven, and a new bride. There was business competition between Mark Iron Works and the Calmensons, who were also in the iron and steel (junk) business, but they eventually merged and became the present day Paper-Calmenson Company, one of the largest of its kind in the country. Both Moses and Cain Calmenson helped to found the Sons of Jacob, the orthodox synagogue (288). Moses Calmenson's descendants became leaders of the Jewish community for many years. Cain's son, Jessie Calmenson, an attorney, was president of the Jewish Educational Center at Holly and Grotto, and active in various Jewish causes for many years. Moses Calmenson was also very prominent in organizing the early Zionist movement, dedicated to the creation of the State of Israel (289). For many years the Moses Calmenson family lived at 650 Reaney on the near East side. The Cain Calmenson family was living at 771 Hague at the time of his death in 1923 (290).

Another early leader in the orthodox community was Gutman Caplan, who, like Aaron Mark, was born in Vilna, Poland. He came from Rabbinical stock and was the son of a rabbi, Reb Nahum Caplan. Gutman Caplan came to America in 1873, and moved to St. Paul as a peddler. He served as an early officer and president of Sons of Jacob in the early 1880s. He married Rikla Blumberg of New York after he left St. Paul and settled in Pittsburgh, Pennsylvania. He became a prominent baker of *matzoh*, the unleavened bread used at mealtime during the commemoration of Passover. Passover celebrates the successful exodus of the Jews from slavery in Egypt. *Matzoh* is directly symbolic of the unleavened bread hastily baked on rocks in the sun during the Jews flight from Egypt to the land of Israel (291).

By 1873, less than 25 years had passed since the first Jews had settled in the little village of St. Paul on the Mississippi River. But Jewish roots were well established in the community. More Jews were coming and staying, despite all the hardships.

Abaham Marks also arrived in 1873 with his family and worked as a peddler (292), and as was common in those days, lived in his small place of business at Fourteenth and Robert. His son Samuel was one of the first Jews to be active in the St. Paul theater, and later developing an active interest when Conley's became the famous old Olympic Theater of the 1890s (293). Abraham's other sons had

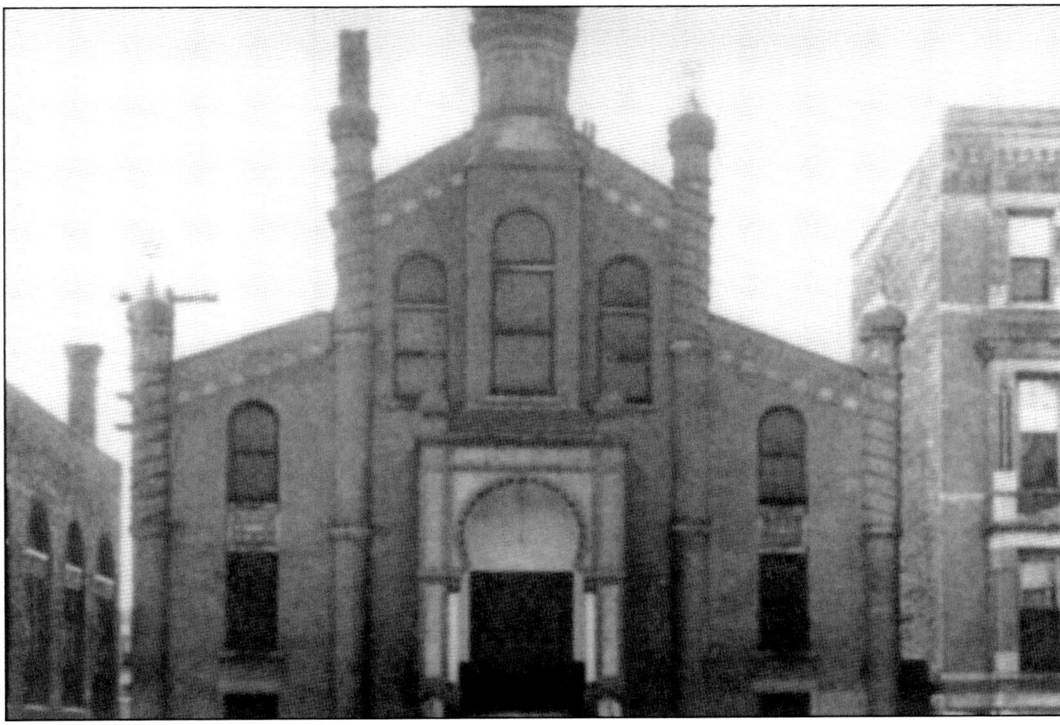

The College Avenue Shul is pictured here. Sons of Jacob Synagogue, located on College Avenue between Wabasha and St. Peter Street, could accommodate 600 people, had a large library, and a Hebrew school. Photo by Geoffrey Marshall. (From the photo archives of Beth Jacob Synagogue, successor to Sons of Jacob Synagogue)

varied careers, with Edward being a bartender for a while, and Himey a waiter (294). Abraham Marks later went into partnership with Mrs. Jennie Koenigsberg in the clothing business. Isaac Koenigsberg was probably her son, and served as an early leader of the new Sons of Jacob (295). Abraham Marks was also in business with Nathan Blumenthal, who was another of the founders of the Sons of Jacob and its first president after its incorporation in 1875 (296).

Among the early pioneers affiliated with the Chevra B'nai Yaakov (Sons of Jacob), the then Orthodox community were: Moses and Samuel Coddon, Aaron Mark, Moses Calmenson, Nathan Blumenthal—who was its first president—Simon Jacobs, David and Wolf Goodman, Abraham Kaufman, Nathan B. Cohen, Charles Polski, Raphael Machinsky, Epraim Skorish, Mayer and Jascha Rosenholtz, Gutman Caplan, Solomon Moses, Robert Burton, Nathan Abrahamson, Isaac Coddon, Louis Pavian, and Samuel Rudowsky. They had begun to meet on the East side of St. Paul at the home of Aaron Mark and later when Aaron Mark moved, at Thirteenth and Robert (today 620 North Robert). On March 20, 1875, 12 of the families formally incorporated (296a). They quickly ran out of space and moved to the Eibert Block at Wabasha and College, and shortly thereafter purchased a large home at Eleventh and Minnesota Streets, which had been used as a private academy. Their first synagogue building at College Avenue (between Wabasha and St. Peter, now the site of the St. Paul Health Department) was constructed in 1881. Its first officers were: Nathan Blumenthal, as president; Simon Jacobs as secretary; and Nathan Coddon, Moses Calmenson, and Moses Polski as trustees (296b).

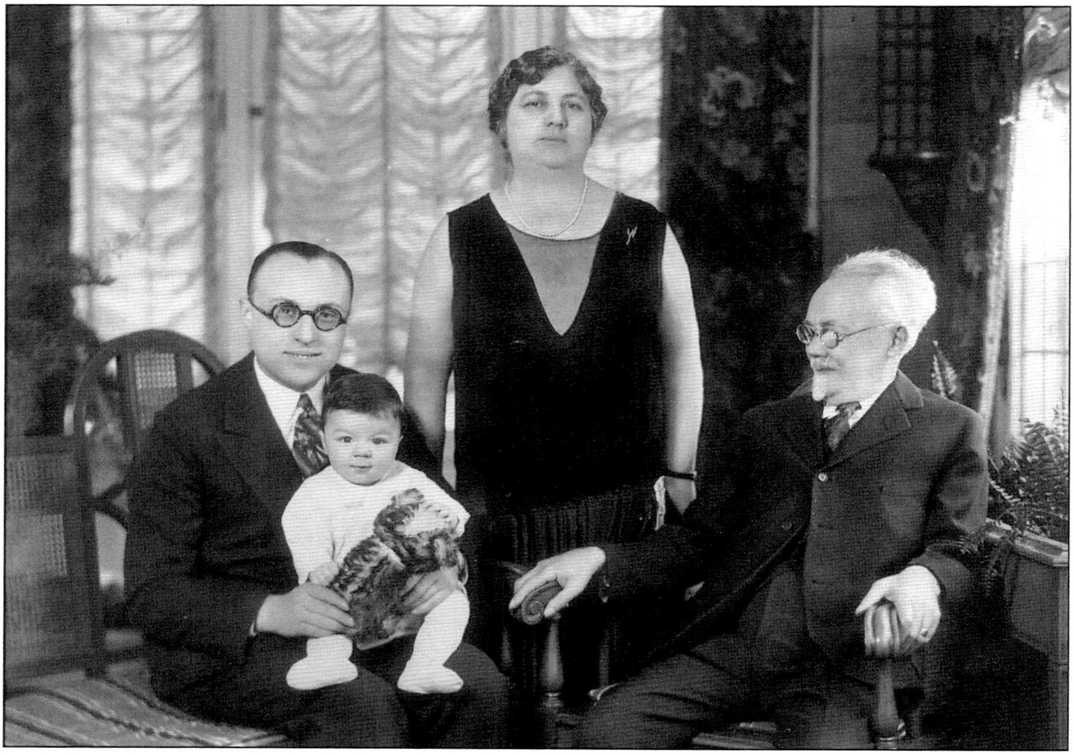

Nathan Blumenthal and his daughter, Rachel (Mrs. Harold Finkelstein (Field)) and her husband Harold Finkelstein (Field). (From the photo archives of Minnesota Historical Society)

The first building immediately became too small, and in 1888 a new Sons of Jacob building was constructed on the same site. It was a large brick structure, which could accommodate 600 people, had a large library, and a Hebrew school and a number of auxiliary organizations (296c). The first pioneer Orthodox religious functionary was Jacob Goldstein, who was *hazaan* in 1875 (296d).

Gustav and Albert Heineman arrived in St. Paul in 1874. Albert had been born in Prussia, and Gustav in Germany. Both were single (297). Albert went to work for Moritz Auerbach. Julius Heineman was probably Gustav's brother and lived with him for a while, and he also worked for Auerbach. Edward Heineman came to live with Albert and may have been another brother. Gustav worked for A.H. Strouse and eventually Gustav and Edward Heineman worked with Esterly and Heineman, a prominent dry goods firm. Gustav started his own dry goods and notion business at Seventh and Jackson, and became a very prominent businessman (298). He served as president of the Dayton's Bluff Building and Loan Association for many years and lived in that community at 652 E. Fifth Street (299). He later lived at 427 Dayton (300). Whether the Heinemans were related to Jacob Heineman, who was here in the early 1860s is unknown (301).

Harry L. Levy was 28 years old when he arrived in St. Paul (302) and went into business with Sigmund Hanauer in the clothing business. His first son, Henry Levy, was born in 1874, and he had three other sons (303). In 1875, he became an active Mason, having joined Ancient Landmark Lodge No. 5, and he remained so his entire life (304). He became active in Mt. Zion and served as trustee in 1874, and recording secretary in 1876, and again in 1896 (305). In between, he spent his lifetime building up a clothing business and then a prosperous wholesale liquor business (306). In 1896, he was also elected as president of Minnesota Lodge of B'nai B'rith (307). He died without a will in 1917, his wife having pre-deceased him (308). One of his sons, Jessie, became a very prominent St. Paul doctor (309).

Sigmund and Gustave Hanauer both arrived in St. Paul in 1874. Sigmund went into partnership with Harry L. Levy and the firm was known as Hanauer and Levy. The Hanauers came from a prominent New York clothing family that had originated the one-price cost of clothing concept. The Hanauer family had one of the largest clothing factories in New York (310). Sigmund was active in Mt. Zion and served as financial secretary in 1890. In 1886, after the departure of his brother Gustave, he organized the Manhattan 1-Price Clothing Store that became one of the largest stores of its kind in St. Paul (311).

Upon his arrival, Gustav Hanauer went into business with Julius Austrian in the clothing business. Gustav's wife, Julia, was a Bernheimer of the New York Bernheimers who were prominent in the clothing business and were intermarried with the Gimbel and Bloomingdale families. Gustav and Julia Hanauer later moved to Spokane, Washington, in the late 1870s. Julia's sister, Adele was married into the Bloomingdale family (312).

Only 25 years had passed since Caroline Bloomingdale's two brothers Edwin and Charles Elfelt became St. Paul's first Jewish settlers. Now, 25 years later, the Jewish community in St. Paul had firmly established its roots and had its identity in what was still a vast wilderness. It had developed cultural, religious, and commercial ties that to this day have remained important parts of St. Paul's diverse ethnic and religious communities. The impact of the Jewish community in St. Paul has been substantial considering its small size. Their struggles, ideals, talents, and achievements enriched the history of St. Paul, Minnesota.

Where They Did Business

Aron Aaronheimer and **Marx (or Max) Marks** had a clothing store on St. Anthony Street (now part of Kellogg Boulevard) near the Presbyterian Church on 3rd Street and St. Peter Street.

Henry Cole (or Cali) owned Elias and Cole Dry Goods and Clothing store across the street from Aaronheimer and Marks on St. Anthony Street (now part of Kellogg Boulevard).

Isaac Ansel and his son had a clothing store on Third Street (now Kellogg Boulevard) between Robert Street and Jackson Street.

Morris Appel had a clothing store on Robert Street between Sixth and Seventh Streets.

Joseph Ullmann had a liquor business and then a fur trading business on Jackson Street at Fifth Street.

Hirsch Heimann and **Benjamin Rose** had a clothing store on Minnesota Street between Sixth and Seventh Streets.

Isadore and **Emmanuel Rose** had a fur business on Jackson Street between Fourth Street and Fifth Street.

Jacob Newman and **Abraham Greenwald** had a clothing store on old St. Anthony Street (now part of Kellogg Boulevard) opposite the city Market at Seventh Street at Wabasha Street. Abraham Greenwald lived over their store.

Henry Marks owned the Peoples Clothing Store on Third Street (now Kellogg Boulevard) between Cedar Street and Minnesota Street.

Morris Marks had a clothing store on Third Street (now Kellogg Boulevard) below Robert Street.

Joseph Bergfeld had a clothing store on Robert Street between Third Street (now Kellogg Boulevard) and Fourth Street.

Kalmon Lion and his son owned a Gents' furnishings store on Third Street, (now Kellogg Boulevard) west of Minnesota Street.

Alexander Sternberg owned a clothing store called the New York Clothing House on Third Street (now Kellogg Boulevard).

Zeigo and **Philip Weiss** were partners in and manufactured and dealt in hoop skirts and women's corsets at 97 East Seventh Street.

George N. Cardozo had both a cigar factory and later a second-hand furniture store on Jackson Street at Fourth Street.

Elfelts had stores at Eagle Street and Upper Levee, Third Street (now Kellogg Boulevard), and Cedar Street and Third Street (now Kellogg Boulevard) and Exchange Street.

Goodkind-Mannheimer's first store was at 7 East Third Street (now Kellogg Boulevard) just below Wabasha Street. Later moved to Mannheimer Block at Third Street (now Kellogg Boulevard) and Minnesota Street.

David Sattler, **Henry T. Sattler**, and **Jacob D. Sattler** had a clothing store at 76 East Third Street (now Kellogg Boulevard) just below Wabasha Street.

Julius Mendelsohn was a partner in Fuller and Mendelsohn whose store was on Robert Street and Fifth Street.

Aaron Meyer had a clothing store on Fourth Street and Jackson Street.

Aaron Mark owned the Aaron Mark Iron Works located on Robert Street between Seventh Street and Eighth Street.

Gustave Heineman had a store on Seventh Street and Jackson Street.

Abraham Marks was a peddler and lived in his place of business at Robert Street and Fourteenth Street.

Others who started out as peddlers were: **Charles Burnstein**, **Jacob Levi**, **Julius Cohn**, **Reuben Goldstein**, **Abraham Goldstein**, **Abraham Marchofsky**, **David Greenblat**, **Moritz Kafka**, **Aaron Mark**, and **Gutman Caplan**.

Bibliography

Andrews, C.C. *History of St. Paul*. 1890.

Birmingham, Stephen. *Our Crowd*. 1967.

Birmingham, Stephen. *The Grandees*. 1971.

Castle. *History of St. Paul and Vicinity*. 1912.

Castle. *Minnesota, Its Story and Biography*. 1915.

Census records of 1857 and 1860. Minnesota Historical Society Archives.

Dashefsky and Shapiro. *The Jewish Community of St. Paul.* United Jewish Fund and Council. Report in cooperation with University of Connecticut Research Foundation. 1971.

Dual Blue Book City Directory *Volumes I & II*. R.L. Polk & Co., 1885-1887.

Empson. *On the Street Where You Live*. 1975.

Fenwick. *Sturdy Sons of St. Paul*. 1899.

Frankel, H.D. *The Jews of St. Paul*. 1907 Edition, Reform Advocate. Chicago, Illinois.

Goodkind, S.B. *Prominent Jews of America*. American Hebrew Publishing Co., 1918.

Hennessy, William B. *Past and Present of St. Paul, Minnesota.* 1906.

"Illustrated St. Paul" *St. Paul Dispatch*. 1892.

Korn. *American Jewry and the Civil War.* 1951.

Kunz. *St. Paul, The Saga of an American City*. 1977.

Little Sketches of Big Folks. R.L. Polk Co., 1907.

Lundeen. *St. Paul's Historic Summit Avenue*.1978.

Microfilm records of St. Paul Pioneer Press, *St. Paul Daily News*, *St. Paul Daily Globe*, *Minneapolis Star, Minneapolis Tribune, Minnesota Historical Society;* also *Crosby Courier, Minnesota Historical Society files.*

Millett. *Lost Twin Cities*. 1992.

Minnesota and its People, Volume III. Chicago: S.J. Clarke Publishing Co., 1924.

Minnesota Gazeteer and Business Directory, 1865, 1867–1868, Hill Reference Library.

Minnesota Historical Society Archives. *Golden Jubilee of A.F. and A.M.* Ancient Landmark Lodge No. 5, 1904.

Minnesota Historical Society Archives. *H.D. Frankel Papers.*

Minnesota Historical Society Archives. *Julius Heilbron papers.*

Minnesota Historical Society Collections. *Early Trade and Traders in St. Paul, Vol. 9*. 1901.

Minnesota Historical Society Library, *Book of Minnesotans.* Marquis, 1907.

Minnesota Historical Society Scrapbooks, 1861-1912.

Minnesota in Civil War and Indian Wars Volume 1; Report of Adjunct-General's Office. Final record, both books in Minnesota Historical Society. 1866.

Minnesota Legislative Manual, 1879.

Morrison. *Industries of St. Paul*. 1886.

Mt. Zion Cemetery Burial Book, Minnesota Historical Society Archive.

Newsom. *Pen Pictures of St. Paul*. 1886.

Pessin. *History of Jews in America*. 1957.

Plaut, Gunther W. *Jews of Minnesota.* 1959.

Plaut, Gunther W. *Mt. Zion, the First 100 Years.* 1956.

Ramsey County, Minnesota, Probate Court Records.

Ramsey County Plat Book.

Rosenbloom. *Biographical Dictionary of Early American Jews*. University of Kentucky Press, 1960.

Shutter. *Progressive Men of Minnesota*.1897.

Stern, Malcolm. *Americans of Jewish Descent.* Cardozo, Seixas, and Cadet Genealogies, 1960.

St. Louis County (Duluth) Minnesota Register of Deeds files.

"St. Paul Architecture," St. Paul Planning Department. August, 1975.

St. Paul City Directories by various publishers. 1857–1885. R.L. Polk Library; Minnesota Historical Society microfilm library. 1886–1915.

St. Paul History & Progress, Principal Men and Industries. St. Paul Pioneer Press, 1897.

Upham. *Minnesota Biographies*. Minnesota Historical Society Collections, 1912.

Various program books of Sons of Jacob. *History of Sons of Jacob*. Private copies.

Voice of Minnesota Lodge, B'nai B'rith. 1953.

Williams. *A History of the City of St. Paul to 1875*. Reprint, 1983.

Williams. *History of St. Paul and Ramsey County*. 1876.

Who was Who in America: 1897–1942. Chicago, 1942.

WPA Historical Research Project, Minnesota Historical Society Archives. 1942.

Annotations

1. "The Jewish Community of St. Paul," Dashefsky and Shapiro; United Jewish Fund and Council Report in cooperation with University of Connecticut Research Foundation (1971) typed copy, page 4.

2. *Ibid*. Also see St. Paul City Directories by various publishers (1865-1883) R.L. Polk Library, Minnesota Historical Society Library.

3. See WPA Historical Research project in Minnesota Historical Society Archives, (1942).

4. The "Jews in Minnesota," W. Gunther Plaut (1959), pages 10-12.

5 Ramsey County Probate Court File No. 783. Petition by Edwin Elfelt, dated August 19, 1869 to sell real estate owned by Simon Elfelt located in Minnesota. The petition gives 1835 as the date of Simon Elfelt's death. Other sources give 1855.

6. The "Jews in Minnesota," W. Gunther Plaut (1959), page 12.

7. "History of St. Paul," C.C. Andrews (1890), page 83.

8. See Ramsey County Plat book for "Elfelt, Bernheimer and Arnold's Addition," page 50.

9. "Jews in Minnesota," Plaut (1959), page 11.

10. "History of St. Paul," C.C. Andrews (1890), page 82.

11. *Ibid*. page 83.

12. City Directories 1874-1886; R.L. Polk Library; Minn. Historical Society Library.

13. Ramsey County Probate Court File No. 4548; Estate of Abram Elfelt.

14. Ramsey County Probate Court File No. 9769; Estate of Charles Elfelt.

15. *Ibid*. Also see "Americans of Jewish Descent," Malcolm Stern (1960) Cadet genealogy, page 22 on Edwin Elfelt. Elfelt's mother's maiden name was Cadet.

15a. Mt. Zion, the first Hundred years, Plaut, (1956) pg 11.

15b. A History of the City of St. Paul to 1875, J. Fletcher Williams, (Reprint) (1983).

15c. Mt. Zion, the First Hundred Years, Plaut, (1956) pages 11, 16, 21, 26.

15d. St. Paul, the Saga of an American City, Kunz, (1977), pages 16 and 38.

15e. Mt. Zion, the First Hundred years, Plaut, (1956) Appendici I and II page 125.

16. "Golden Jubilee of A.F. and A.M. Landmark Lodge No. 5," Minnesota Historical Society files. This book, published in 1904 to celebrate 50th anniversary of Ancient Landmark Lodge No. 5, A.F. and A.M., lists a number of early Jewish settlers who became members.

17. "Jews in Minnesota," Plaut (1959), page 22.

18. "Past and Present of St. Paul, Minnesota," William B. Hennessy (1906), page 443; "Book of Minnesotans," Marquis (1907), page 436; "Jews in Minnesota," Plaut (1959), page 45.

19. Ramsey County Probate Court File No. 4796; Estate of Benjamin Rose; "Golden Jubilee of A.F. and A.M. Landmark Lodge No. 5," (1854-1904); "Jews in Minnesota," Plaut (1959), page 45.

20. "Jews in Minnesota," Plaut (1959), page 45; "Voice of Minnesota Lodge, B'nai B'rith," October, 1953 edition (private copy).

21. *Ibid*. Also see Ramsey County Probate Court File No. 23345; Estate of Isadore Rose; Polk City Directory and St. Paul City Directory by other publishers, R.L. Polk Library, and Minnesota Historical Society Microfilm Library (1856-1915).

22. "Jews in Minnesota," Plaut (1959), page 42; Also see 1857 Census, page 136; "Mt. Zion, the first 100 years," Plaut (1956), page 11.

23. "The Jews of St. Paul," H.D. Frankel, printed in 1907 in the Reform Advocate, Special Edition; "Jews in Minnesota," Plaut (1959), page 42; "Mt. Zion, the first 100 years," Plaut (1956), page 65.

24. Census of 1857, page 136.

25. City Directories, R.L. Polk Library; Minnesota Historical Society Microfilm Library (1856-1898).

26. "Mt. Zion, the first 100 years," Plaut (1956), pages 15-16; 27.

27. *Ibid*. Pages 21-22.

28. "Jews in Minnesota," Plaut (1959), page 42; also see note 7.

29. *Ibid*. Also see Ramsey County Probate Court File No. 791; Estate of Hirsch Heimann.

30. *Ibid*. Page 46.

31. "Americans of Jewish Descent," Malcolm Stern (1960), Cardozo genealogical chart, page 23.

32. *Ibid*. Seixas genealogical chart, page 191.

33. "The Grandees," Stephen Birmingham (1971).

34. *Ibid*.

35. "Our Crowd," Stephen Birmingham (1967), page 30. Also see "Biographical Dictionary of Early American Jews," Rosenbloom (1960), University of Kentucky Press.

36. "Jews in Minnesota," Plaut (1959), page 46.

37. City Directories, Minnesota Historical Society Library Microfilm Library; R.L. Polk Library, (1860-1887).

38. Ramsey County Probate Court File No. 4690; Estate of Isaac N. Cardozo.

39. St. Paul Pioneer Press, November 10, 1887, page 1.

40. "American of Jewish Descent," Malcolm Stern (1960), Seixas family genealogical chart, page 191; City Directories, R.L. Polk Library (1887-1910); Ramsey County Probate Court File No. 17893; Estate of Rachel N. Cardozo (Mrs. Isaac N. Cardozo).

41. "Golden Jubilee of A.F. and A.M." (1904); Minnesota Historical Society Library; "Mt. Zion, first 100 years," Plaut (1956), pages 26, 127; City Directory (1876-1877); Minnesota Historical Society Microfilm Library.

42. City Directories (1881-1895), R.L. Polk Library; Minnesota Historical Society Microfilm Library.

43. Ramsey County Probate Court File NO. 179; Estate of Marks Marks.

44. "Jews in Minnesota," Plaut (1959), page 43; "Mt. Zion, first 100 years," Plaut (1956), page 14.

45. *Ibid*.

46. Ramsey County Probate Court File No. 1878; Estate of Daniel Goodman.

47. Polk City Directory, R.L. Polk Library (1878-1880).

48. Ramsey County Probate Court File No. 3003; Estate of Kalmon Lion.

49. "Jews in Minnesota," Plaut (1959), page 43.

50. 1860 Census Report, page 77; City Directories, R.L. Polk Library, 1863, 1869-1870; "Mt. Zion, first 100 years," Plaut (1956) page 22.

51. "Jews in Minnesota," Plaut (1959), page 41; "Mt. Zion, first 100 years," Plaut (1956), pages 12, 16.

52. "Jews in Minnesota," Plaut (1959), page 41; City Directories, R.L. Polk Library (1863-1868).

53. *Ibid*, pages 39, 43; City Directories, R.L. Polk Library, Minnesota Historical Society Microfilm Library, 1856.

54. "Mt. Zion, first 100 years," Plaut (1956), page 14; Ramsey County Probate Court File No. 375;

"Golden Jubilee of A.F. and A.M. Ancient Landmark Lodge No. 5," (1904), Minnesota Historical Society Files.

55. "Mt. Zion, first 100 years," Plaut (1956), page 125; Mendelsohn struggled to hold Mt. Zion together during the chaotic period of the Civil War. As a result there are no records from 1862–1869 concerning Mt. Zion, which was then the only organized Jewish synagogue in the State of Minnesota.

56. "Golden Jubilee of A.F. and A.M. Ancient Landmark Lodge No. 5," (1904), Minnesota Historical Society Files.

57. "The Jews of St. Paul," H.D. Frankel (1907), Reform Advocate, Special Edition (Chicago), page 42.

58. R.L. Polk Library; Minnesota Historical Society Microfilm Library, City Directory (1863).

59. Ramsey County Probate Court File No. 24264; Estate of Carrie Bernheim (Mrs. Nathan Bernheim); "Mt. Zion, first 100 years," Plaut (1956), page 27.

60. "Minnesota in Civil War and Indian Wars," Vol. 1; "Report of Adjutant-General's office," (1866), Final Record; both books in Minnesota Historical Society Library.

61. City Directories, R.L. Polk Library (1865-1870); Minnesota Historical Society Microfilm Library; R.L. Polk Library (1866-1912).

62. Ramsey County Probate Court File No. 339.

63. "History of Ramsey County," Neill (1881), page 544.

64. "Jews in Minnesota," Plaut (1959), page 311, Appendix.

65. "Mt. Zion, first 100 years," Plaut (1956), page 128; "Voice of Minnesota Lodge, B'nai B'rith," October, 1953 issue (private copy): contains list of all presidents from 1871 through 1953.

66. "Jews in Minnesota," Plaut (1959), page 311, Appendix; A search of Adjutant-General's report of 1866 indicates that Harris, Smith and Neumann did not enter service in Minnesota.

67. City Directory (1864), R.L. Polk Library.

68. "Voice of Minnesota Lodge, B'nai B'rith," October, 1953 (private copy).

69. R.L. Polk Library, City Directories (1866-1898); Mt. Zion Burial Book contained in Minnesota Historical Society Archives; also see oral interview with Bertha Heilbron in 1953, in Julius Heilbron's papers filed in Minnesota Historical Society Archives, which lists members of the Mt. Zion Sunday School classes in the 1880s.

70. "Jews in Minnesota," Plaut (1959), page 230.

71. R.L. Polk Library, Directories (1866-1898).

72. "Jews in Minnesota," Plaut (1959), page 54.

73. "American Jewry and the Civil War," Korn (1951), pages 2–3.

74. "History of Jews in America," Pessin (1957), page 250.

75. "Jews in Minnesota," Plaut (1959), page 56.

76. *Ibid.*

77. "Mt. Zion, first 100 years," Plaut (1956), pages 26-27.

78. R.L. Polk Directory Library.

79. "The Jews of St. Paul," H.D. Frankel, Reform Advocate (1907), page 43; "Mt. Zion, first 100 years," Plaut (1956), page 27.

80. "The Street Where You Live," Empson (1975).

81. "Mt. Zion, first 100 years," Plaut (1956), see appendix for list of Mt. Zion officers, page 129.

82. R.L. Polk City Directories, R.L. Polk Library (1886-1889), Minnesota Historical Society Microfilm Library.

83. Ramsey County Probate Court File No. 9828; Estate of Samuel Sternberg; Ramsey County Probate Court File No. 28493; Estate of Alexander Sternberg; "Book of Minnesotans," Marquis (1907), page 488.

84. "Jews in Minnesota," Plaut (1959), page 160; Ramsey County Probate Court File No. 9828; Estate of Samuel Sternberg.

85. Mt. Zion Cemetery Burial Book, Minnesota Historical Society Archives.

86. "Mt. Zion, first 100 years," Plaut (1956), page 65.

87. "Americans of Jewish Descent," Malcolm Stern (1960), page 191; See Seixas (3) genealogy; also see "A Biographical Dictionary of Early American Jews," Rosenbloom (1960).

88. *Ibid.*

89. R.L. Polk Directory Library; St. Paul City Directories.

90. *Ibid.*

91. *Ibid.*

92. *Ibid.* Campbell's City Directory (1876).

93. Ramsey County Probate Court File NO. 4690; Estate of Isaac N. Cardozo.

94. “Mt. Zion, first 100 years,” Plaut (1956), Appendix, 1889 membership list.

95. R.L. Polk Directory, 1885-1886, R.L. Polk Library; Minnesota Historical Society Library.

96. R.L. Polk Directory, 1903, R.L. Polk Directory Library; Minnesota Historical Society Library.

97. R.L. Polk Directory, 1884-1885, R.L. Polk Directory Library; listed as John C. Seixas.

98. St. Paul Daily Dispatch, June 26, 1877; WPA Historical Research Project, Minnesota Historical Society Archives (1942); Minnesota Historical Society Microfilm Library.

99. Campbell's City Directory (1877), R.L. Polk Directory Library; Minnesota Historical Society Microfilm Library.

100. “Voice of Minnesota Lodge, B'nai B'rith,” October, 1953, private copy.

101. R.L. Polk Directory Library, various directories (1878-1890).

102. R.L. Polk Directory, 1899, R.L. Polk Library; Minnesota Historical Society Library.

103. R.L. Polk Directory Library.

104. *Ibid.*

105. *Ibid.*

106. Mt. Zion Burial Book (old cemetery), Minnesota Historical Society Archives; also see “Americans of Jewish Descent,” Malcolm Stern (1960), page 191; Seixas (3) genealogy.

107. R.L. Polk Directory (1879), R.L. Polk Library.

108. Mt. Zion Burial Book (old cemetery), Minnesota Historical Society Archives.

109. R.L. Polk Directory Library.

110. Edward's Census Report and City Directory (1873), R.L. Polk Directory Library (1868-69).

111. “Mt Zion, first 100 years”, Plaut (1956), See appendix.

112. R.L. Polk Directory Library; Minnesota Historical Society Microfilm Library.

113. *Ibid.*

114. *Ibid.*

115. Edward's Census Report and City Directory, (1873), R.L. Polk Library.

116. City Business Directory (1869-1870), R.L. Polk Library; Minnesota Historical Society Microfilm Library.

117. R.L. Polk Directory Library.

118. *Ibid.*

119. "Voice of Minnesota Lodge, B'nai B'rith," October, 1953 issue, private copy.

120. R.L. Polk Directory, (1898), R.L. Polk Directory Library.

121. "American Jewery and the Civil War," Korn, (1951), page 3.

122. "History of Sons of Jacob," program books, private copies.

123. *Ibid.*

124. "Jews in Minnesota," Plaut (1959), page 13.

125. *Ibid.*; also "Mt. Zion, first 100 years" Plaut (1956) page 28; also see Julius Heilbron papers in Minnesota Historical Society Archives.

126. *Ibid.*

127. "Jews in Minnesota," Plaut, (1959), pages 13-14.

128. *Ibid.*

129. R.L.Polk Directory Library.

130. *Ibid.*

131. *Ibid.*

132. *Ibid.*

133. "Jews in Minnesota," Plaut, (1959), page 57.

134. "Mt. Zion, first 100 years," Plaut, (1956), page 56; also see St. Paul Daily Globe, July 18, 1882, Minnesota History Society Microfilm Library; WPA Historical Research project, Minnesota Historical Society Archives, (1942).

135. Julius Heilbron papers, Minnesota Historical Society Archives; St. Paul Pioneer Press March 20, 1891, page 5, Minnesota Historical Society Microfilm Library; Ramsey County Probate Court File No. 5807; Estate of Julius Austrian; "Voice of Minnesota's Lodge B'nai B'rith, "October, 1953 issue, private copy.

136. R.L. Polk Directory Library.

137. Julius Heilbron papers, Minnesota Historical Society Archives.

138. Edward's Census and City Directory, (1873), R.L. Polk Library.

139. "Jews in Minnesota," Plaut (1959), page 14.

140. *Ibid*.

141. *Ibid*., also see footnote 15.

142. Mt. Zion Burial Book (old cemetery), Minnesota Historical Society Archives.

143. Ramsey County Probate Court File No. 4499, Estate of Abraham Leopold; Edwards Census and City Directory (1873), R.L. Polk Library.

144. Ramsey County Probate Court File No. 1855; Estate of Samuel Levi.

145. "History of Sons of Jacob", Programs books, private copies.

146. Edward's Census and City Directory, (1873), R.L Polk Library.

147. "Voice of Minnesota Lodge, B'nai B'rith," October, 1953 issue, private copy.;

148. "Jews in Minnesota," Plaut, (1959), page 134.

149. Edward's Census and City Directory, (1873), R.L. Polk Library.

150. "Mt. Zion, first 100 years," Plaut, (1956), see Appendix.

151. "Voice of the Minnesota Lodge, B'nai B'rith," October, 1953 issue, private copy.

152. "Mt. Zion, first 100 years," Plaut, (1956), page 41.

153. *Ibid*., page 50.

154. St. Paul Daily Globe, August 25, 1882, "History of New Mt. Zion Building," Minnesota Historical Society Microfilm Library.

155. "Mt. Zion, first 100 years," Plaut, (1956), page 27; Also see Ramsey County Probate Court File No. 1076; Estate of Joseph Abeles; also see R.L. Polk Directory 1883 and later years, R.L.Polk Directory Library.

156. "Mt. Zion, first 100 years," Plaut, (1956), page 27–28.

157. *Ibid*., pages 41 and 63; also Mt. Zion Burial Book (old cemetery), Minnesota Historical Society Archives.

158. "Voice of Minnesota Lodge, B'nai B'rith, October, 1953 issue, private copy.

159. "Mt. Zion, first 100 years," Plaut, (1956) page 41; also information on Mt. Zion Cemetery in WPA Historical Research Project, (1942), Minnesota Historical Society Archives.

160. *Ibid*.

161. R.L. Polk Directory Library.

162. Edward's Census and City Directory, (1873) R.L. Polk Directory Library.

163. *Ibid.*; Mt. Zion Burial Book (old cemetery) Minnesota Historical Society Archives.

164. "Voice of the Minnesota Lodge, B'nai B'rith", October 1953 issue, private copy.

165. "Jews in Minnesota," Plaut, (1959), page 58.

166. Edward's Census Report and Directory, (1873), R.L. Polk Directory Library.

167. "Mt. Zion, first 100 years," Plaut, (1956) see appendix.

168. "Voice of the Minnesota Lodge, B'nai B'rith," October 1953 issue, private copy.

169. St. Paul Dispatch, November 18, 1931, "History of Cardozo Furniture Co.", Minnesota Historical Society Microfilm Library; also St. Paul Dispatch, August 20, 1924, page 1, (Ralph M. Cardozo obituary), Minnesota Historical Society Microfilm Library.

170. St. Paul Dispatch, August 20, 1924, pages 1-2 (Ralph N. Cardozo obituary), Minnesota Historical Society Microfilm Library.

171. R.L. Polk Directory Library.

172. *Ibid.*

173. St. Paul Dispatch, August 20, 1924, pages 1–2 (Ralph N. Cardozo obituary); also see R.L. Polk Directory, (1889), R.L. Polk Directory Library.

174. R.L. Polk Directory Library.

175. *Ibid.*

176. R.L. Polk Directory Library, (1885), Minnesota Historical Society Microfilm Library; R.L. Polk Directory Library.

177. R.L. Polk Directory Library.

178. Ramsey County Probate Court File No. 8036; Estate of George N. Cardozo; Ramsey County Probate Court File No. 9769; Estate of Charles Elfelt.

179. Ramsey County Probate Court File No. 8036; Estate of George N. Cardozo.

180. "Voice of Minnesota Lodge, B'nai B'rith," October 1953 issue, private copy.

181. "Mt. Zion, first 100 years," Plaut, (1956) see appendix.

182. St. Paul Dispatch, July 5, 1911, (story on Mrs. Bessie Greenblat, who lived to 107 years of

age), Minnesota Historical Society Scrapbook No. 59, Minnesota Historical Society Library.

183. R.L. Polk Directory Library.

184. St. Paul Dispatch, July 5, 1911 (Bessie Greenblat story) Minnesota Historical Society Scrapbook No. 59; Minnesota Historical Society Library.

185. R.L. Polk Directory Library.

186. "Jews in Minnesota," Plaut, (1959) page 230; Edward's Census and Directory, (1873) R.L. Polk Directory Library.

187. "Mt. Zion, First 100 Years," Plaut, (1956), see Appendix.

188. "Voice of Minnesota Lodge, B'nai B'rith," October 1953 issue, private copy.

189. See St. Paul Dispatch, June 26, 1877, Minnesota Historical Society Microfilm Library.

190. "Voice of Minnesota Lodge, B'nai B'rith," October 1953 issue, private copy.

191. "Jews in Minnesota," Plaut, (1959), page 232; (Interview with Judge Gustavus Loevinger, now deceased.).

192. "Mt. Zion, First 100 Years," Plaut, (1956), pages 65–66.

193. "Voice of Minnesota Lodge, B'nai B'rith," October 1953 issue, private copy.

194. "Jews in Minnesota," Plaut, (1959), pages 232–233.

195. *Ibid.*

196. "Voice of Minnesota Lodge, B'nai B'rith," October 1953 issue, private copy.

197. "Little Sketches of Big Folks," R.L. Polk (1907), page 140; "Book of Minnesotans," Marquis (1907), page 170; St. Paul Pioneer Press, April 26, 1946, page 4.

198. *Ibid.*

199. "Jews in Minnesota," Plaut (1959), page 154, footnote 16; also see "Mt. Zion, First 100 Years," Plaut (1956), Appendixes.

200. R.L. Polk Directory Library.

201. "Jews of St. Paul," H.D. Frankel, <u>Reform Advocate</u> (1907) special edition, page 51.

202. "Mt. Zion, first 100 Years," Plaut (1956), page 65.

203. See "Jews of St. Paul," H.D. Frankel, <u>Reform Advocate</u> (1907), special edition Minnesota Historical Society, Archives.

204. "Mt. Zion, first 100 Years," Plaut (1956), See Appendixes.

205. "Jews in Minnesota," Plaut (1959), page 230, footnote 1.

206. *Ibid*; page 64; also Appendix "A," page 311; Edwards Census Report and Directory (1873), R.L. Polk Directory Library.

207. "Jews in Minnesota," Plaut (1959), page 64.

208. "Mt. Zion, First 100 Years," Plaut (1956), appendix; "Voice of Minnesota Lodge, B'nai B'rith," October 1953 issue, private copy.

209. "Mt. Zion, First 100 Years," Plaut (1956), pages 47–48.

210. Ramsey County Probate Court File No. 7089; Estate of Benjamin Plechner.

211. R.L. Polk Directory Library.

212. St. Paul Pioneer Press, November 25, 1912, Minnesota Historical Society Scrapbook No. 7, Minnesota Historical Society Library.

213. "History of Ramsey County," Neill (1881), page 544.

214. *Ibid.*

215. R.L. Polk Directory Library.

216. "Mt. Zion, first 100 Years," Plaut (1956), See Appendixes.

217. "History of Ramsey County," Neill (1881), page 544.

218. *Ibid.*

219. R.L. Polk Directory Library.

220. St. Paul Dispatch, February 15, 1904, Minnesota Historical Society Microfilm Library; also see Minnesota Historical Society Scrapbook No. 35, Page 31, Minnesota Historical Society Library.

221. St. Paul Pioneer Press, April 24, 1914, Minnesota Historical Society Microfilm Library; "Book of Minnesotans," Marquis (1907), pages 187–188.

222. St. Paul Pioneer Press, April 24, 1914, Minnesota Historical Society Microfilm Library; also see Minnesota Historical Society Scrapbook No. 80, page 18, Minnesota Historical Society Library.

223. St. Paul Dispatch, July 16, 1926, Minnesota Historical Society Microfilm Library.

224. *Ibid.*

225. "Jews in Minnesota," Plaut (1959), pages 48–50; also footnotes 2 and 3, pages 49 and 50.

226. St. Paul Dispatch, February 27, 1903, Minnesota Historical Society Microfilm Library; also see Minnesota Historical Society Scrapbook No. 28, pages 65–67.

227. St. Paul Dispatch, July 16, 1926, Minnesota Historical Society Microfilm Library.

228. "Past and Present of St. Paul," Hennessey (1906), pages 469–470; "St. Paul History, Progress, Principal Men and Institutions," (1897), Edited by St. Paul Pioneer Press, pages 103–104; also see "Illustrated St. Paul," Edited by St. Paul Dispatch (1892).

229. *Ibid.*

230. "Voice of Minnesota Lodge, B'nai B'rith," October 1953 issue, private copy.

231. "Mt. Zion, First 100 Years," Plaut (1956), see Appendix; "Jews in Minnesota," Plaut (1959), page 59; 160.

232. "Mt. Zion, First 100 Years," Plaut (1956), page 82.

233. "Blue Book. Dual City Directory," R.L. Polk (1887), page 41.

234. "Jews in Minnesota," Plaut (1959), page 158.

235. St. Paul Dispatch, August 10, 1902, Minnesota Historical Society Microfilm Library.

236. "Jews in Minnesota," Plaut (1959), page 292.

237. Emil Mannheimer died in 1899; Jacob and Robert Mannheimer in 1903, and Louis Goodkind in 1904; See Ramsey County Probate Court records.

238. "Jews in Minnesota," Plaut (1959), page 55.

239. R.L. Polk Directory Library; also see Minnesota Inventory of Historic Homes, "St. Paul Architecture," St. Paul Planning Department, August 1975, page 59.

240. See Minnesota Historical Society Scrapbook No. 65, page 45, and St. Paul Pioneer Press, August 28, 1910, Minnesota Historical Society Microfilm Library, on James Oppenheim.

241. "Jews in Minnesota," Plaut (1959), page 225.

242. *Ibid*, page 232, footnote no. 7.

243. Edwards Census Report and Directory (1873), R.L. Polk Directory Library; also see Ansel Oppenheim in "History of St. Paul and Vicinity," Castle (1912), page 1125.

244. *Ibid.*

245. 1879 State Legislative Manual, page 362; Joseph and Ansel Oppenheim's father, Isaac Oppenheim, died in 1879. See "History of St. Paul and Vicinity," Castle (1912), page 1125; also see "Minnesota Biographies" Upham, Minnesota Historical Society Collection (1912), page 568.

246. Campbell's City Directory (1876), R.L. Polk Directory; Plaut erroneously lists him as Julius Oppenheimer in "Jews in Minnesota," (1959), page 59, footnote no. 14.

247. "Voice of Minnesota Lodge, B'nai B'rith," October 1953 issue, private copy.

248. R.L. Polk Directories, 1881–1885, R.L. Polk Directory Library.

249. R.L. Polk Directories 1884–1885, R.L. Polk Directory Library.

250. "Who was Who in America 1897–1942," Chicago (1942), page 917; also see Minnesota Historical Society Scrapbook No. 65, page 45; St. Paul Pioneer Press, August 28, 1910, Minnesota Historical Society Microfilm Library.

251. *Ibid.*

252. R.L. Polk Directory (1885–1886), R.L. Polk Library.

253. "History of St. Paul and Vicinity," Castle (1912), pages 1125–1127; "Illustrated St. Paul," edited by St. Paul Dispatch (1892); "Book of Minnesotans," Marquis (1907), page 388; "Little Sketches of Big Folks," R.L. Polk (1907), page 300.

254. *Ibid.*

255. St. Paul Daily Globe, July 18, 1882, Minnesota Historical Society Micro-film Library.

256. St. Paul Pioneer Press, December 10, 1916, page 1, Minnesota Historical Society Micro-film Library.

257. "Little Sketches of Big Folks," R.L. Polk (1907), page 300; ST. Paul Dispatch, December 18, 1913; Minnesota Historical Society Micro-film Library; Minnesota Historical Society Scrapbook No, 72, page 127, Minnesota Historical Society Library.

258. Edward's Census Report and Directory (1873), R. L. Polk Directory Library; Report of Adjutant General's office (1866); also see "Minnesota in Civil War and Indian Wars," Volume 1, Minnesota Historical Society Library.

259. "Mt. Zion, first 100 years," Plaut (1956), see Appendixes.

260. See St. Louis County, Minnesota (Duluth) Register of Deeds records on "Sattler Brothers" ownership of various downtown Duluth real estate.

261. Mt. Zion Burial Book (old cemetery), Minnesota Historical Society Archives; "Jews in Minnesota," Plaut (1959) page 134.

262. "Mt. Zion, first 100 years," Plaut, (1956) page 50.

263. "Jews in Minnesota," Plaut, (1959) pages 59–60.

264. Edwards Cencus Report and Directory, (1873), R. L. Polk Directory Library, "Mt. Zion, first

100 years," Plaut (1956), pages 42–43.

265. "Jews in Minnesota," Plaut, (1959) page 52, footnote no. 9.

266. R. L. Polk Directory Library.

267. "Jews In Minnesota," Plaut (1959) page 52, footnote no. 9.

268. Campbell and Dawson's City Directory, (1874), R. L. Polk Directory Library, "Voice of the Minnesota Lodge, B'nai B'rith," October 1953 issue, private copy.

269. R. L. Polk Directories (1882–1894), R. L. Polk Library; He served as Vice President of the City Assembly, which was one of the two bodies in St. Paul's earl; bi-cameral form of government. The city Assembly was elected at large, as opposed to Alderman, elected from specific wards of the city.

270. R. L. Polk Directory Library.

271. "Jews in Minnesota," Plaut (1959), pages 54–55.

272. *Ibid*.

273. *Ibid*. pages 56–57 and page 71.

274. *Ibid* page 90, footnote 1; "Minnesota and its People," Volume 3, (1924) S. J. Clarke Publishing Co. (Chicago), page 340; Crosby-Courier, May 14, 1936, page 1, (Abraham Mark obituary) Minnesota Historical Society Micro-film Library.

275. "Jews in Minnesota," Plaut (1959), page 90, footnote no. 1.

276. Crosby Courier, May 14, 1936, Minnesota Historical Society Micro-film Library, (see page 1, obituary of Abraham Mark.)

277. "Jews in Minnesota," Plaut, (1959), page 90, footnote no. 1.

278. See "History of Sons of Jacob" various program books, private copies; also see St.Paul Pioneer Press, December 22, 1930, page 1. for obituary of Mrs. Bessie Mark (Mrs. Aaron Mark); "orthodox community consisted of only five families" when Aaron Mark arrived in St. Paul in 1873; *Ibid*.

279. The "History of Sons of Jacob" contained in various program books of the synagogue's various celebrations and dedications lists 262 Robert as Aaron Mark's address and the early meeting place for members of the Sons of Jacob. In 1883, St. Paul's streets were re-numbered to their present status and this became 620 North Robert (13th and Robert) as the early center of the orthodox Jewish community.

280. "Jews in Minnesota," Plaut. (1959) page 90, footnote no.1 also see obituary of Mrs. Bessie (Aaron) Mark, St. Paul Pioneer Press, December 22, 1930, page 1; Minnesota Historical Society Micro-film library.

281. "Jews in Minnesota," Plaut (1959), pages 197–198.

282. "Minnesota and its People," Volume 3, (1924) S.L. Clarke Pub. Co., (Chicago, IL) page 34.

283. Crosby Courier, May 14, 1936, page 1, obituary of Abraham Mark, Minnesota Historical Society Micro-film Library.

284. "Jews of St. Paul," H.D. Frankel, (1907) Reform Advocate, (Chicago,IL) special edition page 43; Minnesota Historical Society Archives; also St. Paul Pioneer Press, December 22, 1930, obituary of Mrs. Bessie (Aaron) Mark, Minnesota Historical Society Micro-film Library.

285. *Ibid.*

286. R. L. Polk Directory Library.

287. "Jews in Minnesota," Plaut, (1959) page 55, 56 footnote no. 3.

288. St. Paul Pioneer Press June 7, 1923, page 1, obituary of Cain Calmenson, Minnesota Historical Society Micro-film Library.

289. "Jews in Minnesota," Plaut, (1959) page 90, footnote no. 1; page 178, footnote no, 18.

290. R. L. Polk Directory Library.

291. "Prominent Jews of America," S. B. Goodkind, (1918) American Hebrew Publishing Co., page 37.

292. R. L. Polk Directory Library.

293. *Ibid.*

294. *Ibid.*

295. "Jews in Minnesota," Plaut (1959) Appendix C, page 312.

296. R. L. Polk Directory Library; "History of St. Paul," C.C. Andrews (1890) page 509; "History of Sons of St. Paul and Vicinity," Castle, (1912) Volume 2, page 543, History of Sons of Jacob" Program book, private copy (1969).

296a. The Jews in Minnesota, Plaut (1959) pages 57, 115–116.

296b. *Ibid.*

296c. *Ibid.*

296d. *Ibid*: (see Appendix C page 312, 313).

297. Edward's Census Report and Directory, (1873) R. L. Polk Directory Library.

298. R. L. Polk Directory Library; "Industries of St, Paul," Morrison, (1886).

299. R. L. Polk Directories, (1886–1892), R. L. Polk Directory Library.

300. R. L. Polk Directory Library.

301. See St. Paul City Directories, 1856 and 1863, R.L. Polk Directory Library;

302. Ramsey County Probate Court File no. 26818; Estate of Harry L. Levy.

303. *Ibid.*; R.L. Polk Directory Library.

304. "Golden Jubilee of A. F. and A.M. Ancient Landmark Lodge No. 5 (1904) program book, Minnesota Historical Society Library. Contains lists of a number of early Jews and when they joined the Masonic movement in St. Paul.

305. "Mt. Zion, first 100 years," Plaut (1956) See Appendixes.

306. "Jews of St. Paul," H.D. Frankel, Reform Advocate (1907) Special Edition, page 51; Minnesota Historical Society Archives.

307. "Voice of Minnesota Lodge, B'nai B'rith," October 1953 issue private copy.

308. Ramsey County Probate Court File No. 26818; Estate of Harry L. Levy.

309. St. Paul Dispatch, June 10, 1944, page 5, obituary of Dr. Jesse Levy; "Book of Minnesotans, Marquis, (1907) page 307, Minnesota Historical Society Library.

310. "Industries of St. Paul," Morrison, (1886); R.L. Polk Directory Library.

311. "Mt. Zion, first 100 years," Plaut, (1956), See Appendixes; "Industries of St. Paul," Morrison, (1886).

312. R. L. Polk Directory Library; Ramsey Court Probate File no. 9815; Estate of Herman Bernheimer; Ramsey Court Probate Court File No. 783; Estate of Simon Elfelt.